More Praise for *Negotiation Genius*

"Invaluable. Whether in business, politics, or the nonprofit sector, leaders must rely on the power to persuade, and Malhotra and Bazerman unlock the secrets of how to do so strategically, ethically, and successfully."

—Bill Shore, Founder and
Executive Director, Share Our Strength

"Whether your passion is sports, politics, or business, negotiations are an integral part of your world. *Negotiation Genius* offers an insightful and entertaining perspective on the negotiation process, plus—even more important—highly effective and relevant advice for conducting negotiations day-to-day."

—Andy Wasynczuk, former Chief Operating Officer,
three-time Super Bowl champion New England Patriots

"For both the novice and the master, *Negotiation Genius* is the single, *most essential source* for the basic understanding of this increasingly important skill set."

—Warren Bennis, Distinguished Professor of Management,
University of Southern California; coauthor of
Judgment: How Winning Leaders Make Great Calls

NEGOTIATION
GENIUS

How to Overcome Obstacles and Achieve
Brilliant Results at the Bargaining Table and Beyond

DEEPAK MALHOTRA
MAX H. BAZERMAN

Harvard | Business | School

BANTAM BOOKS

NEGOTIATION GENIUS
A Bantam Book / October 2007

Published by
Bantam Dell
A Division of Random House, Inc.
New York, New York

Book design by Robert Bull

Library of Congress Cataloging-in-Publication Data
Malhotra, Deepak, 1975-
Negotiation genius : how to overcome obstacles and achieve brilliant results at the
bargaining table and beyond / Deepak Malhotra and Max Bazerman.
p.   cm.
ISBN: 978-0-553-80488-1 (hardcover)
1. Negotiation in business.   2. Negotiation.   3. Miscommunication.
4. Interpersonal communication—Moral and ethical aspects.   5. Conflict
management.   I. Bazerman, Max. H.   II. Title.

HD58.6.M35 2007   2007019718
658.4/052 22

Printed in the United States of America
Published simultaneously in Canada

www.bantamdell.com

BVG   10   9   8   7   6   5   4   3   2   1

Dedicated to Shikha and Marla

Your ideas and encouragement influence everything we do.

CONTENTS

Becoming a
Negotiation Genius

What is a negotiation genius? Let's start with the simple observation that you often know a negotiation genius when you see one. You can see genius in the way a person thinks about, prepares for, and executes negotiation strategy. You can see genius in the way a person manages to completely turn around a seemingly hopeless negotiation situation. You can see genius in the way a person manages to negotiate successful deals—consistently—while still maintaining her integrity and strengthening her relationships and her reputation. And, in all likelihood, you know who the negotiation geniuses are in your organization. This book will share with you their secrets.

Consider the following stories, in which negotiators faced great obstacles, only to overcome them to achieve remarkable levels of success. But we will not reveal *how* they did it—yet. Instead, we will revisit these stories—and many others like them—in the chapters that follow, as we share with you the strategies and insights you need to negotiate like a genius in all aspects of life.

A FIGHT OVER EXCLUSIVITY

Representatives of a Fortune 500 company had been negotiating the purchase of a new product ingredient from a small European supplier. The parties had agreed to a price of $18 per pound for a million pounds of product per year, but a conflict arose over exclusivity terms. The supplier would not agree to sell the ingredient exclusively to the U.S. firm, and the U.S. firm was unwilling to invest in producing a new product if competitors would have access to one of its key ingredients. This issue appeared to be a deal breaker. The U.S. negotiators were both frustrated and surprised by the small European firm's reticence on the issue of exclusivity; they believed their offer was not only fair, but generous. Eventually, they decided to sweeten the deal with guaranteed minimum orders and a willingness to pay more per pound. They were shocked when the European firm still refused to provide exclusivity! As a last resort, the U.S. negotiators decided to call in their resident "negotiation genius," Chris, who flew to Europe and quickly got up to speed. In a matter of minutes, Chris was able to structure a deal that both parties immediately accepted. He made no substantive concessions, nor did he threaten the small firm. How did Chris manage to save the day? We will revisit this story in Chapter 3.

A DIPLOMATIC IMPASSE

In the fall of 2000, some members of the U.S. Senate began calling for a U.S. withdrawal from the United Nations. Meanwhile, at the United Nations, the United States was on the verge of losing its vote in the General Assembly. The conflict was over a debt of close to $1.5 billion, which the United States owed to the UN. The United States was unwilling to pay unless the UN agreed to a variety of reforms that it felt were long overdue. Most important, the United States wanted a reduction in its "assessments"—the percentage of the UN's yearly regular budget that the United States was obligated to pay—from 25 percent to 22 percent. The problem was this: if the United States paid less, someone else would have to pay more.

There were other serious complications as well. First, UN regulations stipulated that Richard Holbrooke, U.S. ambassador to the UN, had to convince all 190 countries to ratify the changes demanded by the United States. Second, Holbrooke faced a deadline: if he could not strike a deal before the end of 2000, the money set aside by Congress to pay U.S. dues would disappear from the budget. Third, no nation seemed willing to increase its assessments in order for the United States to get a break. How could Holbrooke convince even one nation to increase its assessment when they all claimed this was impossible? As the end of 2000 approached, Holbrooke decided on a different strategy. He stopped trying to persuade other nations to agree to his demands. What he did instead worked wonders: the issue was resolved, and Holbrooke was congratulated by member states of the UN as well as by members of both political parties in the U.S. Congress. How did Holbrooke resolve this conflict? We will revisit this story in Chapter 2.

A LAST-MINUTE DEMAND

The CEO of a construction company was negotiating a deal in which his firm would be contracted to build midsize office buildings for a buyer. After months of negotiations had finally concluded—but just before the contract was signed—the buyer approached the builder with an entirely new and potentially costly demand. The buyer wanted to include a clause in the contract that would require the builder to pay large penalties if the project's completion was delayed by more than one month. The builder was irritated by this sudden demand; it seemed as though the buyer was trying to squeeze a last-minute concession from him. The builder weighed his options: he could accept the buyer's demand and seal the deal; he could reject the buyer's demand and hope this would not destroy the deal; or he could try to negotiate to reduce the proposed penalties. After considering these options, the builder decided on an entirely different approach. He negotiated with the buyer to *increase* the amount of penalties he (the builder) would have to pay if the project was delayed—and the revised deal made *both* parties better off. How? We will revisit this example in Chapter 3.

A CAMPAIGN CATASTROPHE

It was 1912, and former president Theodore Roosevelt was campaigning for a third term. The campaign was tough; every day seemed to present new challenges. But here was a challenge that no one had anticipated. Three million copies of Roosevelt's photograph had already been printed for circulation with a campaign speech when Roosevelt's campaign manager discovered a catastrophic blunder: the photographer had not been asked permission for the use of Roosevelt's photograph. To make matters worse, it was soon discovered that copyright law allowed the photographer to demand as much as $1 per copy to use the photograph. Losing $3 million in 1912 would be equivalent to losing over $60 million today. No campaign could afford that. The alternative was almost equally unattractive; reprinting three million brochures would be tremendously costly and could cause serious delays. The campaign manager would have to try to negotiate a lower price with the photographer, but how? The photographer seemed to hold all the cards. The campaign manager, however, had something better: an effective strategy that he used to negotiate an almost unbelievable deal. We will reveal the deal—and the strategy—in Chapter 1.

As we hope to persuade you, people are rarely born "negotiation geniuses." Rather, what appears to be genius actually reflects careful preparation, an understanding of the conceptual framework of negotiation, insight into how one can avoid the errors and biases that plague even experienced negotiators, and the ability to structure and execute negotiations strategically and systematically. This book will provide you with this framework—and with an entire toolkit of negotiation strategies and tactics that you can put to work immediately. As you begin to apply the framework and strategies in the many negotiations you encounter—in business, in politics, or in everyday life—you will begin to build your own reputation as a negotiation genius.

OUR APPROACH

Just twenty-five years ago, courses on negotiation were rarely taught in management schools or in executive education programs. Now they are one of the most sought-after courses in business schools throughout the world. Negotiation courses are also tremendously popular in law schools and schools of public policy and government. Why? Because in our increasingly complex, diverse, and dynamic world, negotiation is being seen as the most practical and effective mechanism we have for allocating resources, balancing competing interests, and resolving conflicts of all kinds. Current and future managers, lawyers, politicians, policy makers, and consumers all want and need to know how to get better outcomes in their negotiations and disputes. Negotiation is, perhaps now more than ever, an essential skill for success in all areas of life.

Why, then, do so many people continue to negotiate ineffectively? In our work as educators and consultants, one of the biggest problems we've encountered is the pervasive belief that people are either good or bad at negotiation, and little can be done to change that. *We could not disagree more.* In addition, too many people—including many seasoned dealmakers—think of negotiation as being all art and no science; as a result, they rely on gut instinct or intuition as they negotiate. But gut instinct is not a strategy. Nor is "shooting from the hip" or "winging it."

We offer a more systematic and effective approach. This approach leverages the latest research in negotiation and dispute resolution, the experience of thousands of our clients and executive students, and our own experience as negotiators, consultants, and educators. It has been challenged and refined in our MBA and executive education courses at the Harvard Business School and in our work with over fifty major corporations in more than twenty-five countries. The resulting framework will help you minimize your reliance on intuition, increase your understanding and use of proven strategies, and achieve superior negotiated outcomes consistently.

We also aim to dispel the notion that negotiating effectively is as simple as achieving "win-win agreements." If you're like many of the executives we've worked with, you've had the experience of wanting to bargain in good faith for a mutually rewarding outcome, only to find that the other party is playing hardball, behaving unethically, or negotiating entirely in their own self-interest. Or you may have found yourself negotiating from a position of weakness, dealing with someone who was not sophisticated enough to negotiate effectively, or sitting across from someone who did not have the authority to negotiate the kind of deal you wanted. How does the "win-win" principle help you in these situations? In complex negotiations, which might include multiple parties, great uncertainty, threats of litigation, heightened emotions, and seeming irrationality, it may not even be clear what "win-win" really means. Because such complexities are commonplace, you must deal with them systematically. This book will provide you with the tools you need to do exactly that. In other words, while preserving the virtues of a win-win mind-set, we will help you understand how to strategize effectively when "win-win" won't save you.

Following is a brief outline of what you will find in this book.

PART I: THE NEGOTIATOR'S TOOLKIT

In Part I, we develop a framework that you can use to analyze, prepare for, and execute almost any negotiation you might encounter. Part I also offers a toolkit of comprehensive principles, strategies, and tactics that will help you execute each stage of the deal, from before the first offer is ever made to the final agreement. It turns out that a significant percentage of the million-dollar problems that our executive clients confront have solutions that are contained in these initial chapters. Because we develop the framework and the toolkit methodically, we recommend that you read Part I straight through in the order presented.

Chapter 1: Claiming Value in Negotiation. We begin by focusing on a topic of great importance and appeal to all negotiators: how do I get the best possible deal for my side? We build our negotiation framework by analyzing a straightforward two-party negotiation in which a buyer and seller are bargaining over one issue: price. This chapter covers, among other topics: negotiation preparation, common negotiator mistakes, whether to make a first offer, responding to offers from the other party, structuring your initial offer, finding out how far you can push the other party, strategies for haggling effectively, and how to maximize not only your outcome, but also the satisfaction of both parties.

Chapter 2: Creating Value in Negotiation. Here we expand the "claiming value" framework by examining the more difficult—and more critical—task of *value creation*. A key insight of this chapter is that negotiators who focus only on claiming value reach worse outcomes than do those who cooperate with the other side to improve the deal for both parties. To demonstrate this, we consider a more complex negotiation in which parties are negotiating multiple issues and facing greater uncertainty. This chapter covers topics such as: strategies for value creation, a framework for negotiating efficient agreements, preparing for and executing complex negotiations, how and when to make concessions, how to learn about the other side's real interests, and what to do after the deal is signed.

Chapter 3: Investigative Negotiation. Much of what negotiators must do to create and capture value depends on their ability to obtain information from the other side. This chapter presents a powerful approach to information gathering that we call "investigative negotiation." The principles and strategies of investigative negotiation will help you discover and leverage the interests, priorities, needs, and constraints of the other party—even when that party is reluctant or unwilling to share this information.

PART II: THE PSYCHOLOGY OF NEGOTIATION

Even experienced negotiators make mistakes when preparing and executing negotiation strategy. After all, even seasoned dealmakers are human, and all human beings are vulnerable to *psychological biases*—systematic and predictable departures from rationality—that can derail an otherwise sound negotiation strategy. Part II builds on cutting-edge research on the psychology of negotiation and decision-making. We distill theory into the practical tools you will need to avoid these costly mistakes, and to recognize and leverage mistakes when they are made by the other side.

Chapter 4: When Rationality Fails: Biases of the Mind. In this chapter, we focus on *cognitive biases*—the mistakes that even the best of negotiators make because of the ways in which our minds operate. As we will illustrate, the human mind is accustomed to taking shortcuts that, while often useful for making decisions quickly, can also lead to disastrous strategic moves in negotiation.

Chapter 5: When Rationality Fails: Biases of the Heart. Next we look at *motivational biases*—the mistakes we make because of our desire to view the world the way we wish it were rather than how it truly is. Unfortunately, it is possible to have a weak negotiation strategy and still feel good about yourself and your prospects for success. It is also possible to continue down the wrong path and never allow yourself to discover how and when a change in strategy is critical. Chapter 5 will help you to identify and avoid these potential pitfalls, and to see the world through a more objective and realistic lens.

Chapter 6: Negotiating Rationally in an Irrational World. Here we offer still more strategies for overcoming your own biases and for leveraging the biases of others. We also explain when it is in your best interest to help the other side be *less* biased. Why? Because their irrationality often hurts you as well as them.

PART III: NEGOTIATING IN THE REAL WORLD

Finally, we turn to a variety of topics that are all too often ignored in negotiation seminars and books, but which are crucial for success in real-world negotiations. How can you tell if someone is lying? How do you persuade reluctant negotiators to agree to your demands or proposals? How should you negotiate when you have little or no power? How should you incorporate ethical considerations into your negotiation strategy? How should you negotiate with your competitors, opponents, and enemies? As in the first part of the book, our insights and advice on these topics emerge from the experience of thousands of real-world negotiators and from years of systematic and scientific research on negotiation, strategic decision-making, psychology, and economics. Each of these chapters can be read as a stand-alone entity, so feel free to choose first the topics that are most relevant to your situation.

Chapter 7: Strategies of Influence. It is often not enough to have a good idea, a well-structured proposal, or a great product or service to offer. You also need to know how to sell it to the other side. This chapter presents eight proven strategies of influence that will increase the likelihood that others will accept your requests, demands, offers, and proposals. Note that these strategies do not improve the merits of your case; rather, they make it more likely that the other side will say "yes" without requiring you to change your position. Of course, you will also be the target of the other side's influence strategies, so we provide detailed defense strategies that will defuse their attempts to manipulate your preferences and interests.

Chapter 8: Blind Spots in Negotiation. Many negotiators focus too narrowly on a negotiation problem and fail to adequately consider how the context, the decisions of the other side, and the rules of the negotiation game will affect their strategy and their prospects for success. They also miss out on opportunities for changing the rules of the game to achieve better results. In this chapter, we provide specific advice on how to broaden your focus to ensure that you consider all of the elements that might come into play as you negotiate.

Chapter 9: Confronting Lies and Deception. While many people identify with the notion that "honesty is the best policy," most people admit to having lied at some point in their negotiations and virtually everyone believes that others have lied to them. In this chapter we address questions such as: What might motivate someone to lie in a negotiation? What are some of the strategic costs of lying? How can you tell if someone is lying? How can you deter people from lying to you? What should you do if you catch someone in a lie? If you are interested in telling the truth, but don't want to lose your shirt at the bargaining table, what are some smart alternatives to lying?

Chapter 10: Recognizing and Resolving Ethical Dilemmas. Many people believe that ethics are too personal and idiosyncratic to be discussed broadly or categorically. This is undoubtedly true—to a degree. Yet recent research suggests that people often behave less ethically than they *themselves* consider appropriate. In other cases, they are not even aware of the damage they are inflicting on others when they pursue certain strategies. And in the shadow of major corporate scandals, there's a renewed emphasis on maintaining integrity while still achieving negotiation success. We provide a framework for thinking more carefully and comprehensively about these issues.

Chapter 11: Negotiating from a Position of Weakness. This chapter is about power—and the lack of it. Most negotiators will at some point find themselves in a position of weakness with seemingly few, if any, alternatives. (Indeed, many of our executive students and clients complain that they are *always* negotiating from a position of weakness vis-à-vis their customers, their boss, or their spouse!) Such negotiations require careful analysis, creative thinking, and insights into how such situations can be turned around. We show how you can effectively negotiate when you lack power, and how you might be able to upset the balance of power so that you move from a position of weakness to a position of strength.

Chapter 12: When Negotiations Get Ugly: Dealing with Irrationality, Distrust, Anger, Threats, and Ego. How do you negotiate when the other side appears to be entirely irrational? How do you negotiate when trust has been lost and the other party is unwilling to come to the table? How can you defuse hardball tactics such as ultimatums and threats? How should you deal with a party that is angry or one that is too proud to admit that their strategy was flawed? Our approach in this chapter recognizes that most important negotiations include at least some of these difficulties and that ignoring them is not only extremely ineffective, but often entirely impossible.

Chapter 13: When *Not* to Negotiate. There are occasions when negotiation is *not* the answer. If you have limited power and few prospects for success, you might do surprisingly better by giving up what little power you have. Or, if the costs of negotiating are high, you might want to find cheaper alternatives to making the deal or resolving the dispute. In other instances, negotiation itself may be a barrier to creating the kind of relationship you want with the other side. But what should you be doing instead? In this chapter, we provide you with a framework for distinguishing between the times when you should be playing the negotiation game and the times when you should be changing the game.

Chapter 14: The Path to Genius. Genius in negotiation requires knowledge, understanding, and mindful practice. This book can give you the first and help you with the second, but the third will be largely up to you. We end by considering what happens when you turn the last page and head back into the real world. Which mind-set will maximize your ability to put your learning into practice? What habits will you want to cultivate in the weeks and months ahead? What expectations should you have of yourself and others? How might you help others in your organization negotiate more effectively?

A sentiment once expressed by Ralph Waldo Emerson captures the essence of our message: "Man hopes; Genius creates." When the task is difficult, when obstacles arise, when negotiations are unraveling, and when it looks as if the deal is lost, most negotiators will panic or pray. Negotiation geniuses, in contrast, will only strengthen their resolve to formulate and execute sound negotiation strategy. We hope that this book convinces you to do the latter, and provides you with the insights and tools you will need to negotiate like a genius at the bargaining table—and beyond.

PART I

THE NEGOTIATOR'S TOOLKIT

CHAPTER 1

Claiming Value
in Negotiation

The year was 1912, and the U.S. presidential election was in full swing. Former president Theodore Roosevelt had decided to return to the political arena due to his frustration with the way his successor, President William Howard Taft, had been running the country. It was a tough campaign, and every day seemed to present a new challenge. But here was a challenge that no one had anticipated: three million copies of Roosevelt's photograph had already been printed for circulation with a campaign speech when Roosevelt's campaign manager discovered a catastrophic blunder—the photographer had not been asked for permission to use the photograph. To make matters worse, copyright law allowed the photographer to demand as much as $1 per copy of the photograph. In 1912, a loss of $3 million would be equivalent to a loss of more than $60 million today. No campaign could afford this price. The alternative was almost equally unattractive; reprinting three million brochures would be tremendously costly and could cause serious delays. The campaign manager would have to try to negotiate a better deal with the photographer. If you were the campaign manager, how would you handle this negotiation?

Now consider how Roosevelt's manager dealt with the situation. After carefully analyzing the problem, he sent the following telegram to the photographer: "Planning to distribute three million copies of campaign speech with photographs. Excellent publicity opportunity for photographers. How much are you willing to pay to use your photographs? Respond immediately."

The photographer did not take long to issue a reply. He sent back a telegram with the following message: "Appreciate opportunity, but can only afford $250."[1]

Most people, when they hear this story, are taken aback. How did the campaign manager turn around such a hopeless situation so completely? The reason for this reaction is that even the most seasoned negotiators may not think systematically about negotiations, nor prepare for and execute negotiations strategically. Our goal is to make the manager's solution to the negotiation problem appear obvious to you. By understanding and applying the principles and strategies of value claiming covered in this chapter, you, too, will be able to handle difficult negotiations with the kind of genius demonstrated by Roosevelt's campaign manager.

STRATEGIES FOR CLAIMING VALUE IN NEGOTIATION

Throughout this book, we will talk a lot about value. How do we define the term, exactly? *Value* is whatever people find useful or desirable. You may measure value in dollars, utility, happiness, or a variety of other metrics. Negotiation helps to create value through agreements that make both parties better off than they were without an agreement. But *how much better off* is each party? This depends, in part, on which party managed to claim (or capture) more of the value that was created. For example, if a buyer negotiates a very low price for an item, she claims more value; the seller claims more of the value (created by the deal) when the price is high.

For many people, learning to negotiate more effectively means one thing above all else: "How can I get a better deal for myself?" Or, put another way, "How can I claim the lion's share of the value in any negotiation?" While *Negotiation Genius* takes a much broader view of negotiation, we, too, start with this basic goal: getting the best possible deal for yourself.

We begin by considering a negotiation over the sale of real estate that allows us to address key issues that you will face in virtually all negotiations. The Hamilton Real Estate case is a relatively simple negotiation: two parties (a buyer and a seller) are negotiating over one issue (price). Within this framework, we cover all of the following aspects of negotiating: preparing to negotiate, avoiding common negotiator mistakes, deciding whether to make the first offer, responding to the other side's offers, structuring your initial offer, finding out how far you can push the other side, haggling effectively, claiming maximum value without sacrificing the relationship, and managing your own satisfaction.

When we use the Hamilton Real Estate case in our negotiation courses with executives and MBA students, we assign half of the participants to the role of "seller" and the other half to the role of "buyer." Each side is given confidential information regarding its needs and interests, and is asked to prepare its strategy for the negotiation simulation. The two sides then meet and try to negotiate an agreement over the sale price of the property.

As you read the case from the perspective of the seller, think about how you would approach this negotiation.

HAMILTON REAL ESTATE[2]

You are the executive vice president of Pearl Investments, a holding company that specializes in real-estate investments. Among your many real-estate holdings is a large piece of property located in the town of Hamilton. The Hamilton real estate is earmarked for divestment, and you are responsible for negotiating its sale.

The amount that a potential buyer will pay for the Hamilton property depends on a number of factors, including the buyer's ability to pay and their planned use of the property. Each of these factors is critical. For example, your experts have estimated that if the land were developed for commercial use (e.g., a set of office buildings), the land might be worth 1.5 to 2 times as much as if it were developed for residential use (e.g., apartment buildings). Unfortunately, commercial developers are unlikely to be interested in the property because Hamilton zoning laws do not allow for commercial development.

While some local politicians have recently discussed allowing commercial development in Hamilton, they have taken no action in this direction. As a result, Hamilton has fallen off the radar for commercial developers.

Over the last few weeks, you have entertained offers from a few potential buyers. All but one of these offers has fallen substantially short of your expectations. The offer of most interest to you is from Quincy Developments, a developer that is planning to construct a set of high-end apartment buildings on the Hamilton property. The offer is for $38 million.

Apart from being the highest offer you have received, this deal interests you because of Quincy Developments' reputation for bargaining in good faith. While this gives you some confidence that the offer is reasonable, you are not necessarily ready to accept it as is. You expect that you could negotiate the price up an additional 10–15 percent if you chose to pursue the offer. You do not think that Quincy Developments would go any higher than that.

For now, however, you have chosen not to negotiate with Quincy Developments. Why? Because Estate One, a premier real-estate company in the region, has just sent word that it is also interested in the Hamilton property. You believe that Estate One would develop the property for the construction of luxury condominiums, as it does with virtually all of its properties. You should be able to negotiate a higher selling price for the Hamilton property if the land is to be used for luxury condominiums rather than for apartment buildings.

You have decided to meet with the CEO of Estate One, Connie Vega, to negotiate a sale. If these talks are not successful, you plan to return to Quincy Developments and finalize a deal. You will not wait for other offers. Quincy Developments has said that its offer expires in three days.

Here is what you know about Estate One: It is a midsize company that is one of the biggest regional developers of residential real estate. Estate One's CEO has been with the company since its founding twenty years ago and is known to be extremely well connected politically, linked to knowledge brokers at all levels of state and local government. Estate One is not a competitor of yours.

To prepare for the negotiation, you have collected as much data as possible. The following information is public knowledge, and is certainly known to the CEO of Estate One:

- Pearl Investments purchased the Hamilton property seven years ago at a price of $27 million.
- Since the purchase, land value in Hamilton has increased substantially. An evaluation of recent sales of somewhat comparable properties suggests that the Hamilton property could be worth $36–44 million if developed for residential use.
- If the land is used for the construction of luxury condominiums instead of apartment buildings, it is probably worth an additional 20 percent.

The impending Hamilton negotiation raises many questions. What would you do first in this negotiation? How would you approach the CEO of Estate One, Connie Vega? Would you make the first offer or would you let her make it? What information, if any, would you share with her? What information, if any, would you try to acquire from her? How much would you expect to earn on the Hamilton sale? How would you know if you got a good deal?

PREPARING TO NEGOTIATE

Over the course of training and consulting with tens of thousands of negotiators and dealmakers, we have become aware that, by far, the most common and costly mistakes in negotiation take place before talks even begin. Interestingly, the problem is usually not *faulty* preparation, but a *lack* of preparation altogether! Under the false assumption that negotiation is "all art and no science," most people fail to prepare adequately for negotiation. When coupled with the belief that the "real action" begins at the bargaining table, even smart, thoughtful, and motivated people walk into substantive negotiations ill-prepared.

Thus, it is critical that you adopt a thorough methodology to help you prepare to negotiate. Our five-step pre-negotiation framework offers a simple yet effective approach. (In the chapters that follow, we will add to this list as we confront more complex negotiations.)

Step 1: Assess your BATNA. The first step in any negotiation is to ask yourself, "What will I do if the current negotiation ends in no deal?" In other words, you need to assess your *BATNA*, or *best alternative to negotiated agreement*—the course of action you will pursue if and when the current negotiation ends in an impasse.[3] Without a clear understanding of your BATNA, it is impossible to know when to accept a final offer and when to walk away in order to pursue other options. Your BATNA assessment requires the following three steps:

1. Identify all of the plausible alternative options you might pursue if you are unable to reach an agreement with the other party.
2. Estimate the value associated with each alternative.
3. Select the best alternative; this is your BATNA.

In the Hamilton case, you have a number of alternatives if the negotiation with Connie Vega ends in impasse: you might wait for other offers, you might approach Quincy Developments to finalize the deal, or you might decide not to sell at all. The information available to you strongly suggests that your BATNA would be to finalize a deal with Quincy.

Step 2: Calculate your reservation value. An analysis of your BATNA is critical because it allows you to calculate your *reservation value* (RV), or your walk-away point in the current negotiation. As the seller in the Hamilton case, your reservation value is the lowest offer you would be willing to accept from Connie Vega. What might this offer be? If the negotiation ended in impasse, you would return to Quincy and finalize the sale. Quincy has offered $38 million. Is $38 million your reservation value? Not quite, because you could negotiate this price further with Quincy. Specifically, you believe that you could negotiate a 10–15 percent increase in the offer, yielding an amount ranging from $41.8–$43.7 million. Your reservation value should fall within this range.

What determines your exact reservation value within this range? If you are risk averse, you might be inclined to lean toward the lower end of the range. But if you are optimistic about your ability to negotiate with Quincy, you might lean toward the upper end. Let's say that you decide on the midpoint of this range and set $42.65 million as your reservation value. If Connie Vega's final offer falls below this amount, you will walk away from the deal. If it is higher than this amount, and you are sure that you cannot negotiate a still higher price with Connie, you will accept the deal. Another way to think about your reservation value is to consider it your *indifference point*. If Connie's final offer is exactly $42.65 million, you are indifferent between accepting this offer and rejecting it in favor of pursuing your BATNA.

As you can see, a careful assessment of your BATNA is essential if you are going to establish a rational reservation value that is based on a realistic assessment of your alternatives. Unfortunately, people often make strategic mistakes when they confuse their BATNAs with other elements of the negotiation. Keep in mind that your BATNA is *not* what you think is fair, or what you originally paid for the item you are selling, or the price that you hope to achieve. Your BATNA is the *reality* you will face if you reach no deal in the current negotiation.

Step 3: Assess the other party's BATNA. Now that you have assessed your BATNA and calculated your reservation value, you know the lowest offer you would be willing to accept in the Hamilton negotiation. Of course, you do not want to settle for a low sale price, so you will need to figure out how high a price you might be able to negotiate. In other words, you have to figure out the *other party's* reservation value. Connie Vega's reservation value is the highest amount that Estate One would be willing to pay for the Hamilton property. How can you determine this amount? How will you know how far you can push the other side? You figure this out by assessing the other party's BATNA. This critical step can make the difference between getting a good deal and getting a great deal. Sometimes it even marks the difference between phenomenal success and utter failure.

Remember Roosevelt's campaign manager? Had he focused only on his own BATNA (reprint three million brochures) and his own reservation value (pay the photographer thousands of dollars), the negotiation would have been a disaster. The manager's genius lay in his decision to assess the photographer's BATNA. In other words, he asked, "What would the *photographer* do if the negotiation ended in impasse?" If no deal could be struck and Roosevelt decided not to use the photograph, the photographer would make little or no money on the photograph; the photographer would also lose the opportunity for national publicity. In other words, while the campaign manager's BATNA was quite poor, so was the photographer's! As a result, the photographer could be induced to accept little or no money at all.

Similarly, in the Hamilton negotiation, thinking through Connie Vega's alternatives can help you to discover her BATNA. Presumably, if she is unable to purchase the Hamilton property, Connie will want to invest Estate One's dollars in a different development project; her preferred alternative may be to try to find another piece of property on which to build luxury condominiums. If such properties are in short supply in the town of Hamilton, her BATNA may be to build elsewhere— or to wait until other properties become available. You will want to think through each of these alternatives carefully—from Connie's perspective. For now, let us presume that your analysis suggests that Connie's BATNA is to wait it out. In other words, if she is unable to reach an agreement with you, Estate One will hold on to their cash and wait for new opportunities to arise in the future.

Step 4: Calculate the other party's reservation value. Now that you have evaluated Connie's BATNA, a reasonable way to determine her reservation value is to consider what she is likely to do with the Hamilton property. You know that Estate One tends to develop its properties for residential construction. Furthermore, you believe that Estate One will build condominiums on the property rather than rental apartments, which makes the property more valuable to them than it would be to Quincy. Specifically, development for the construction of condominiums would increase the value of the property by 20 percent. To assess Estate One's reservation value (or highest willingness to pay), the following reasoning may be appropriate:

- Estimates suggest that the property is worth $36–44 million if used for apartment buildings.
- The midpoint of this range is $40 million.
- A 20 percent increase (due to development for condominiums) over $40 million yields a value of $48 million.
- Thus, it is reasonable to expect that Connie Vega's reservation value is $48 million (assuming the valuation has already factored in the costs of development).

Step 5: Evaluate the ZOPA. Once you have an idea of each party's reservation value, you can evaluate the *zone of possible agreement,* or ZOPA. The ZOPA is the set of all possible deals that would be acceptable to both parties. Put another way, the ZOPA is the space between the seller's reservation value and the buyer's reservation value. In the current negotiation, the ZOPA is any offer that falls between $42.65 million and $48 million:

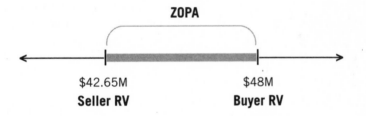

Figure 1.1: The Zone of Possible Agreement

The ZOPA contains all possible agreements because any point in this range is a possible final deal to which both parties could agree; any point outside of this range will be rejected by one of the two parties. You will reject any offer below $42.65 million; Connie Vega will reject any price above $48 million.

The ZOPA gives you the lay of the land, but tells you little about where exactly the negotiation will actually end. You will want to make a deal at a high price that is as close to Connie's reservation value as possible, while Connie will want the price to be as low as possible. And so the negotiation begins. Your task in this negotiation is not simply to get a deal, but to claim as much value as possible. Now that you have an idea about how much value is up for grabs ($48M–$42.65M = $5.35M), you are ready to do your best at claiming the lion's share of it.

MAKING THE DEAL

If you were a student in one of our negotiation courses, you would have approximately twenty minutes to negotiate this deal. This would give you enough time to reach an agreement because this is a relatively simple (price-only) negotiation. After the twenty minutes were up, we would collect all of the agreements—that is, the price agreed to by each buyer-seller pair—and then put them on the board for everyone to see. The reason for doing so is that it allows us to consider, during the class discussion, which strategies led to better (or worse) outcomes. But there is an additional benefit to making the results public: you would be amazed at how seriously most MBA and executive students take an exercise when their performance will be judged by a group of their peers!

To set up our own analysis of the case, let's consider how your negotiation with Connie might have unfolded:

You met with Connie and engaged in some small talk. You were glad to learn that Connie was indeed very interested in the property. As substantive discussions began, you took control and started to make the case for a high sale price. You also mentioned that you had received several other offers and that you were seriously considering one of them. To leverage the momentum you had created, you then made an aggressive opening offer: "Considering the fact that multiple parties are showing an interest in this property, and the fact that the land is worth 20 percent more when used for condominium development, we believe that a $49 million sale price is both fair and acceptable." Connie seemed taken aback; she shook her head as she responded: "Well, that is certainly not what we had expected." Just as you began to wonder whether you had asked for too much, Connie, to your great relief, decided to make a counteroffer: $45 million. This offer already exceeded your RV (excellent!), but you wanted to make as much profit as you could, so you continued to haggle. At the end of the day, you were able to convince Connie to accept a price of $46 million.

How would you feel at the end of this negotiation? What did you do right? What, if anything, could you have done better? How can you evaluate whether you got a good deal, a great deal, or a bad deal?

NEGOTIATION POSTMORTEM

One way to evaluate your performance is to ask whether you surpassed your reservation value: clearly, you did. While this is certainly good news, it may not be a great measure of negotiation success. Why? Because it's possible to surpass your RV and yet only claim a small portion of the total value up for grabs. Another way to evaluate your performance is to consider the entire ZOPA. The price you negotiated ($46 million) seems closer to Connie's RV than yours, suggesting that you claimed significantly more than 50 percent of the value that was up for grabs (though not all of it). Depending on how high your aspirations were at the outset of this negotiation, you might be happy or displeased with this outcome.

While these two metrics are useful, they both suffer from one important drawback: they evaluate your performance relative only to what you knew *before* the negotiation. A more complete measure would evaluate your outcome according to what you could have discovered *during* the negotiation. How would you feel if you discovered that Connie's RV was not $48 million but $46 million? Presumably, you would feel that you did even better than you had originally thought: you captured all of the ZOPA. Alternatively, how would you feel if Connie's RV was much higher—$55 or $60 million? In that case, Connie would have captured the lion's share of the value. As you can see, how well you actually performed in this negotiation depends on an evaluation of how well you *could* have done.

Now consider some information that only Connie knew at the outset of the negotiation:

- Estate One was actually *not* interested in developing the Hamilton property for residential construction; they hoped to use this property to enter the commercial development industry.
- Connie Vega, with her strong political ties, was among the first to know that zoning laws in Hamilton were scheduled to change in the coming months, making commercial development possible.
- Estate One would have been willing to pay up to $60 million to purchase the Hamilton property.

Given this new information, how should we evaluate the deal you negotiated? Clearly, the $46 million sale price looks a lot less impressive! In this new light, the outcome you negotiated is much closer to *your* RV than it is to Connie's. It looks as if Connie captured most of the value that was up for grabs. You could have done much better! But then again, is it really fair to evaluate your outcome relative to information that you did not even have during the negotiation?

We think so. Negotiation geniuses are not bound by their circumstance nor limited by the information with which they are endowed. Negotiation geniuses know how to act on information they have, acquire information they do not have, and protect themselves from information they cannot obtain. As a result, they evaluate their performance by the strictest of standards.

COMMON NEGOTIATOR MISTAKES

Now that you have more information about what was happening on the other side of the table, take another look at your negotiation with Connie Vega. In hindsight, what mistakes did you make? What might you have done differently? How could you have claimed a larger share of the ZOPA?

To start, here are a few clear mistakes:

1. You made the first offer when you were not in a strong position to do so.
2. You made a first offer that was not sufficiently aggressive.
3. You talked but did not listen.
4. You tried to influence the other party but did not try to learn from her.
5. You did not challenge your assumptions about the other party.
6. You miscalculated the ZOPA and did not reevaluate it during the negotiation.
7. You made greater concessions than the other party did.

As it turns out, these mistakes are among the most common that negotiators make as they attempt to claim value in a deal. In the following sections, we will introduce you to a better approach to the Hamilton negotiation—and to negotiations more generally—by answering a series of questions that executives, students, and clients have asked us hundreds of times. In doing so, our goal is not only to equip you with effective negotiation strategies, but also to provide you with an understanding of important psychological principles that will help you anticipate and respond to the negotiation behaviors of others.

SHOULD YOU MAKE THE FIRST OFFER?

When we pose this question to the executives in our classes, most insist that you should *never* make the first offer. Instead, they say, let the other party make the first offer; this provides valuable information and tells you where they are coming from. But there are also many executives who believe you should *always* make the first offer; by doing so, they argue, you take control of the dialogue and negotiate "on your terms." The right answer—hardly surprising to those who know a trick question when they see one—is "it depends."

The primary benefit of making a first offer in negotiation is that it establishes an *anchor*. An anchor is a number that focuses the other negotiator's attention and expectations. Especially when the other party is uncertain about the correct, fair, or appropriate outcome, they are likely to gravitate toward any number that helps them focus and resolve their uncertainty. As it turns out, first offers tend to serve this purpose well: they anchor the negotiation and strongly influence the final outcome.

For example, imagine that you calculated Connie's reservation value to be $48 million and that you expected her to make an aggressive first offer of about $40 million. If, instead, she makes a first offer of $32 million, you are likely to start questioning your assessment of Connie's RV. Would Connie start so low if she could actually pay as much as $48 million? Is Estate One planning to build apartments, not condominiums? Perhaps their maximum willingness to pay is much lower than $48 million. When the other party sets an anchor, it influences not only your perceptions of their RV (and, hence, of the ZOPA), but also your counteroffer. You may have planned to start the negotiation at $50 million, but given Connie's surprisingly low first offer, you now begin to think that you should start a little lower. An offer of $50 million now seems extreme, carrying with it the risk of impasse. Instead, you counter the $32 million offer with a more reasonable-sounding offer of $45 million. Connie's anchor has worked.

The power of anchors is substantial. Research has shown that anchors affect even those with negotiation experience and expertise. In one remarkable demonstration of the power of anchors, professors Greg Northcraft and Margaret Neale invited real-estate agents to evaluate a house that was for sale.[4] The agents were allowed to walk through the house and the neighborhood, and were given a Multiple Listing Service (MLS) information sheet that provided details about the house, including its size and dimensions, the year it was built, the amenities included, et cetera. They were also given detailed information about other properties located in the same neighborhood. The information provided to each agent was identical with one exception: the "list price" on the MLS sheet that was given to the agent was randomly picked from one of the following: (a) $119,000, (b) $129,000, (c) $139,000, or (d) 149,000.

In real estate, the list price is the "first offer" made by the seller. Thus, this study manipulated the first offer to see whether it would affect the perceptions of experienced real-estate agents. After seeing the house and reading all of the information, agents were asked to evaluate the house on four dimensions:

1. What is an appropriate list price for this house? *(Appropriate List Price)*
2. What do you estimate is the appraisal value of this house? *(Appraisal Value)*
3. As a buyer, what is a reasonable amount to pay for the house? *(Willingness to Pay)*
4. What is the lowest offer you would accept for this house if you were the seller? *(Lowest Acceptable Offer)*

Figure 1.2 graphs the responses to these questions by agents who were provided each of the list prices. As you can see, agents were strongly influenced by whichever list price they were arbitrarily assigned! On every measure, those given a higher list price thought the house was worth more than did those given a lower list price. Furthermore, when the agents were asked whether their answers had been influenced *at all* by the list price given to them on the information sheet, more than 80 percent of them said no.

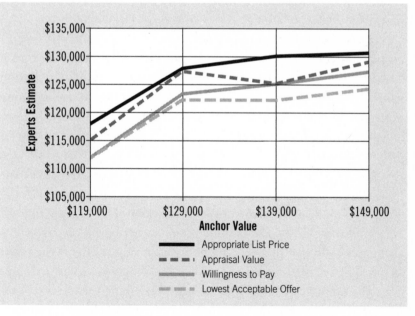

Figure 1.2 The Powerful Effects of Anchoring

Given the powerful effects of anchoring, it becomes clear that there may be an advantage to making an aggressive first offer in a negotiation. Why, then, is it sometimes better to let the other party make the first move?

When made prematurely, a first offer can be extremely costly. Consider what happened in the Hamilton negotiation. Your "aggressive" first offer of $49 million was based on your belief that Connie's reservation value was $48 million. As it turns out, your perception was incorrect, and the first offer was disastrously low. (No wonder Connie looked taken aback when you made it!) Because Connie's actual RV was $60 million, you probably could have negotiated a much higher sale price than you actually did. However, the moment you made a first offer of $49 million, you set the upper limit for what you could possibly capture. In other words, you lost your claim to a large portion of the ZOPA by making a first offer that was well below the other party's reservation value. It's not every day that you lose $11 million simply by opening your mouth! Yet even experienced negotiators who stand to lose thousands or millions of dollars often err by making a first offer when they are not in a position to do so wisely.

As this discussion suggests, whether you should make the first offer or not depends upon how much information you have. If you believe you have sufficient information about the other side's reservation value, it pays to make a reasonable (i.e., *sufficiently* aggressive) opening offer that anchors the discussion in your favor. If you suspect that you may not have enough information about the ZOPA, you'd be wise to defer an opening offer until you have collected more information. In this case, it may even be a good idea to let the other party make the first offer. You might forgo the opportunity to anchor the negotiation, but you also avoid the downside of not anchoring aggressively enough. Notice that a lack of information can also lead you to anchor *too* aggressively, demanding an amount that might offend the other side and drive them away. In other words, asking for too little diminishes the amount of value you can capture; asking for too much diminishes your chances of consummating the deal. As we will discuss shortly, negotiation geniuses know how to balance these two concerns, and they know which factors to consider when structuring their initial offer.

HOW SHOULD YOU RESPOND
TO THEIR INITIAL OFFER?

When the other party makes the first move, you become vulnerable to the effects of anchoring. Because anchoring effects can be very subtle, this is likely to be true even if you are aware of these effects. However, there are a number of ways you can protect yourself from being overly influenced by the other side's anchor:

STRATEGY 1: IGNORE THE ANCHOR

The best thing to do in the event that the other party makes an aggressive first offer—whether high or low—is to ignore it. This doesn't mean you should pretend you didn't hear it. Rather, respond to this effect: "Judging by your offer, I think we might be looking at this deal in very different ways. Let's try to bridge that gap by discussing . . ." In this manner, you can shift the conversation to an entirely different topic, one that allows you to reassert control of the discussion.

STRATEGY 2: SEPARATE INFORMATION FROM INFLUENCE

Every offer is a combination of *information* and *influence*. The other party's offer tells you something about what she believes and what she wants (information), but it also has the power to derail your strategy (influence). Your task is to separate the information contained in the particulars of the offer (and the way in which it was made) from the other side's attempt to influence your perceptions. The best way to stave off influence is to stick to your original game plan. If you walked in with a prepared first offer, don't allow the other side's anchor to soften it. This does not mean that you should ignore substantial information that changes your beliefs about the actual ZOPA. For example, if the other side has just provided credible evidence that she has an attractive offer from a competitor of yours, this might be reason to adjust your counteroffer. However, it is important to realize that anchors will affect perceptions and counteroffers even in the absence of any real information provided to you. For example, the negotiator's mind can sometimes fail to distinguish between these two statements:

- *Information and Influence:* "We have received a better offer from Company X. As a result, we think your initial offer is low. We would like you to increase it to $7 million."
- *Influence Only:* "As you know, there are other companies with whom we do business. We have spoken with them. As a result, we think your initial offer is low. We would like you to increase it to $7 million."

The first statement provides some (but not much) substantive information that should prompt you to think about whether to accept, challenge, or question the statement being made. The second statement simply reiterates what you already knew, but uses phraseology that helps the other side emphasize its anchor. Thus, you have every reason to ignore this statement.

STRATEGY 3: AVOID DWELLING ON THEIR ANCHOR

Many negotiators believe that if someone anchors aggressively, you should push them to justify the anchor, thereby exposing the frivolous nature of their extreme demands. This is a dangerous strategy. Why? Because the more an anchor is discussed in a negotiation, the more powerful it becomes. If you ask the other party to justify their offer or discuss it further (e.g., "How did you come up with that number?"), you increase the power of that anchor to define the negotiation parameters. Almost always, your counterpart will find a way to frame the negotiation such that their offer makes at least a modicum of sense.

On the other hand, you do not want to miss out on the opportunity to learn something new about the deal or about your counterpart's perspective. To resolve this dilemma, try the following: if you are surprised by their offer, probe a little to find out if there is in fact any substantive new information that you can obtain. If no such information is forthcoming, quickly shift attention away from the anchor by sharing your own perspective and defining the negotiation in your terms.

STRATEGY 4: MAKE AN ANCHORED COUNTEROFFER, THEN PROPOSE MODERATION

Finally, if it is not possible to ignore or dismiss the other party's anchor, you should offset its influence by making an aggressive counteroffer. In doing so, you retain the ability to capture as much of the ZOPA as possible. However, countering aggression with aggression comes at a risk: the possibility that both parties will become entrenched and reach an impasse. To mitigate this risk, you should offset their anchor with an aggressive counteroffer, and then suggest that you need to work together to bridge the gap. In addition, you should offer to make the first move toward moderation by discussing your own perspective (i.e., by justifying your aggressive counteroffer). This allows you to deflate their anchor while shifting from an aggressive exchange to a quest for common ground. For example, in response to an aggressive anchor, you might say:

> Well, based on your offer, which was unexpected, it looks like we have a *lot* of work ahead of us. From our perspective, a fair price would be closer to $X [your counter-anchor]. I will explain to you how *we* are valuing this deal, but it appears to me that if we are to reach any agreement, we will both have to work together to make it happen.

STRATEGY 5: GIVE THEM TIME TO MODERATE THEIR OFFER WITHOUT LOSING FACE

If the other party's initial offer is *very* extreme—far outside the ZOPA—you may need to inform them that their offer is not even a basis for starting the discussion. This assertion should be followed by information regarding your own perspective and a candid invitation to reopen negotiations from a very different starting point.

Of course, it may not be easy for them to quickly reduce their demands so drastically—doing so would reveal that they were simply posturing when they made their initial offer. As a result, you may want to give them some time to "think about it." If they decide to moderate their demands, they will need time to save face. They can return to the bargaining table in a day or a week, after "having figured out a way to make this happen," "having re-crunched the numbers," or "having fought it out with our constituents." In other words, when reacting to very extreme offers, your foremost goal should be to re-anchor successfully, not to convey your outrage. And re-anchoring successfully often means helping the other side find a way to retract earlier demands and arguments.

WHAT SHOULD MY FIRST OFFER BE?

Suppose you have collected enough information before and during the negotiation to make an appropriate first offer. How aggressively should you anchor? There are four factors to consider:

1. Keep the entire ZOPA in play. How can you meet the goal of making an offer that keeps the entire ZOPA in play? By making an offer that falls *outside* the ZOPA—one that you know the other side will not accept. In this manner, when substantive negotiations begin, you will still have the ability to claim as much value as possible. The idea is to force the other party to *negotiate their way into* the ZOPA. If your first offer is already inside the ZOPA, you have given up the ability to claim value that lies between your offer and the other party's RV from the very start. In the Hamilton negotiation, your first offer ($49 million) was well within the actual ZOPA (as revealed to you after the fact), thereby eliminating the possibility of any agreement between $49 million and $60 million.

2. Provide a justification for your offer. How far outside the ZOPA should your offer be? Should your offer in the Hamilton negotiation have been $61 million? $70 million? $100 million? On the one hand, the higher your first offer, the more likely it is that *if* you reach an agreement, it will be closer to the other side's reservation value than to yours (and hence more profitable for you). However, the more aggressive your first offer, the more likely it is that the other party will be offended by it, think that you are not serious, or believe that there is no way of reaching an agreement with you.

How can you balance these concerns? First, consider the context: the degree of aggressiveness should be appropriate to the situation. In most real-world negotiation contexts, you will not want to be *too* far outside the ZOPA; otherwise, you lose credibility. In other situations (business disputes involving a mediator, contentious labor-management negotiations, haggling with a street vendor, et cetera), it is normal and expected for both parties to open with extreme demands. It would be unwise in these cases to moderate your demands too much because the other side is still likely to anchor aggressively.

To determine your exact offer, ask yourself the following question: "What is the most aggressive offer that I can *justify*?" You should never make an offer so extreme that it cannot be stated as follows: "I would like to propose X, because ..." If you cannot finish this sentence in any meaningful way, you are probably asking for too much.

In the Hamilton negotiation, you could have leveraged a variety of information to justify increasingly aggressive offers to Connie Vega, as follows:

- "We think **$48** million is a fair price because the *average* of recent sale prices in the area suggests that the land is worth $40 million and because condominium development makes the land worth 20 percent more."
- "We think **$52.8** million is a fair price because recent sale prices in the area suggest that the land is worth *as much as* $44 million and because condominium development makes the land worth 20 percent more."
- "We think **$60** million is a fair price because the land can be used for commercial development, which makes it worth *at least* one and a half times what it is worth if used for residential development (which is $40 million on average)."
- "We think **$88** million is a fair price because the land can be used for commercial development, which makes it worth *as much as* two times what it *might be* worth if used for residential development (which is $44 million)."

While Connie would surely respond to these different offers with varying levels of receptivity or apprehension, the inclusion of the justification would make it difficult for her to dismiss your offers out of hand. She may want to challenge your assumptions—but that's not a problem, as it increases the amount of time that you spend dwelling on your perspective and your anchor. Connie might want to aggressively bargain down the price—also okay, because you have opened high enough that she *should* work to negotiate into the ZOPA (and you should allow her to do so!).

Finally, the most aggressive offers ($60 and $88 million) are smart even if you do not believe that the property will be used for commercial development—and even if both of you know that it won't. Regardless, the anchor has been set, and the other side's counteroffer will likely be less aggressive than it otherwise would have been.

3. Set high, but realistic aspirations. In our negotiation seminars, we ask participants to write down their *target price*—that is, the outcome they *hope* to achieve—before the negotiation begins. After the simulation has concluded, we analyze the relationship between negotiators' target price and final negotiated price. These two correlate *highly;* that is, those who have more aggressive targets tend to achieve more favorable outcomes than do those with more modest goals.

Why? First, those who set high aspirations tend to make more aggressive first offers in order to reach their target. Thus, aspirations influence first offers, which in turn influence final prices. Second, those with aggressive targets work harder at haggling once both parties' opening offers are on the table. High aspirations serve as self-fulfilling prophecies; they motivate the kinds of behaviors that help us achieve aggressive targets.

This simple advice—"Always reach for the stars!"—is nonetheless often ignored by negotiators; few set explicit targets prior to negotiation. But targets that are inspired by high aspirations and yet grounded in reality (i.e., in your assessment of the ZOPA) are effective because they motivate behavior and minimize your susceptibility to influence tactics.

4. Consider the context and the relationship. The most important thing to consider when making *any* offer is the context of the negotiation. What type of relationship do you have with the other side? Will hard bargaining be ill-received? Are reputations at stake? What norms drive your interactions? For example, you might have evaluated the ZOPA perfectly and justified your offer brilliantly, but if you lose sight of the fact that your tactics could affect the relationship, you might lose the deal—or worse, lose the deal, damage the relationship, and ruin your reputation all at the same time. Thus, your offer and your justifications should be informed by your understanding of the needs and sensitivities of the relationship. Your goal should not simply be to get the best possible deal while preserving the relationship, but to get the best deal while *strengthening* the relationship and your reputation. You may have to forgo some short-term gains to meet this goal, but this sacrifice will almost always be worth the price.

HOW FAR CAN I PUSH THEM?

Knowing the other side's walk-away point tells you just how far they can be pushed—and how much value you can capture. Of course, the other side has no incentive to reveal their reservation value to you. How, then, can you obtain the information that will help you estimate their RV with greater accuracy? Here are the steps to follow:

Step 1. Exhaust all pre-negotiation sources of information. There are often dozens of ways to collect information that do not entail guessing or asking the other party directly. For example, in a real-world Hamilton negotiation, the seller should begin by talking to state and local politicians to assess the likelihood that commercial zoning laws will change. Connie Vega gained this information from her political ties, but that doesn't mean it is confidential. (And, note that your own confidential role information raised this issue as well.) You could have saved millions on the deal by seeking out this information. Here are other potential sources of information in the Hamilton case:

- Estate One board members or executives with whom you or others in your organization have ties.
- Individuals and firms that Estate One has dealt with in the past.
- Commercial developers who might be tracking proposed changes in zoning laws.
- Businesses near or in Hamilton that might be affected by proposed changes in zoning laws.
- Residents of Hamilton who may have heard about proposed changes in the zoning laws.

Consider another situation in which such background information is key: negotiating a job offer. Often, when MBA students come to us seeking advice regarding negotiations with prospective employers, they are confused about what is negotiable, the degree to which each issue is negotiable, and how much is reasonable to demand. When we ask them what they have done to resolve this uncertainty, they usually tell us that they have only discussed these questions informally with their classmates. That is certainly not enough of an effort. We encourage them to talk to students from their program who were hired the previous year by the same firm, friends and acquaintances who have worked in (or who have offers from) firms in the same industry, and staff in the MBA placement office. They can also obtain information from industry publications or from websites that provide hiring and salary data for a wide variety of professions. More generally, in any negotiation, once you know what you do not know, it is important to seek out all potential sources of information.

Gaining a clearer understanding of the ZOPA and the other side's interests is just one benefit of acquiring information prior to negotiation. Information also helps you to avoid being manipulated or lied to during the negotiation. If the other party perceives that you have done your homework, their willingness to deceive you decreases. Yet another potential benefit of gathering information prior to negotiation is that you are likely to be taken more seriously. Your counterpart may benefit from your ignorance, but do they really want to make a deal with someone who is completely unprepared? This is unlikely. Prepared negotiators not only make fewer strategic mistakes, they also command greater respect both during and after the negotiation.

Step 2. Identify your assumptions prior to the negotiation. Socrates is believed to have said: "I am likely to be wiser to this small extent, that I do not think I know what I do not know." Such wisdom about one's limitations is critical in negotiation. For example, you are unlikely ever to know the other side's exact reservation value. As a result, you do not know the ZOPA; you can only estimate the ZOPA—and revise that estimate as you gather more information.

Wise negotiators create a comprehensive list of what they are assuming and what they do not know prior to negotiation. In the Hamilton negotiation, you *assumed* that commercial development was not an option. What other assumptions did you make? Perhaps you assumed that Estate One does not know about your offer from Quincy. But what if they do? What if Connie knows the CEO of Quincy—and you have lied about the size of Quincy's offer?

Of course, in any negotiation, each party makes an infinite number of assumptions. You cannot keep track of each one—and you don't have to. But you *do* need to identify and be aware of all of the assumptions that underlie your planned course of action. For example, if you do not plan to refer to Quincy's bid, you don't have to worry about assumptions regarding Quincy. But because your plan *does* require an assessment of the other party's RV, you must keep in mind your assumptions regarding Estate One's plans for the land.

Step 3. Ask questions that challenge your assumptions. The wrong way to approach a negotiation is to start bargaining as if your assumptions are correct. Instead, ask questions to clarify matters. Consider these three alternative approaches to starting the Hamilton discussion:

A. "We understand that you might be interested in developing this land for the construction of luxury condominiums. We think that's great. Of course, we both understand that this makes the land quite valuable."

B. "Perhaps we should begin by discussing your needs. What are
your plans for this excellent piece of real estate?"
C. "If the land is used for *commercial* development, that will make
it quite valuable. With that in mind, let's discuss some specifics.
What are your plans for this excellent piece of real estate?"

Approach A has the merit of preparing the discussion for an aggressive anchor; the mention of the land's high value is a nice touch.
However, the problem with this approach is that it potentially gives
away $11 million. Even if Connie had been willing to truthfully an-
swer every question regarding Estate One's plans, the fact that you
didn't ask her any direct questions makes it easy for her to let you persist in your ignorance. Approach B potentially saves you up to $11 mil-
lion because it forces Connie to explicitly lie if she wants to convince
you that Estate One is not planning commercial development.
Approach C combines and improves on the merits of the previous approaches; here, you take an anchoring position and also ask a direct
question about Estate One's plans. This approach is even more powerful because it frames the question in terms of commercial development. This makes it difficult for Connie to lie, as it now sounds as if
you already know of Estate One's plans (even if you do not). Thus, this
approach—*anchoring, interrogating,* and *sounding sufficiently informed*—
encapsulates all the characteristics of an effective approach in the face
of uncertainty.

Step 4. Ask indirect questions. Naturally, the other party will sometimes refuse to answer questions that could help you determine their
reservation value. In that case, you need to ask questions that are less
direct—and less threatening. For example, you might ask Connie
about the challenges her company faces, what Estate One hopes to accomplish in the next ten years, what kinds of projects you might be
able to help them with in the future, or how the Hamilton purchase
fits into their portfolio of projects. Given that Estate One is not a
competitor of yours, these are reasonable questions for you to ask and
for her to answer.

Similarly, consider the questions that our MBA job candidate might ask prospective employers to determine the hiring manager's likely reservation value:

- How many hours do employees typically work each week?
- What kinds of projects will I be working on?
- Who will my clients be?
- Whom does the firm typically hire?
- With whom does the firm typically compete for hiring?
- What, if any, are the formal constraints on compensation for new hires?

Step 5. Protect yourself from lies and uncertainty with contingency contracts.
Suppose you have done everything right: you have identified what you do not know, you have exhausted all sources of information prior to negotiation, and you have done everything you possibly can to obtain information from the other side. Yet you remain uncomfortable because you still lack certain vital information. For example, imagine that Connie has told you that Estate One will *not* use the Hamilton property for commercial development. Although you have no way of knowing with any certainty, you believe this is a lie. What should you do now?

Consider the use of a *contingency contract*. Contingency contracts are agreements that leave certain elements of the deal unresolved until uncertainty is resolved in the future. In the Hamilton negotiation, a contingency contract might state: "The sale will be made at a base price of $46 million, with the condition that if the land is used for commercial development in the next seven years, Estate One will pay an additional $10 million to Pearl Investments." The moment this clause is included in the agreement, Estate One no longer has a motivation to lie! Because the sale price is now tied to Estate One's plans, they cannot benefit from deceiving you. Furthermore, even if Connie was *not* lying (i.e., Estate One is not currently planning commercial development), the contingency contract protects you against a future change of plans by Estate One.

Notice that if Estate One *is* planning to use the land for commercial development, and if Connie wants to keep this a secret, she will likely resist the inclusion of your proposed contingency contract.

What then? Her unwillingness to agree to the contingency should be a warning sign that something could be very wrong! Why would she resist this clause if Estate One were entirely uninterested in commercial development? Thus, contingency contracts not only protect you from lies, but also help you detect lies.

EFFECTIVE HAGGLING STRATEGIES

When most people think about negotiation, they think about *haggling*—the iterative give-and-take that takes place after each party has made its initial offer. Haggling is a necessary component of every negotiation. Why? Because it is not sufficient that parties discuss options that exist within the ZOPA; to reach a specific negotiated agreement, they must coordinate and ratify a mutually acceptable final deal. Since neither party wants to concede more than the other, each tends to concede slowly and, typically, only in response to the other side's concessions. Nonetheless, some negotiators are excellent hagglers, while others fall prey to the other side's influence tactics and end up conceding too much. In addition, some negotiators fail to take basic steps to ensure that the other party will not take advantage of them. Here we consider each of these issues and offer specific advice about effective haggling.

STRATEGY 1: FOCUS ON THE OTHER PARTY'S BATNA AND RESERVATION VALUE

Think back to when Roosevelt's campaign manager discovered that he might owe as much as $3 million to a photographer. Instead of focusing on his own weak BATNA (reprint millions of brochures), the manager focused on the photographer's weak BATNA (make no money and lose a publicity opportunity). In doing so, the manager not only avoided paying a high price, but also made some money on the deal. Negotiators who focus on their own BATNA (i.e., "What can I do without the other party?") tend not to set high aspirations and are happy getting anything better than their RV. Meanwhile, those who focus on the other party's BATNA ("What will they do without me?") are paying attention to the amount of value they bring to the other party. These folks tend to set higher aspirations and capture more value in the deals they negotiate.

STRATEGY 2: AVOID MAKING UNILATERAL CONCESSIONS

Once each party has made an initial offer, it's time to take measured steps toward a mutually acceptable agreement. Negotiation geniuses are willing to be flexible and to make concessions, but they also demand reciprocity. It is important to avoid making unilateral concessions. Luckily, a *norm of reciprocity* pervades most negotiation contexts: parties widely expect and understand that they will take turns making concessions. If the other party violates this norm, you should rectify this problem immediately. The next five points show how to do so.

STRATEGY 3: BE COMFORTABLE WITH SILENCE

Many people are uncomfortable with silence. As a result, they speak when they should not. A particularly dangerous time to speak is after you have made your offer and the other side is considering it. If the other side seems to be taking too long to respond, negotiators often grow nervous and start bargaining against themselves. Before your counterpart has even voiced a concern or a grievance, you might be tempted to retract your offer or to make further concessions.

Experienced negotiators have told us that they use silence to their advantage in exactly this way. Instead of responding negatively to an offer, they simply wait it out. Very often, the party that has made the offer will begin to qualify it, moderate it, or simply signal a greater willingness to concede. Effective negotiators understand not only the power of silence, but also the need to be comfortable with it. Just remind yourself that if you speak when it is *their* turn, you will be paying by the word.

STRATEGY 4: LABEL YOUR CONCESSIONS

According to the norm of reciprocity, negotiators should reciprocate the concessions made by others. Because people are hardwired to feel obligated when someone has provided them something of value, this norm is a powerful motivator of behavior. Yet people are also motivated to undervalue or ignore the concessions of others in order to *escape* feelings of obligation. Our research has shown that it is easy for people *not* to reciprocate when the other party's concessions are not top of mind.[6] For this reason, it is critical to label your concessions. Instead of simply giving something away or moderating your demands, make it clear that your action is costly to you. Because labeled concessions are hard to ignore, it becomes difficult for recipients to justify nonreciprocity.

STRATEGY 5: DEFINE WHAT IT MEANS TO RECIPROCATE

Reciprocity is even more likely if you not only label your concession, but specify what you expect in return. This strategy eliminates another piece of ambiguity. Even if the other side acknowledges your concession, they might still reciprocate with something of low value unless you make it clear that such a move does not fulfill their obligation to reciprocate. For example, your concession might take the following form: "I understand that we are still millions of dollars apart. I'm willing to moderate my demands, though this will be very costly to me. I'm making a concession with the understanding that you will reciprocate with concessions of similar magnitude. This is the only way we will be able to reach an agreement we both can accept."

STRATEGY 6: MAKE CONTINGENT CONCESSIONS

Contingent concessions explicitly tie your concessions to specific actions by the other party. In other words, you can phrase your concessions in a quid-pro-quo manner to clarify that you will only make them if the other party does their part. For example: "I can pay a higher price if you can promise me early delivery."

While such concessions are among the safest a negotiator can make, that doesn't mean they are always appropriate. The more conditions you place on your concessions and your willingness to cooperate, the more difficult it may be to build trust and strengthen the relationship. Thus, contingent concessions should be used as needed, but not overused.

STRATEGY 7: BE AWARE OF THE EFFECTS OF DIMINISHING RATES OF CONCESSIONS

In most negotiations, concession rates follow a pattern: early concessions are larger in size than later concessions. In other words, negotiators tend to offer diminishing rates of concessions over the course of the negotiation. For example, at the car dealership, the salesperson might start at $45,000, then go to $44,000, then to $43,500, then to $43,300. This may be a reasonable trend; as a negotiator gets closer to his reservation value, there is less room for large concessions. As a result, most negotiators expect this pattern and take it as a signal that the other party's RV is approaching. But it's also possible that the other party could use this expectation strategically. That is, a party that is far from his RV might suggest that he is running out of room by offering concessions that quickly diminish in size. It is important to consider this possibility when updating your beliefs regarding the true size of the ZOPA.

NEGOTIATING THE RELATIONSHIP

Many people believe that you can either get a great deal for yourself, or you can play nice and make the other side happy. As it turns out, this is not the way it works. Whether the relationship is strengthened, weakened, or destroyed in the negotiation *does* depend on how satisfied each party is with the final outcome—but satisfaction has less to do with how well someone *actually* negotiated and much more to do with how well they *think* they negotiated. With this in mind, negotiation geniuses not only manage their own outcomes, they also manage the other side's satisfaction. Put simply: you are negotiating not just the deal, but also the relationship.

The people with whom you negotiate will be satisfied to the degree that they believe they got a good deal, the degree to which they felt respected, and the degree to which they felt the outcome was equitable. This means that your reputation as a negotiator hinges on your ability to manage the other party's perceptions. Lest this advice be viewed as Machiavellian, keep in mind that we are not recommending that you surreptitiously take advantage of the other side. Indeed, some negotiators will get a *bad* deal for themselves (by giving up too much value) and yet manage the process so poorly that they also destroy their relationship with the other party. What we want you to keep in mind is that you always have two distinct goals in any negotiation: to get a good deal and to strengthen your relationship. Ignoring either one can be disastrous. Here are some of the ways that this plays out at the bargaining table.

1. Responding to an offer that you love—one approach. Imagine that you have done your homework and carefully evaluated the ZOPA. You have thought hard about your first offer and have come up with one that you believe to be aggressive; it falls outside the ZOPA and should serve to anchor the negotiation effectively. You make the offer. The response? The other party grins and accepts your offer immediately! How do you feel? In all likelihood, you feel terrible. It dawns on you that you have misjudged the ZOPA, made a poor first offer, and failed to capture much of the value that was up for grabs. You blew it!

Now turn the situation around. Imagine that the other side has made a first offer that you find surprisingly attractive. How should you respond? If you accept too quickly or too enthusiastically, you are likely to upset the other party. To increase their satisfaction from the deal, you might take some time to ponder the offer. Then, when you eventually accept the offer without enthusiasm, they are likely to feel that they got a great deal. The outcome is the same in both cases, but the latter approach makes the other side happier.

2. Responding to an offer that you love—another approach. If you really want to increase your counterpart's satisfaction from the deal, you might want to do more than simply wait before you respond. If you accept their first offer, even begrudgingly, they are likely to feel some regret and wonder whether they could have gotten more from you. This suggests a different strategy: make a counteroffer and ask for additional concessions. That is, if you *really* want the other side to feel satisfied with the negotiation, take more of their money! Even if they have to make some nominal concessions, they will be happier than if you accepted their first offer. This interesting result wonderfully illustrates the dissociation between outcomes and satisfaction in negotiation:

satisfaction has everything to do with how well you think you did, and often little or nothing to do with how well you actually did.

3. Responding to an offer that you love—yet another approach. Consider the following anecdote from Professor Richard Shell's book *Bargaining for Advantage*.[7] When, in the early 1930s, the Institute for Advanced Study at Princeton University was recruiting Albert Einstein, the head of the institute wrote to Einstein asking him how much he expected to be paid. Einstein wrote back: "$3,000 (annually), unless you think I can get by with less." Now, this seems like a surprisingly dim-witted first offer from a man as smart as Einstein. But look at Princeton's response: "We'll pay you $15,000 a year." Einstein accepted and the deal was done.

Why didn't Princeton accept Einstein's low offer or, better yet, negotiate an even lower salary? For one thing, as the adage proclaims, "Time reveals truth." Writing from Austria, Einstein may not have known how much he was worth to Princeton, but this would change when he joined the faculty in the United States. In other words, Einstein's perception of the ZOPA may have been inaccurate while negotiations were under way; eventually, however, he would update his assessment. When he did, he might feel as if Princeton had negotiated in bad faith by accepting his uninformed initial offer. In addition, by offering Einstein five times what he requested, Princeton administrators sent a strong signal about the school's integrity, their interest in his well-being, and their desire to negotiate in good faith. By declining to take advantage of his attractive first offer, they might have cheaply "purchased" the kind of loyalty and strong relationship that is hard to come by at the bargaining table.

More generally, this story suggests that sometimes the smartest response to an offer that you love is to *give something back*. If you have been given an opportunity to strengthen the relationship or enhance your reputation, and all you need to do is reciprocate in kind to a generous (i.e., not aggressive) opening offer, it may be foolish to do otherwise.

4. Responding to an offer that you love—a caveat! So far we have looked at this issue under the assumption that the other party has made a

poor first offer that allows you to capture most of the value in the negotiation. But this assumes that *your* evaluation of the ZOPA is the
correct one! As we have discussed earlier, such assumptions can be
costly. If the other side makes an offer that appears to give you everything you could hope for and more, it is critical that you stop and ask
yourself: "What do they know that I don't?"

For example, if the other side offers to buy something from you for
more than you could have dreamed, you should ask yourself whether
you made a mistake in estimating their reservation value. Maybe the
item you are selling is more valuable than you thought. Maybe they
are more desperate than you expected, or have a lot more money than
you thought. In short, *if you are surprised by an offer, don't celebrate—
think!* You might still decide that they have made too generous an offer, but it is better to postpone your counteroffer until you are sure
you know where things stand.

MANAGING YOUR OWN SATISFACTION

Earlier, we stated that one way to obtain better outcomes is to have
high aspirations; those who set aggressive targets tend to capture
more value. Here's something we neglected to mention: those who set
aggressive targets and get better outcomes as a result also tend to be
less satisfied with the deals they negotiate![8] Why? Because when the
negotiation is over, they compare their final outcome to their high initial aspirations. Naturally, those with high aspirations will be more
likely to fall short, even though they achieved better outcomes than
those who set low aspirations.

Thus, increasing your satisfaction with a deal requires a simple
change of mental habits: focus on your target *during* the negotiation;
when it is over, shift your focus to your reservation value. By doing so,
you will negotiate effectively (thanks to your high aspirations) and
still be satisfied with your outcome afterward (because you are now
comparing it with your RV). Because your satisfaction with a deal depends on your point of comparison, or *reference point*, it pays to pick a
low reference point when there is nothing more that you can do to
change the outcome.

BEYOND CLAIMING VALUE

So far, our focus has been almost exclusively on claiming value at the bargaining table. But claiming value is simply the tip of the iceberg in negotiation. In the next chapter, we begin to focus on a much more critical topic—one that is all too often ignored by even the most experienced negotiators: how to *create* value in negotiation. Negotiators who ignore this vital aspect of bargaining do so to their great disappointment and disadvantage.

CHAPTER 2

Creating Value
in Negotiation

By October 2000, Richard Holbrooke, U.S. ambassador to the United Nations, was facing a rapidly deteriorating situation. Members of the U.S. Senate were calling for a U.S. withdrawal from the United Nations. Meanwhile, at the UN, U.S. representatives were being sidelined in committee meetings, and the United States was on the verge of losing its vote in the General Assembly. The conflict was over a large sum of money—more than $1 billion. The United States owed this amount in arrears to the UN, but was unwilling to pay unless the UN agreed to a variety of reforms.

The conflict could be traced back to the founding of the United Nations. In 1945, the United States had agreed to pay 50 percent of the UN's yearly regular budget. The amount owed by each country was recalibrated several times over the ensuing years as other nations began to develop economically and wanted more influence in the UN. The most recent adjustment affecting the United States had been in 1972, when the U.S. assessment was reduced to 25 percent of the regular UN budget. The U.S. was also paying approximately 30 percent of the peacekeeping budget, which, due to conflicts in Somalia, Rwanda, and Bosnia, was increasingly seen as an unpredictable and hefty commitment. As a result, by the end of the decade, the United States was demanding another recalibration of assessments. Feeling that the United States was paying too high a share of the dues, Congress decided to hold the nearly $1 billion debt hostage. The U.S. demand (as manifested in the Helms-Biden bill) was this: the United States would pay what it owed if the UN agreed to a variety of reforms, in particular a reduction of the U.S. assessment from 25 percent to 22 percent.

There were three serious problems with this demand. First, other nations viewed it as unfair: the United States was essentially asking for a concession in return for something it already owed. Second, this was not a two-party negotiation in which the United States simply had to convince a UN delegation. Because UN regulations stipulated that such a change could only be approved with the consensus of all UN member states, Ambassador Holbrooke would have to convince all 189 countries to agree to the U.S. demands. Third, Holbrooke was facing a deadline. The Helms-Biden bill had appropriated $1 billion toward payment of arrears, but this money would disappear from the budget on January 1, 2001.

It became clear early in the process that negotiations between the UN and the United States would not be easy. Holbrooke's team had hoped that Japan and the Europeans would pick up most of the slack created by the reduction in U.S. assessments. The Japanese, however, made it clear that not only were they unwilling to increase their dues, but that if the U.S. received a reduction, they, too, would demand one. Japan was the second-highest contributor to the UN, paying a little over 20 percent of the regular budget. The Japanese felt this amount was too high given that Japan did not even have a seat on the UN Security Council. The Europeans also appeared extremely hesitant to approve an increase in their assessments.

In the face of such resistance, how could Holbrooke and his team convince even one nation to increase its assessment? How could they avoid an impasse?

As the year 2000 wore on, Holbrooke and his team decided to start from scratch. They drew up a chart of every UN member state and determined how much each was currently paying. They then began to visit representatives from every single country—not to convince them, but simply to understand their perspective. They quickly confirmed that no country wanted an increase in its assessment. But that was not the whole story. Holbrooke pushed further in his discussions to discover *why* they could not pay more. The reasons varied widely, but one important—and unforeseen—reason soon became salient. One of the problems faced by many countries—that would otherwise agree to increase their contributions—was the fact that fiscal year 2000 was coming to an end, and their federal budgets for 2001 were already fixed. Holbrooke was asking for a change in assessments before January 1, 2001. This deadline was making the deal unworkable.

As the reason underlying the reticence of these UN member states became apparent, so did the solution. Holbrooke proposed that the U.S. assessments be reduced from 25 percent to 22 percent immediately to meet the Helms-Biden deadline, but that other nations not be asked to increase their contributions until 2002. "That made a fantastic difference," recalled Ambassador Holbrooke, "that really worked."[1]

On the surface, the negotiation with UN member states appeared to be a *zero-sum negotiation:* whatever one party gained resulted in an equivalent loss to another. As in the Hamilton Real Estate case discussed in Chapter 1, there appeared to be only one salient issue—in this case, assessments—and the parties were making incompatible demands. Holbrooke's genius lay in discovering that the dispute entailed not one but two issues: the *size* of assessments and their *timing.* Only when the negotiators stopped haggling over one divisive issue (assessment size) and broadened their focus to include the issue of timing could they strike a deal.

While the final agreement required compromise by both sides, it also allowed each side to get what it wanted most on the issue it cared about most: the U.S. got the assessment size it wanted, and other countries got the timing they wanted. You might still wonder how such a deal was possible, given that it would create a shortfall in dues for the year 2001. As it turns out, thanks to another successful negotiation by Ambassador Holbrooke, philanthropist Ted Turner agreed to cover the one-year budget shortfall with a personal donation of over $30 million, and the Republicans in Congress, though initially reluctant to permit a donation from a politically liberal contributor, eventually accepted the deal.

A MULTI-ISSUE NEGOTIATION

In Chapter 1, we looked at a relatively simple, one-issue negotiation that allowed us to begin developing our negotiation framework and to answer some important questions regarding negotiation strategy. As the Holbrooke negotiation suggests, however, dealmaking is often more complicated than it was in the Hamilton Real Estate case. Effective negotiators need to prepare to execute complex negotiations that entail multiple issues, complex analysis, and considerable uncertainty.

The case in this chapter contains many more variables and identifies additional tactics and strategies that should be part of your negotiation toolkit. Specifically, we will address questions such as these: How should you prepare for a multi-issue negotiation? Should you negotiate the easiest issues first, the hardest issues first, or neither? How should you structure your offers? How should you handle sharp differences in beliefs or expectations regarding the value of the deal? What is the role of compromise in negotiation? What should you do after negotiating an agreement?

The following case, entitled "Moms.com," concerns the sale of syndication rights for a television program. As in Hamilton Real Estate, you have been assigned the role of seller and given a packet of background information. How would you approach this negotiation?

MOMS.COM[2]

You are Terry Schiller, the syndicated sales representative for Hollyville, Inc., a multimedia corporation that specializes in producing television shows and motion pictures. You represent the company in negotiating the sale of syndicated programs to local television stations. Programs in syndication are typically sold to local stations after having run as regular shows on one of the major networks. While few shows ever make it into syndication, revenue from the sale of syndication rights can be a major component of a producer's revenue.

Your firm, Hollyville, has just decided to release its one hundred episodes of *Moms.com,* a popular situation comedy ("sitcom"), to syndication this year. The plot of *Moms.com* revolves around three women who are trying to balance their lives as business executives and mothers of teenage children. The show has received strong ratings and appeals primarily to women in the 25–54 age bracket. This makes the show potentially quite valuable, as advertisers are willing to pay a great deal to reach this market.

Your current negotiation is focused on the Chicago market, in which two local stations are potential buyers. WWIN has already made you an offer. However, WCHI is the more attractive buyer because it has a stronger audience base in the 25–54 age bracket. How much a potential buyer is willing to pay for *Moms.com* depends on its expected advertising revenue from the show. Expected revenue, in turn, will depend on the ratings that the show receives. You estimate that the show will produce $7 million in net revenue over the life of the five-year contract if ratings fall within the 2–3 point range. (Rating points signify the percentage of all television households that are watching a particular show.) Advertising revenue would likely increase by $1 million with each point increase above a 3-point rating.

To evaluate the show's expected revenue to the buyer, you have estimated the likelihood of various ratings that it might receive. Your analysis appears in Table 2.1.

Table 2.1

Ratings	Likelihood	Ad Revenue Generated
2–3	10%	$7 million
3–4	10%	$8 million
4–5	10%	$9 million
5–6	50%	$10 million
6–7	20%	$11 million

You estimate that the show will likely receive a rating of 5–6, making it quite profitable for WCHI (even after taking into account the costs they will incur to market and run the show); thus, the station should be willing to pay you handsomely for *Moms.com.* The *licensing fee* that you negotiate with WCHI is the primary determinant of how much you make from the sale of *Moms.com.* You are hoping to negotiate a licensing fee close to $7 million for the five-year contract.

While licensing fee is a salient feature of the agreement, for the deal to be finalized, you and the seller must also agree on another important issue: *runs per episode.* The show's expected revenues (as calculated above) assume that the buyer has the right to run each of the one hundred episodes six times over the term of the contract. (Six runs per episode is the current industry standard for this particular market.) However, WCHI has already alerted you that it wants the right to run each episode eight times. You want to avoid "overexposing" the show and prefer that runs per episode be limited to four. If the same episode of the show is aired too often, the residual value of the show diminishes. When the contract term ends, and the rights to *Moms.com* return to Hollyville, it will be a much less valuable show if all of the episodes have already been shown many times.

The financial impact of this diminishing residual value is significant. Table 2.2 shows how the number of runs will affect your expected revenue from the show after the contract term ends. Your analysts project that for each additional run per episode above six that you allow you will lose an estimated $250,000. If you can limit the number of runs to less than six, you can save up to $500,000.

Table 2.2

Runs per Episode	Effect on Your Revenue
4	Save $500,000
5	Save $250,000
6	No effect
7	Lose $250,000
8	Lose $500,000

While your goal in this negotiation is to get the best deal possible, you also want to maintain a good working relationship with WCHI because it is possible that you (Hollyville) would do more business with the station in the near future. For example, Hollyville is very interested in selling a new show, *Juniors*, for the upcoming season. (Another Chicago station has already offered you $1 million for *Juniors*, however, an offer you are inclined to accept.)

Your assigned task in the current negotiation, then, is to structure an agreement for the sale of *Moms.com* that maximizes profit, preserves the relationship, and is superior to pursuing your BATNA. Your BATNA is to sell *Moms.com* to WWIN; the deal you have negotiated with that station is worth $3.5 million (you have agreed to six runs per episode with WWIN). If you are to finalize the deal with WCHI instead, you must agree on both the licensing fee and the number of runs. Hollyville management has asked you to report back after the negotiation with the agreed-upon terms on both of these issues and on any other terms of the signed contract. You will be negotiating with Kim Taylor, the general manager of WCHI.

Take some time to think about how you would approach this negotiation. How would you prepare? Which issue would you discuss first? How would you structure your offer? What information, if any, would you plan to share? What information, if any, would you try to acquire? How would you incorporate the lessons of Chapter 1 into your negotiation strategy? Once you have thought through these questions and others that may occur to you, read ahead as we narrate how your negotiation might have unfolded.

MAKING THE DEAL

You and Kim met and quickly got down to the business at hand. You suggested that while there were many issues to discuss, licensing fee had the biggest financial impact and should be discussed first. You had thought ahead about WCHI's BATNA and RV, and felt comfortable making an aggressive first offer. You asked for $9 million and justified this figure using selective precedents involving prior shows you had sold. Kim made it clear that he did not like your offer at all, but he stayed at the table. The two of you discussed the licensing fee for the next hour. Kim argued that *Moms.com* would probably receive ratings of 3–4 and that advertising revenues would likely be much lower than the licensing fee you had proposed. You responded that your projections suggested the show would receive higher ratings (5–6). Privately, you were unsure whether Kim was being honest about his projections; it was in his interest to convince you that the show would earn low revenues in order to justify paying you less. At one point, Kim alluded to the possibility of purchasing *Juniors* from you. Because he seemed to be mentioning his interest in purchasing *Juniors* only as a way of softening your demands for *Moms.com*, you suggested that the *Juniors* discussion be kept separate. The rest of the negotiation focused on *Moms.com*. Eventually, you reached an agreement of $5.5 million for the licensing fee and turned your attention to number of runs. Kim opened aggressively on this issue, but you convinced him that you simply could not accept seven or eight runs; eventually you settled on six runs. In retrospect, any other outcome would have required one of you to make a larger compromise than the other, which could have soured the relationship. Having reached agreement on both issues, you submitted a report to Hollyville management that contained the following financial analysis:

Licensing fee received from WCHI:	$5,500,000
Revenue adjustment based on six runs:	No effect
Net revenue:	$5,500,000
Value of the BATNA (sell to WWIN):	– $3,500,000
Net value of the negotiated agreement:	$2,000,000

How would you feel at the end of this negotiation? What do you think you did right? What, if anything, could you have done better? How could you evaluate whether you got a good deal, a great deal, or a bad deal?

NEGOTIATION POSTMORTEM

The best way to evaluate how well you did is to systematically analyze how well you *could have* done. We do so by focusing on each issue in the negotiation from the perspective of both the buyer and the seller.

ISSUE 1: LICENSING FEE

You entered the negotiation hoping to negotiate a licensing fee close to $7 million. What you did not know was that Kim's reservation value was $6.5 million. In other words, WCHI would have been unwilling to pay any amount greater than this. Meanwhile, assuming six runs per episode, you would have been unwilling to accept any amount less than $3.5 million (the value of your BATNA). This means that there was $3 million of value up for grabs on this issue ($6.5 million−$3.5 million). Because you anchored sufficiently aggressively (at $9 million), you were able to capture much of the ZOPA by securing a $5.5 million licensing fee. When MBA students and executives participate in this exercise, we observe an extremely wide range of outcomes on this issue; some sellers successfully negotiate fees close to the reservation value of the buyer, while others agree to accept very low licensing fees. Much of the variance in outcomes is explained by the aggressiveness of opening offers and counteroffers. Another reason for different outcomes on this issue, of course, is that it is affected by how the other issue is handled.

ISSUE 2: RUNS PER EPISODE

The buyer pushed aggressively for seven or eight runs, but you would lose money if you allowed WCHI to air each *Moms.com* episode more than six times. You negotiated six runs and are fairly certain that you could not have pushed the buyer any lower on this issue. The agreement of six runs entailed a perfect compromise; you met in the middle of each side's opening demand. Sounds good, right?

Well, it isn't. To understand the critical mistake you made, consider Table 2.3, which reveals the financial impact of increasing the number of runs on Hollyville (which you knew) *and* on WCHI (which you did not know). Notice anything interesting? Clearly, this issue has a significant effect on revenue for both parties—but it has a *greater* impact on WCHI than on Hollyville. For each additional run granted, WCHI revenue increases by $800,000, but Hollyville revenue decreases by only $250,000. In other words, increasing runs helps WCHI more than it hurts Hollyville. What are the implications of this?

	Table 2.3	
Runs per Episode	*Effect on Hollyville's Revenue*	*Effect on WCHI's Revenue*
4	Save $500,000	Lose $1,600,000
5	Save $250,000	Lose $800,000
6	No effect	No effect
7	Lose $250,000	Save $800,000
8	Lose $500,000	Save $1,600,000

CREATING VALUE THROUGH LOGROLLING

Rational negotiators should agree to grant eight runs per episode to WCHI. By providing eight runs instead of six, the negotiators can *create* $1.1 million in total value ($1.6 million benefit to WCHI minus $500,000 cost to Hollyville). WCHI will obviously agree to this, but why should Hollyville? Because it is in Hollyville's best interest as well. Hollyville should agree to eight runs *in exchange for* other things that it values, such as a higher licensing fee. Let's see how this works by comparing your agreement with an alternative agreement that you could have negotiated:

Your original agreement (Agreement O):
  ➤ Licensing fee of $5.5 million, six runs per episode
Alternative agreement (Agreement X):
  ➤ Licensing fee of $6.5 million, eight runs per episode

Agreement X forces you to give up two additional runs but provides you with a higher licensing fee. What is the net impact of these changes? You lose $500,000 by giving up two additional runs but gain $1 million from the higher licensing fee. The result: you are better off by $500,000. How would this alternative agreement affect WCHI? WCHI would lose $1 million by giving you a higher licensing fee, but would gain $1.6 million from additional runs. The result: WCHI is better off by $600,000. In other words, Agreement X makes *both parties* better off!

Negotiations such as *Moms.com* differ fundamentally from negotiations such as Hamilton Real Estate in Chapter 1. One-issue negotiations such as Hamilton Real Estate, in which the two sides have directly opposing interests, are zero-sum (when one party gains something, the other side loses an equivalent amount). Negotiations with multiple issues, such as *Moms.com,* can be *non-zero-sum negotiations:* it is often possible for one party to achieve gains without hurting the other party. In short, negotiating multiple issues allows for *value creation.* In the *Moms.com* negotiation, negotiators maximize the "size of the pie" (i.e., the value of the deal) when they agree to eight runs. Table 2.4 shows the effect on value creation of revising your agreement.

		Value to	Total Value
Agreement	Value to You	WCHI	Created
Original (O)	$2,000,000	$1,000,000	$3,000,000
Revised (X)	$2,500,000	$1,600,000	$4,100,000

Table 2.4

As Table 2.4 suggests, the total value of the deal (when you reach Agreement X) is $4.1 million. By contrast, in your original deal (Agreement O), the total value is only $3.0 million. In other words, agreeing to eight runs creates $1.1 million in value. Meanwhile, negotiators who do not agree to sell eight runs end up with an outcome that *burns* money; these dollars cannot be recovered.

Note that the amount to which you agree for the licensing fee does not affect how much value is *created;* it only determines who captures a bigger piece of the pie. Because both parties value the licensing fee equally, any change in the fee helps one party to the same degree that it hurts the other party. In other words, this negotiation is not just about value creation; claiming value is still an important element. However, negotiation geniuses do not let the value-claiming component derail their value-creation strategies.

As the *Moms.com* case suggests, effective negotiators look for opportunities to create value by making trades across multiple issues—for example, giving up runs in exchange for a higher licensing fee. The act of trading across issues is called *logrolling*. Logrolling requires that you not only know your own priorities, but that you learn about the priorities of the other side. If the other side values something more than you do, you should give it to them in exchange for reciprocity on issues that are a higher priority for you. In his negotiations with the UN member nations, Ambassador Holbrooke demonstrated this knowledge implicitly. Once he discovered that the size of assessments was relatively less important to other nations than the timing of assessments, he structured a deal that gave the United States what it valued most (change in assessment amount) and gave other contributing nations what they valued most (delay in implementation).

Now imagine how negotiations might proceed if you intensely dislike Kim Taylor, WCHI's representative. You think he is selfish and arrogant and cares only about his own negotiated outcome. In this case, how many runs per episode should you prefer? If you answered four—or even six—you might want to think again. In negotiation, you should consider giving up something that you value—even to someone you do not care about—if that person values it more than you do. This is not a matter of altruism or kindness, but of value creation. If you create value, you have the opportunity to capture a portion of this created value for yourself, as happened when we moved from Agreement O to Agreement X.

This insight is critical: negotiators should seize every opportunity to create value. If the other party values something more than you do, let them have it—but don't *give* it away, *sell* it. Of course, if you *do* care about the other side, all the more reason to create value. But remember that creating value is not just what a "nice" negotiator does when she cares about the other side. It's what a negotiation genius will do categorically.

CREATING VALUE BY ADDING ISSUES

The only issues you were required to negotiate in this deal were licensing fee and runs. However, you had the potential to bring up other issues that could create additional value for both parties. Specifically, you were interested in selling *Juniors* at a price higher than $1 million (the amount of your other offer for this show). Kim signaled to you during your negotiation that WCHI might be willing to purchase the show, but you set aside that discussion. What would have happened if you had engaged Kim in a discussion about their interest in *Juniors*? You may have discovered that WCHI was willing to pay up to $2 million for the show! In this case, failure to negotiate the sale of *Juniors* resulted in a net loss of $1 million for the two parties. Put another way, the ZOPA for *Juniors* consisted of all prices between $1–2 million—yet both parties walked away from the negotiation without agreeing to a sale.

How might the sale of *Juniors* have impacted final outcomes? Table 2.5 builds on Table 2.4 by including an agreement (Agreement Y) in which the buyer and seller agree to sell *Juniors* for $1.5 million. This agreement provides an additional $500,000 to each party. (Notice that if the parties had agreed to a higher price for *Juniors*, you [the seller] would have captured more value; if the price was lower, WCHI would have captured more of the value. In either case, the total value created by including the sale of *Juniors* would be $1 million.)

		Value to WCHI	Total Value Created
Agreement	Value to You		
Original (O)	$2,000,000	$1,000,000	$3,000,000
Revised (X)	$2,500,000	$1,600,000	$4,100,000
Agreement Y	$3,000,000	$2,100,000	$5,100,000

Table 2.5

The *Juniors* issue highlights an important difference between a good negotiator and a negotiation genius. A good negotiator will do whatever it takes to *close the deal*, while a negotiation genius will do whatever it takes to *maximize value* in the deal. A good negotiator plays the game well; a negotiation genius changes the nature of the game itself. In this case, that means identifying and pursuing opportunities for value creation that are not obvious.

Adding issues to a negotiation is an important tactic for value creation because of a simple formula: *more issues = more currency*. The more issues you have to play with, the easier it will be to find opportunities for logrolling. Imagine that you have agreed to seven runs and a licensing fee of $6.5 million. You know that moving to eight runs will create additional value, but you are only willing to do so if the buyer gives you something in return. Unfortunately, WCHI has reached its limit on the licensing fee issue; it cannot pay more than $6.5 million. Does this mean that you must forgo the opportunity to create value? Yes—if there are only two issues in the negotiation. But if you add another issue—*Juniors*—you can engineer the value-creating trade. "It's costly for me to give up any more runs," you might tell Kim. "However, depending on the kind of deal we can structure for *Juniors*, I may be able to give you the additional runs you want." If Kim agrees to purchase *Juniors* for any price between $1.25 million and $2.8 million, in return for adding the eighth run, both of you will be better off! Notice that Kim may be willing to pay even more for *Juniors* than it is worth (up to $800,000 more), because doing so allows WCHI to gain $800,000 in revenue on the issue of runs. As this example reveals, the goal of negotiation is not to get the best possible outcome on any *one* issue, but to negotiate the best possible *package deal* based on a consideration of all of the issues.

This discussion also highlights an important distinction between logrolling and compromise. Many negotiators, including some seasoned dealmakers, believe that negotiation is about compromise. This is not true. Negotiation often *entails* compromise, but it is not *about* compromise. For example, when our executive students negotiate *Moms.com*, they often compromise across all issues. "We started at four runs versus eight runs," someone might argue, "and compromised at six runs, which is a win-win outcome that makes both people happy." Yet both parties could have been *happier* if they had been sophisticated enough to realize that logrolling to achieve eight runs is better for both parties than compromising to achieve six runs. Our goal here is not simply to help you reach agreements that both parties *consider* to be "win-win"; our goal is to help you maximize value. What does that require?

As it turns out, even a desire to make the other side happy is not enough to help maximize value creation. People in close relationships (such as spouses) often negotiate *worse* outcomes than do people who care less about their counterpart.[3] Why? Because those in close relationships compromise across the board in order to avoid being perceived as greedy or overly self-interested. As a result, they often ignore opportunities for logrolling and, instead, destroy value rather than create it! Excellent partners—in personal and business relationships alike—master the ability to communicate openly and share information about their real needs and priorities. In doing so, they identify all of the potentially relevant issues and cooperate to create maximum value. And, once you have created the conditions for value maximization, you can focus on capturing as much of that value for yourself as you deem appropriate given your relationship with the other party and your desire to be fair.

Adding issues to the negotiation may be most critical when the deal is centered on one divisive issue and no one is willing to compromise. For example, in the United States in the early 1800s, when the northern and southern states were embattled over the issue of slavery, they argued over whether states newly admitted to the Union would be "free" states or "slave" states. In 1819, the country was in balance (numerically, certainly not morally), with eleven free and eleven slave states. But when Missouri petitioned to join the Union, a major dispute arose between pro-slavery and anti-slavery forces. Because giving numerical dominance to one side on the issue of slavery would upset the balance of power in the U.S. Senate, no deal seemed possible. Eventually, a deal *was* structured—the "Missouri Compromise"—but only after Maine petitioned to join the Union in 1820. The two issues were purposely linked: both sides agreed to allow Maine to enter as a free state and for Missouri to enter without restrictions on the issue of slavery.

In business negotiations, price is often the divisive issue. Smart negotiators recognize the limitations of one-issue deals and work to broaden the scope. Here are a few of the negotiable issues that you can introduce into the discussion the next time the other side appears entirely focused on price:

- delivery date
- financing
- quality
- contract length
- last-look provisions
- arbitration clauses
- exclusivity clauses
- level of service support
- warranties
- future business

The more issues there are available to play with, the more likely it is that each party will obtain what it values most and become willing to compromise on issues of relatively less importance.

YOUR GOAL SHOULD BE TO MAXIMIZE VALUE

Table 2.5 demonstrates how both parties can be made better off when an additional issue is added to the negotiation. In technical terms, such a revision of the agreement is referred to as a *Pareto improvement:* changes to a deal that make at least one person better off without making anyone worse off. As you can see, Pareto improvements create value in negotiation. One of your goals in *every* negotiation should be to look constantly for Pareto improvements until you have reached an agreement that is *Pareto efficient:* that is, until there is no way to make one party better off without hurting the other. According to Table 2.5, the only Pareto-efficient outcomes are those that create a total value of $5.1 million.

The virtue of Pareto efficiency is that it ensures that no money is left on the table (i.e., burned) at the end of the deal. But notice that Pareto efficiency says nothing about how the created value is divided between parties. It is possible to have an efficient agreement in *Moms.com* where all of the created value goes to one party. An agreement in which you get $1 million and WCHI gets $4.1 million is still Pareto efficient because, at this point, there is no way to make one of you better off without hurting the other. In other words, the parties may jointly agree to eight runs and a sale of *Juniors,* but the party that does a better job of haggling over the licensing fee and the price for *Juniors* will capture the lion's share of the value. For this reason, Pareto efficiency is seldom your *only* goal; you will also strive to capture as much of the value for yourself as possible. Or, if your priority is to reach a "fair" deal and build a strong relationship, you may choose to give up some of the created value to the other side.

How do you know whether you have reached a Pareto-efficient outcome? Unfortunately, there is no definitive answer; bells will not sound and flowers will not fall from the sky. But one good test is to consider how well you understand the concerns of the other side. If you leave the negotiation table without knowing very much about their interests and priorities, you have probably left value on the table.

This brings us back to *Moms.com.* Guess what? You missed another opportunity to create value in that negotiation.

CREATING VALUE THROUGH CONTINGENCY CONTRACTS

In your *Moms.com* negotiation, recall your disagreement with Kim regarding how much revenue the show is likely to bring to WCHI. Kim argued that the show was likely to receive low ratings (3-4). You suspected he was lying; your research showed expected ratings of 5-6. What did you do when that difference of opinion surfaced? You essentially ignored it, decided to "agree to disagree" on the issue, and moved ahead with other substantive discussions. Is that the best way to handle such disagreements? Very often, it is not. Let's consider a better, more systematic approach for handling disagreements regarding expectations about the future success, quality, or performance of a good or a service that you might be negotiating.

First, try to figure out who is right and who is wrong. For example, you might share your research with each other and work together to analyze the data. You might agree to conduct additional research together, or you might bring in a disinterested third party whom you both trust to do the research. Any of these approaches will help you resolve your differences and allow you to negotiate based on shared assumptions and analyses. You hope, of course, that the additional research will support your contention (in this case, that the show's ratings will be high). If both parties can agree that expected ratings and expected revenue are high rather than low, you stand to make more money in the sale.

Another solution to the disagreement is for both parties to compromise. In other words, you might agree to assume that both sides are probably somewhat incorrect and that an average (4–5) is a reasonable best estimate of ratings. The benefit of this approach is that you do not have to waste extra time or money gathering additional data or hiring a third party. A problem with this approach is that if you truly believe that your numbers are correct—and that the other side is either incompetent or dishonest—you will not want to compromise. Why would you throw away your own numbers simply because the other party (who has an incentive to lowball the estimate) is telling you that you are wrong?

This brings us to a third solution, one that avoids the costs of gathering more data, avoids the hassle of trying to convince the other side that you are correct, and avoids capitulating to the desires of a party you do not trust: negotiate a contingency contract. As discussed in Chapter 1, contingency contracts allow negotiators to avoid arguing about the likelihood of some future event (in this case, the show's ratings) and instead wait to see what actually transpires. In the *Moms.com* negotiation, the negotiators could agree to the following deal:

Agreement Z:	
Licensing fee:	$6.5M
Runs:	8
Price for *Juniors*:	$1.5M

Contingency clause:

- If the ratings next year are less than 4, WCHI receives a $1 million rebate.
- If the ratings next year are greater than 5, WCHI pays a $1 million surcharge to Hollyville.

In other words, if the show does very well (as you suspect it will), WCHI will owe Hollyville an additional sum of money. But if WCHI's projections are correct, Hollyville will refund some of the money paid in the licensing fee. Would both parties agree to such a clause? If they truly believe their own projections, they should!

Table 2.6

Ratings	Likelihood Based on Hollyville's Projection	Likelihood Based on WCHI's Projection
2–3	10%	20%
3–4	10%	50%
4–5	10%	10%
5–6	50%	10%
6–7	20%	10%

Let's examine this issue in more detail. Table 2.6 displays rating projections for each party. (Going into the negotiation, you only knew Hollyville's projections.) As the table reveals, the buyer and seller had a genuine difference of opinion regarding the show's likely success. Given these different beliefs, how would each party have evaluated the contingency clause described above? Hollyville believes it has a 70 percent chance of being correct and "winning the bet" because ratings will be greater than 5, a 20 percent chance of being wrong and "losing the bet" because ratings will be less than 4, and a 10 percent chance that no money will change hands because ratings will be 4. Meanwhile, WCHI *also* believes that it has a 70 percent chance of winning the bet, a 20 percent chance of losing the bet, and a 10 percent chance of being unaffected. Based on these projections, the expected value of the contingency clause to each party can be calculated as follows:

	Rating > 5	Rating = 4	Rating < 4	
Hollyville	(.70 x $1M) +	(.10 x $0) +	(.20 x -$1M) =	$500,000
WCHI	(.20 x -$1M) +	(.10 x $0) +	(.70 x $1M) =	$500,000

In other words, *both* parties expect to receive an additional $500,000 as a result of this clause, and both should be willing to agree to it. Table 2.7 compares the value created by Agreement Z (which includes the contingency clause) with the value created in the other agreements we have considered.

Table 2.7

Agreement	Value to You	Value to WCHI	Total Value Created
Original (O)	$2,000,000	$1,000,000	$3,000,000
Revised (X)	$2,500,000	$1,600,000	$4,100,000
Agreement Y	$3,000,000	$2,100,000	$5,100,000
Agreement Z	$3,500,000	$2,600,000	$6,100,000

In Chapter 1, we showed you how contingency contracts can protect you from dishonest negotiators. That same benefit exists here as well. If Kim was being dishonest about WCHI's projections and knew that the show would receive higher ratings, he would never accept the contingency contract. His unwillingness to "put his money where his mouth is" could alert you to possible deception.

The *Moms.com* contingency contract reveals another benefit of such contracts: they can create value by allowing negotiators to stop arguing about their different beliefs and instead leverage their differences through bets that *both* sides expect to win. In this case, both parties are better off (in terms of expected revenue) when the contingency contract is signed because both are confident in their projections. Technically, this contingency clause does not actually "create" value in the way that logrolling or adding issues creates value. This is because when the ratings are revealed next year, the contract will simply force one party to transfer $1 million to the other party. Although essentially a zero-sum transfer, the contingency contract does create *expected* value. At the time of the deal, both parties *are* made better off in terms of expected revenue from the deal—a Pareto improvement.

Such clauses are of even greater value and consequence when the beliefs of each party are *extremely* different and no deal is possible unless these different expectations are managed. For example, if a client doubts her lawyer's ability to win in court, she may choose to hire the lawyer based on a contingency contract: the lawyer will be paid a large sum if the client wins and not at all if she loses. Similarly, book publishers typically pay the author a sum of money up front, followed by a fixed percentage of sales revenue. If the publisher is skeptical about the author's ability to write a best seller, it should be willing to pay the author a higher percentage of sales revenue (or offer a bonus if the book becomes a best seller) in exchange for less money up front. If the author is confident, he will agree.

As a final example of the ability of contingency contracts to salvage deals, consider the 1997 negotiations between basketball star Dennis Rodman and the Chicago Bulls. Rodman was known for his superior ability to rebound and play defense; he was also known for his unpredictability, his disdain for professional norms, and his propensity to miss games. In the previous season alone, he had missed twenty-seven of eighty-two games. As a result of his guaranteed contract, the Bulls paid Rodman close to $3 million for games he did not even play! Determined not to repeat the mistake, the team negotiated an unprecedented contingency-laden contract with Rodman. He would have the ability to earn as much as $10.5 million, but he would be guaranteed only $4.5 million. The rest of the salary was tied to various clauses, including $1 million for playing in all playoff games, $500,000 for winning another rebounding title, and $185,000 for each game he played above fifty-nine. What was the result? Rodman won his seventh consecutive rebounding title and played in eighty of the season's eighty-two games (he missed two games due to injury), and the Bulls won another championship.

While contingency contracts are powerful tools for creating value and motivating performance, they are not always desirable. Here are some caveats to keep in mind:

- Contingency contracts are dangerous if the other party is more knowledgeable than you. For example, if WCHI has access to better ratings data than Hollyville, and WCHI is offering to bet on the basis of ratings, Hollyville should be wary.

- Contingency contracts are useful only if uncertainty will be resolved in ways that can be measured objectively. If you hire an employee and offer to promote her "if she performs well," make sure that both parties understand what "performs well" means. Will you base performance on revenue generated? Hours worked? Projects completed? A good work ethic? Not all of these standards are easy to measure objectively. A rule of thumb: if you're going to argue about who won the bet, it's not worth betting in the first place. In the *Moms.com* negotiation, parties could agree to base the contingency clause on ratings reported from a specific source (e.g., Nielsen Media Research).

- Make sure you understand the effect of contingency contracts on the incentives of the other party. Imagine that your contingency clause in *Moms.com* was not for $1 million but $20 million. If you were to calculate your expected value for the clause, you would discover that your expected revenue is $10 million. Sounds great! But there's a *big* problem. You have just bet a lot on the possibility that the show will receive high ratings—but who now has the incentive, and the *ability*, to make sure the show receives extremely poor ratings? WCHI. They can choose not to advertise the show, to air it on an unpopular day, or to air it in the middle of the night. While this would hurt their revenues (worth approximately $7 million), it would help them receive $10 million from you based on the contingency clause. For this reason, make sure your contingency contracts are *incentive compatible*. That is, the clause you negotiate should provide incentives for the other party to behave in ways that are compatible with the spirit of your agreement.

PREPARATION STRATEGIES FOR VALUE CREATION

Now that we have considered the logic of value creation and highlighted some key methods for doing so, let's step back and consider how negotiators who are interested in creating value and achieving efficient agreements should prepare for negotiation. In the previous chapter, we discussed the necessity of assessing your BATNA, calculating your reservation value, and evaluating the ZOPA prior to every negotiation. In this section, we add to this list of preparation tasks.

STRATEGY 1: IDENTIFY YOUR MULTIPLE INTERESTS

Most negotiators take the domain of negotiation as given. For example, they enter talks thinking, "Today we're going to be haggling over salary," or "We're meeting with the client to negotiate an extension of the contract length," or "This negotiation is about the sale of our company." A more effective strategy is to think about *all* of the things that you value that the other party might have the ability to provide. For example, in addition to negotiating your salary, perhaps you should also negotiate your start date, vacation days, signing bonus, job description, promotion schedule, and stock options.

The goal is not to overwhelm the other party with demands, but to give them a lot of different ways to compensate you and make you happy. If they cannot increase your salary but they can make you equally happy with some combination of signing bonus, change in job description, and more aggressive promotion opportunities, *both of you* stand to gain. They get to hire their preferred candidate (you) without paying a high salary, and you get a compensation package that makes you happy. Similarly, when approaching the sale of your company, it is critical that you think about everything that you value. For example, you might care about the preservation of your company's legacy, maintaining a seat on the board, having a minority stake in the company, or safeguarding the continued employment of your workers. It may be that you are unwilling to accept the price offered when it is the only issue being negotiated, but the price becomes acceptable if you can retain some shares, are given a seat on the board, and have the ability to protect your workers. Unfortunately, some such issues never see the light of day because the seller assumes that "they will never agree to give me a seat on the board" or that "they've already decided whether they will keep or lay off my employees."

STRATEGY 2: CREATE A SCORING SYSTEM

Identifying issues is only the first step. Next, you need to think about your relative priorities over the many issues. For example, how much are you willing to give up on price to get more favorable financing terms or a better delivery date? How do you trade off salary against stock options, starting date, or promotion track? How much would you be willing to give up in salary to work in a specific division of the firm?

A scoring system offers a way to organize your interests and priorities so that you can answer these questions efficiently. To create a scoring system, list each issue and weight it according to its importance using a computer spreadsheet program. You will need to think of a common metric for evaluating each issue. For example, you might start with a hundred points and distribute these points across the issues (and across potential outcomes for each issue) in proportion to their relative importance. Another easy metric involves converting everything into dollar values (e.g., each additional day of vacation equals $600 in salary). Having a common metric across all issues will help you evaluate the package offers the other party makes and also help you structure your counteroffers more carefully and strategically.

STRATEGY 3: CALCULATE A PACKAGE RESERVATION VALUE

Instead of having a reservation value for each issue ("The lowest salary I will accept is $X, the lowest signing bonus is $Y, and the lowest number of stock options is Z"), you should use your scoring system to calculate an overall reservation value. For example, if your BATNA is to accept an offer from Company A, entering the specifics of the offer from Company A into your scoring system will give you the total value (in points or dollar terms) of that offer. This is your *package reservation value* (PRV). Now, in your current negotiation, you know not to accept any offer that gives you a total value less than your PRV.

The problem with having a separate reservation value for each issue is that your options become limited. You may not *want* a salary below $X, but are you sure you would not be willing to accept a lower salary if the other side made significant concessions on many or all of the other issues you value? Often, negotiators set arbitrary limits on individual issues (such as salary, bonus, stock options, delivery dates, closing dates, up-front payment, et cetera) because they think that anything beyond that limit would be "unfair" or "unreasonable." But doing so only limits the negotiator's flexibility. If the other party cannot stay within your limit on that one issue, but can more than make up for it with other concessions and guarantees, you both may stand to lose because of the limit you have set.

For example, a consultant or contractor may not be able to lower their price enough to beat all other offers, but if that consultant or contractor can provide much better service, give more comprehensive guarantees, and throw in additional work for free, you might want to reconsider the reservation value you placed on the issue of price. Unfortunately, far too many firms, organizations, and governments will make purchases or hire contractors and consultants entirely based on the service provider's ability to compete on only one issue (price). This practice can be highly inefficient.

STRATEGY 4: IDENTIFY THE OTHER PARTY'S MULTIPLE INTERESTS

In negotiation, there often will be issues that you do not care about—but that the other side cares about very much! It is critical to identify these issues. For example, you may be indifferent between whether you start your new job in June or July. But if your potential employer strongly prefers that you start as soon as possible, that's a valuable piece of information. Now you are in a position to give them something that they value (at no cost to you) and get something of value in return. For example, you might start a month earlier and re-ceive a larger signing bonus for doing so. Similarly, when Deepak was purchasing his home, he discovered that the seller was very interested in closing the deal as soon as possible. With far fewer constraints on his ability to close the deal early or late, Deepak was more than willing to oblige. He agreed to close one month earlier than originally offered, and the seller agreed to a lower price.

EXECUTION STRATEGIES FOR VALUE CREATION

Once talks begin, it is common for negotiators to focus primarily on value-claiming strategies and to forgo opportunities for value creation. This is not surprising. Most people view negotiation as a battle in which the object is to outwit, out-think, and out-negotiate the other side. This mentality leads to the dangerous belief that *they lose = you win*. As we saw in the *Moms.com* negotiation, this is simply not the case. In fact, almost all negotiations entail the possibility of at least some—and often a lot of—value creation. In Part II, we will look more closely at the psychological biases that can lead to a *they lose = you win* mentality and discuss ways in which to overcome these biases. For now, we focus on the correct approach for executing negotiations so that you create value and reach efficient agreements, while still capturing much of that value for yourself.

STRATEGY 1: NEGOTIATE MULTIPLE ISSUES SIMULTANEOUSLY

We often ask seasoned negotiators the following question: when you are involved in a complex, multi-issue deal, which issues do you negotiate first, the easiest or the toughest? Most negotiators respond that it's best to start with the easy issues. According to this logic, starting with easy issues allows negotiators to build trust and gather momentum toward an agreement; if you start with a difficult issue, you might derail the negotiation from the start. Another benefit of starting with an easy issue is that it allows you to make a low-cost concession early and set the stage for the other side to reciprocate later on issues of more value to you. While this strategy seems reasonable, some negotiators tell us that it is a better idea to start with the tough issues first. They point out that some issues are "make or break"; if you can't reach agreement on them, there's no point in wasting time on other, less important issues. Finally, a third group of negotiators responds with the seemingly fail-safe answer "It depends."

As it turns out, we disagree with all three responses. While negotiators typically find it more natural (and easier) to negotiate one issue at a time, a much better strategy is to negotiate multiple issues simultaneously. Why? Because negotiating one issue at a time eliminates the possibility of logrolling. For example, in the *Moms.com* negotiation, if you have already reached agreement on the licensing fee and are now negotiating the number of runs, it will be extremely difficult to agree to eight runs. The only way Hollyville will allow eight runs is if WCHI concedes on a different issue—but if you have already put aside the other issues, this is not possible. Notice that, when considered *separately*, both issues in the *Moms.com* negotiation are effectively zero-sum; the buyer and seller have diametrically opposed interests on each issue. Only when they negotiate these issues simultaneously can they create a non-zero-sum negotiation that allows for value creation. In other words, although the buyer and seller will be in conflict on each issue, they are not equally passionate about each issue. The relative importance of each issue to each party only becomes apparent when the issues are discussed simultaneously.

STRATEGY 2: MAKE PACKAGE OFFERS

Negotiating multiple issues simultaneously does not mean that you must literally talk about every issue at the same time. It *does* mean that you should avoid reaching final agreement on any one issue until you have had the opportunity to discuss every issue. Especially when there are many complex issues to discuss, a particularly productive approach is to begin with a discussion of each side's perspective and preferred outcome on each issue. Once you have shared preliminary information, you can begin comparing relative preferences across issues. Finally, when it is time to exchange offers, make package offers. That is, instead of making an offer or demand on one issue (such as price or salary), propose a package deal that communicates to the other side your preferred outcome across all of the issues. This helps the other party isolate aspects of the offer that are particularly problematic and propose counteroffers that do not simply ask for more on each issue. Instead, your counterpart can signal flexibility on some issues while making demands on others.

Consider the following two approaches for negotiating the price of a service agreement between your firm and a potential client. Which approach is likely to create more value in the end?

A. "Thank you for providing me with a detailed list of the services that your firm requires and for explaining that you would like to begin the service period in July. We can provide these services at a cost of $650,000."

B. "Thank you for providing me with a detailed list of the services that your firm requires and for explaining that you would like to begin the service period in July. Thank you also for signaling that you have some flexibility on when the service period begins and for your interest in exploring the 'premium' service option that I described. This gives us a number of different ways to price the services you value. Here are two options:

"*Option 1:* If the service period begins in July, and without the premium service, we can provide these services at a cost of $650,000. If you would like to add the premium service, that will come at a cost of $50,000, for a total price of $700,000.

"*Option 2:* If the service period begins earlier, in March, and without the premium service, we can lower the price to $635,000. If you would like to add the premium service, that will come at a cost of $45,000, for a total price of $680,000."

Approach B helps your potential client understand what trade-offs are possible, and makes it much more likely that the two of you will reach an efficient agreement.

STRATEGY 3: LEVERAGE DIFFERENCES OF ALL TYPES TO CREATE VALUE

Because people are different, conflict is natural. We have different perspectives, interests, needs, constraints, careers, educational backgrounds, and experiences. But while differences often lead to conflict, they also provide a means of resolving conflict. The reason logrolling creates value, for instance, is that parties have *different priorities*. If their priorities were identical, there would be no way for one person to concede on Issue A in return for more of Issue B. Similarly, consider the essence of contingency contracts: they create value because the two parties have *different expectations about the future*. If their expectations were identical, they would have no opportunity to introduce clauses that increase both parties' expected value.

Negotiation geniuses understand this crucial insight: you can leverage differences of all types to create value. For example, consider *differences in risk preferences*. If you are risk averse and someone else is risk neutral, you are in a position to pay that person to take on your risk. Sounds funny, right? But that is exactly what an insurance company does. You pay your health, automobile, or home insurance company a premium to cover your losses in case something goes wrong. On average, you will lose money when you buy insurance. But because you are risk averse, you are willing to lose some money in exchange for paying the risk-neutral company to take away your risk. This makes both of you better off and no one worse off—which means value has been created!

As another example, consider *differences in time preferences.* If you are not currently using something you own, but another party needs it right away, you can give them what you have in return for a payment. If this sounds familiar, it's because this is what happens when you deposit some of your money with a bank. You give your money to the bank because you do not need to spend it immediately. In return, the bank gives your money to its borrowers and pays you for the use of your money in the form of interest. This exchange makes both of you better off.

When negotiating, rather than trying to ignore, reconcile, or overcome your differences with the other party, you should try to *seek out* differences, and then find ways to leverage them to create value. For example, the next time someone strenuously objects to a particular aspect of your proposal, do not be dismayed. Instead, try to discover how much the other side values getting their way on this aspect of the deal. If they value it sufficiently, they may be in a position to make the deal even sweeter for you by making other concessions in return for your flexibility.

POST-NEGOTIATION STRATEGIES FOR VALUE CREATION

Negotiation geniuses do not stop after having created value during the negotiation; they continue to seek out Pareto improvements even after the deal is signed. A powerful tool for value creation is the use of *post-settlement settlements (PSS),* settlements that are reached after the initial agreement is signed.[4] Imagine the following:

> After weeks of negotiation, you have just signed a complex deal with the CEO of Firm X. You are satisfied with the deal and so is the other party. You want nothing more than to go home,

take a shower, and pop open some champagne. But you reconsider, deciding to try something a little different. You ask the CEO of Firm X whether she would be willing to take another look at the agreement and see if it can be improved. She is surprised by the suggestion and asks if you're having second thoughts about the deal.

Often, the last thing you want to do after a long negotiation is to open up a can of worms and potentially derail the agreement. You do not want to appear to be reneging on the deal you just signed, nor do you want to suggest that you held back in your ability to make concessions earlier. You are also unwilling to give away any more ground to the other party.

Why, then, might you propose a post-settlement settlement? Because, for a variety of reasons, a PSS can lead to Pareto improvements. First, the already-signed agreement confirms the parties' ability to work together to reach value-creating deals and creates an environment of optimism. Second, once a signed agreement exists, parties feel less anxious and are often more willing to share information. Third, if presented correctly, both sides will understand that they will only accept a PSS if it improves both of their outcomes. In other words, the recently signed agreement becomes the new BATNA for *both* parties.

This is a crucial point: you don't want the other side to perceive the PSS as your attempt to renege or squeeze last-minute concessions out of them. On the contrary, you should present the idea of a PSS as an opportunity for both parties to benefit. Indeed, state this ground rule explicitly at the outset: either we both benefit, or we stick with what we have agreed to already.

Consider the following story, recounted by one of our former executive students, the CEO of a small firm in the pharmaceutical industry:

"I had agreed ... to sell the rights to eight different drugs I have in development ... I had negotiated for five straight days on this deal and it closed ... before the Harvard course. After your classes I call up the pharmaceutical company that is buying the rights and said that I needed more money up-front. The company was taken aback by my call.

However ... I used this opportunity to explain exactly *why* I wanted different terms. Once they heard my rationale—that I wanted the money to start more projects, that I wanted the money to help me with cash flow, and that I wanted the money to be able to go to some angel investors to raise even more money—they understood. All they wanted in return was a right of first refusal on any future projects I develop with the additional cash flow in the next two years.

Now instead of using a line of credit to support all these development programs, I have three or four more projects that I will start this summer versus end of '04. And both sides have a better value under these terms ..."

As the story suggests, the pharmaceutical company was initially surprised (and not particularly thrilled) by the executive's request to reopen negotiations. This was largely due to the perception that the executive was simply coming back for more money without concern for the other side's interests. The situation improved once the executive shared more information regarding his interests and communicated a willingness to give the pharmaceutical company something in return. PSSs not only facilitate logrolling, they can also help to identify and add issues that were not even part of the initial negotiation; in the above example, the parties had never discussed a right of first refusal in the formal negotiations that preceded the PSS.

It is easy to see how a PSS might have improved the outcome in the *Moms.com* negotiation. Had the parties continued to negotiate and share information after the initial agreement was signed, they might have discovered the value of shifting to eight runs, making a deal on *Juniors,* and/or including a contingency clause that leveraged different ratings expectations.

Despite these potential benefits, post-settlement settlements are a severely underutilized tool. Many people have never heard of PSS, others are wary of the risks associated with renegotiating, others doubt that a PSS can really be of benefit, and still others do not know how to propose a PSS. We have addressed the first three issues. Now let's consider how you might propose a PSS:

Step 1: Start by acknowledging the progress that was already made in reaching the initial agreement.

Step 2: Suggest that there are aspects of the deal that you wish could be improved; acknowledge that they probably feel similarly.

Step 3: Suggest that you may have already conceded everything that you can afford, but that you are willing to try to think "outside the box" if that will help the other party.

Step 4: State that it is important for both of you to realize that you are not looking for a *new* agreement, but for an *improved* agreement that both parties prefer to the current agreement.

As an example, you might say the following:

"Congratulations! I think that our hard work has really paid off in a great deal. We're probably both ready to call it a day. I'm wondering, though, whether you might be open to an idea. Though we're both satisfied with the agreement, there are inevitably aspects of the deal that I wish could have been better for me, and you probably feel the same way about other aspects. What if we spent a few more minutes talking about potential improvements to the deal that would make both of us better off? Maybe we've already exhausted those possibilities—but it might be a good idea to see if there are any stones left unturned. Of course, if we can't find ways to make both parties happier, we'll be even more confident that our signed agreement is the right one for everyone. If you're up for it, let's give it a try …"

Keep in mind that it is not necessary for you to have this conversation immediately upon signing the initial deal. You might want to sleep on it. You might even wait a week or a month before revisiting the deal. The key, however, is to realize that your negotiation should not end when the deal is signed—it should end when you feel that you have exhausted all options for value creation.

THE GENIUS OF VALUE CREATION

As the ideas, strategies, and tactics we've presented in this chapter suggest, getting a good deal in negotiation is not simply about claiming as much value as you can. Often, a much more important (and difficult) task is to create value and increase the size of the pie. Unfortunately, too many negotiators focus most of their energy on claiming value. In doing so, they leave money on the table and walk away confident, satisfied—and also poor. As you finish this chapter, consider the following question: would you rather claim 70 percent of a $100 pie, or 70 percent of a $200 pie? That is the type of choice you will face in most of your real-world negotiations. Even if you get a slightly smaller portion of a large pie (say, 50–60 percent), this trade-off may be very profitable for you.

It is important to realize that we are not preaching the gospel of altruism and benevolence, but rather teaching the art and science of value creation. Even the most self-interested negotiators must rely on others to satisfy their own interests. Remember: to *take* what is there, you must work with the other side to *make* what is there. And if you care about your reputation and your relationship with the other party, all the more reason to exercise the genius of value creation.

CHAPTER 3

Investigative Negotiation

One of us works closely with a Fortune 500 executive named Chris who is widely regarded within his firm as a negotiation genius. Chris's reputation has been built on a host of stories like this one: Some years ago, Chris's firm was negotiating to buy a new health-care product ingredient from a small European company. The parties had agreed to a price of $18 per pound for a million pounds of product per year, but a conflict developed over exclusivity terms. The European supplier would not agree to sell the ingredient exclusively to the U.S. firm, and the U.S. firm would not invest in manufacturing a new product based on an ingredient to which competitors would have access. This issue appeared to be a deal breaker.

The U.S. firm's negotiators were frustrated and surprised by the small European firm's reticence on the issue of exclusivity. After all, there was no way the supplier could hope to sell even close to one million pounds of the product elsewhere. Eventually, though with understandable hesitation, the U.S. firm's negotiators decided to sweeten the deal with guaranteed minimum orders and a willingness to pay more per pound. They were shocked when the supplier still refused to provide exclusivity! As a last resort, the U.S. team called Chris and asked him to fly to Europe to join them.

When Chris arrived and took a seat at the bargaining table, the argument over exclusivity continued. After listening briefly to the two sides, he interjected one simple word that changed the outcome of the negotiation. With it, he was able to structure a deal that both firms found agreeable. The word was "why."

Chris simply asked the supplier *why* he would not provide exclusivity to a major corporation that was offering to buy as much of the ingredient as he could produce. The supplier's answer was unexpected: exclusivity would require him to violate an agreement with his cousin, who currently purchased 250 pounds of the ingredient each year to make a locally sold product. With this information in hand, Chris proposed a solution that helped the two firms quickly wrap up an agreement: the supplier would provide exclusivity with the exception of a few hundred pounds annually for the supplier's cousin. Chris was on the next plane home.

Chris's colleagues still tell the story of how Chris (the genius) saved the deal through his amazing detective work and creativity. What does Chris say? "All I did was ask them why they didn't want to provide exclusivity." Why didn't the other U.S. negotiators ask this simple question? Because, based on their prior business experience, they assumed they already knew the answer: either the supplier was holding out for more money, or he was worried that exclusivity would eliminate the possibility of more profitable future business deals. Anchored to these assumptions, the U.S. negotiators tried to "sweeten" the deal at a potentially high cost to their own firm. Of course, the deal was never going to be sweet enough because their assumptions were wrong. Chris succeeded where his team had failed because he was willing to challenge assumptions and gather as much information as possible about the other side's perspective. In short, Chris employed the first principle of a method we call *investigative negotiation*.

THE SEVEN PRINCIPLES OF INVESTIGATIVE NEGOTIATION

Investigative negotiation is both a mind-set and a methodology. Investigative negotiators approach negotiations the same way a detective might approach a crime scene: the goal is to learn as much as possible about the situation and the people involved. Here are the key principles for negotiators:

PRINCIPLE 1: DON'T JUST ASK WHAT—ASK *WHY*

Many experienced negotiators believe that the purpose of listening to the other side is to find out what they want. This sounds reasonable. After all, unless you know what the other side wants, how can you structure a deal that they will be willing to accept? Similarly, negotiators tend to spend most of their own speaking time telling others what they themselves want or need. Unfortunately, this approach—finding out what each side wants—often *derails* negotiations. The reason: too much focus on *what* people want distracts your attention from discovering *why* they want it.

In his negotiation with the supplier, Chris understood that for progress to be made both sides had to stop talking about *what* they wanted (exclusivity versus no exclusivity) and begin talking about *why* they wanted it. While there was no room for compromise on *what* they wanted, a clear solution emerged when the focus shifted to *why*. Once the supplier explained that he was resisting exclusivity because it would force him to renege on his promise to his cousin, Chris had the information he needed to structure a value-creating deal.

Ambassador Holbrooke employed the same approach in his negotiations with UN member states (see Chapter 2). Rather than accepting their stated demands ("We don't want an increase in our assessments"), Holbrooke probed further by asking *why* they did not want an increase. When some states explained that they were constrained by their annual budgeting process, but were otherwise willing to increase their contributions, the outlines of a deal became visible.

The same tactic—asking why—can do wonders even in mundane negotiations. For example, Shikha, Deepak's wife, recently found herself in a predicament. In downtown Boston on an extremely cold winter day, she needed to hail a cab. But it was rush hour, and as literally dozens of occupied cabs drove by, she began to consider the possibility that she might get frostbite. Finally, she spotted an empty cab waiting at a red light. But there was a problem: the cab's "for hire" light was off. She asked for a ride anyway. As expected, the cabdriver refused her request with a dismissive wave of the hand. Undeterred, she asked the driver *why* he would not take her. The driver explained that he was not in service because he needed to get home. "Well, maybe we're going in the same direction. Would you drop me off if we're going to the same area?" she asked. As it turned out, their destinations were mere blocks from each other. She jumped into the warm cab and made it home quickly, and the driver made a few extra dollars without having to change his plans.

PRINCIPLE 2: SEEK TO RECONCILE INTERESTS, NOT DEMANDS

One of the biggest mistakes a negotiator can make is to focus exclusively on trying to reconcile the *demands* of each party. Investigative negotiators move beyond demands and instead focus on each side's *underlying interests*. In Chris's case, the buyer and the supplier were making irreconcilable demands: one wanted exclusivity; the other did not. Only when Chris shifted attention away from stated demands (exclusivity versus no exclusivity) toward each side's underlying interest (protection from competitors versus a promise made to a cousin) was a deal possible. The demands of the two parties were incompatible, but their interests were entirely reconcilable. Moreover, neither party had to make a substantive concession or compromise to make the deal happen.

The key insight: negotiation geniuses are not discouraged when the demands of each party seem incompatible. Instead, they probe deeper to find out each side's real underlying interests. This strategy allows them to think more broadly and creatively about agreements that might satisfy the interests of both sides.

This is exactly how some political activists responded to an impending crisis in the 2000 U.S. presidential elections. Democratic candidate Al Gore was in close competition with Republican candidate George W. Bush. Unfortunately for Gore, what would normally have been a two-party battle for votes (with Gore on the political left and Bush on the political right) became a three-party contest when Green Party candidate Ralph Nader entered the race and generated interest from voters on the political far left. Having two contenders on the left clearly benefited the Republicans; every vote for Nader would be a loss for Gore, and Bush faced no serious competition on the far right. Not surprisingly, relations between Gore and Nader supporters quickly soured. Gore supporters berated the Nader campaign for organizing what they viewed as a suicide mission. Nader was polling at less than 4 percent in most of the country and had no chance of winning the election, but his ability to siphon votes from Gore could help elect Bush, the Nader and Gore campaigns' common enemy.

In the midst of this heated campaign, a small group of supporters from the Nader and Gore campaigns had a brilliant idea. They devised a plan that might simultaneously benefit both Nader and Gore at the expense of Bush. They did so by examining each candidate's underlying interests.

Clearly, both Gore and Nader wanted as many votes as possible, but they wanted votes for different reasons. Gore was hoping to win the election in 2000. To do so, he did not need to win large majorities of the popular vote in each state; he simply needed majority support in enough states so that his electoral votes exceeded Bush's electoral votes. (In most states, the candidate with the highest number of popular votes receives that state's entire share of electoral votes.)

Meanwhile, Nader had no hope of winning the presidency in 2000. However, he knew that if he could obtain 5 percent of the *popular* vote nationwide (not statewide), his party would qualify for federal matching funds in the *next* presidential campaign. Knowing that his only chance (albeit slim) of being elected president in the future hinged on receiving matching funds, Nader was campaigning hard in 2000.

On the surface, the conflict between Gore and Nader was irreconcilable—they were competing for votes from the same group of supporters. A closer look, however, revealed that they were actually trying to satisfy very different—and perhaps compatible—interests: Gore wanted electoral votes, whereas Nader wanted popular votes. If Gore supporters who lived in states where Gore was certain to get a large majority of popular votes could "trade" some of their votes with Nader supporters in "battleground states" (i.e., those states where the race between Bush and Gore was extremely tight), both Gore and Nader could benefit. For example, if a Gore supporter in California (where Gore was expected to win) voted for Nader, and if a Nader supporter in Florida (where the Bush-Gore competition was fierce) voted for Gore, then Nader would still receive the *popular* vote he needed, and Gore would increase his chances of obtaining the additional *electoral* votes he needed. To facilitate such trades, a number of websites emerged to pair Gore and Nader supporters from different states. Each voter in the pair would commit to vote for the other's candidate. The entire transaction would be governed by the honor system.

The genius of this strategy is perhaps most evident in the response it garnered from Bush supporters, some of whom began to argue that vote-trading is illegal in the United States. The ensuing threat of prosecution from election officials forced some operators to shut down the vote-trading websites. Both Nader and Gore subsequently failed to accomplish their goals. Although Gore won the most popular votes nationwide, he did not receive enough electoral votes to win the presidency, and Nader fell short of the 5 percent popular vote he needed to receive matching funds in 2004.

Consider a more commonplace example of the same principle: A job candidate demands a high salary from his potential employer, only to find that the employer is constrained by budget restrictions. If the two parties focus only on the demands involved, few options remain; the candidate can accept the job as is, or he can look for a different job. But what happens when the employer focuses on *why* the candidate is demanding a higher salary? Presumably, it is because he wants a more comfortable lifestyle, greater purchasing power, more freedom and flexibility, higher status, and better health. Once they begin to focus on these underlying interests, the employer and the candidate may discover that they have more options. Instead of an increase in salary, the employer might offer more vacation days, a better job title, a choice of work locations, improved health benefits, and/or a signing bonus.

PRINCIPLE 3: CREATE COMMON GROUND WITH UNCOMMON ALLIES

It is tempting to believe that Gore and Nader supporters were able to negotiate an agreement in 2000 because they shared an overarching goal: defeating Bush. What happened four years later, however, suggests otherwise. In the 2004 presidential campaign, Democratic candidate John Kerry challenged Republican President George Bush. Again Nader entered the fray. Knowing that Nader's candidacy had likely cost them the 2000 election, Democrats were in an uproar. Many who had supported Nader in 2000 begged him not to run. Nader refused to abandon his campaign, despite polls showing he had the support of less than 2 percent of voters.

In the summer of 2004, it was revealed that Nader had begun to receive—and to accept—a number of large donations. But these donations did not come from his supporters on the far left—they came from Republicans! Clearly, Republicans were supporting Nader's candidacy to take votes away from their more dangerous competitor, Kerry. As in 2000, the bargain was consummated in the midst of a seemingly zero-sum game between competitors. This time, it was an implicit pact between Nader supporters (who benefited by receiving additional money with which to attract votes) and Bush supporters (who benefited by diminishing the votes available to their primary opponent, Kerry). Despite the clear-as-day nature of this transaction, Nader's running mate, Peter Camejo, defended the acceptance of Republican donations by saying, "We have no way to know what the intent of the money is."[1]

As these two stories from the 2000 and 2004 elections suggest, value-creating opportunities can emerge even between competitors who abhor each other. This fact speaks to the power of understanding and leveraging underlying interests. Professors Adam Brandenburger and Barry Nalebuff coined the term *co-opetition* to describe the mixed motives we often do (and *should*) have when engaging with those whom we view as our competitors.[2] According to the principle of co-opetition, it is possible to simultaneously cooperate and compete with others. You saw this principle at work in Chapter 2, where we developed a framework for simultaneously creating and claiming value in negotiation. Here the power of co-opetition becomes even clearer: those who view their relationship with the other side as one-dimensional ("He is my enemy") forgo opportunities for value creation, whereas those who appreciate complex relationships and explore mutual interests are able to create common ground.

It is worth considering what might have occurred if, between 2000 and 2004, Democrats had made an effort to build common ground with Nader and his supporters. For example, Democrats might have promised to work with the Nader candidacy on shared issues and in states that were not hotly contested. In return, Nader supporters could have committed not to campaign as hard in battleground states. If this had happened, it is imaginable that Nader and his supporters would have aimed their fiery rhetoric more at Bush than at Kerry. Instead, a Bush-Nader coalition emerged in 2004.

PRINCIPLE 4: INTERPRET DEMANDS AS OPPORTUNITIES

An executive student, the CEO of a successful construction company, related the following story in one of our classes. The CEO was negotiating a deal in which a buyer would contract with his company to build midsize office buildings. After months of negotiations finally concluded—but just before the contract was signed—the buyer approached the executive with an entirely new and potentially costly demand: a clause in the contract that would require the builder to pay large penalties if the project's completion was delayed by more than one month. The builder was initially outraged by this sudden demand; it seemed as though the buyer was trying to squeeze some last-minute concessions from him.

The builder weighed his options: he could accept the buyer's demand and seal the deal; he could reject the buyer's demand and hope this would not destroy the deal; or he could try to negotiate to reduce the proposed penalties. Then he thought more deeply about the situation. What did the buyer's demand reveal? At the very least, it revealed that the buyer was concerned about delays and that he valued timely (and perhaps *early*) project completion. With this in mind, the executive approached the buyer with the following proposal: he would pay even *higher* penalties than the buyer had demanded if the project was delayed, but the buyer would give the construction company a bonus if the project was completed *earlier* than scheduled. After working out the details, both parties agreed to this clause, and both were happier with the deal. The builder was confident that he would finish on time and receive the bonus, and the buyer was able to minimize his downside risk.

The genius of the CEO's approach lay in his ability to focus on the other party's needs and interests rather than on his own predicament. Typically, when facing demands from the other party, negotiators adopt a defensive posture: "How can I avoid accepting this demand?" Investigative negotiators confront demands the same way they confront any other statement from the other party: "What can I learn from this demand? What does it tell me about the other party's needs and interests? How can I use this information to create and capture value?"

PRINCIPLE 5: DON'T DISMISS ANYTHING AS "THEIR PROBLEM"

While our own constraints are highly visible to us, it's easy to overlook those of the other party. In fact, negotiators often adopt the attitude "It's their problem, not mine." Unfortunately, in negotiation, their problem quickly becomes your problem. For example, if one party faces a deadline, the amount of time available to negotiate diminishes for both parties. Similarly, if one party is unable to fulfill her responsibilities, she may be legally liable, but both parties may stand to lose profit.

A former student's experience inspired this example: The CEO of "HomeStuff," a well-established and profitable producer of household appliances, was negotiating the purchase and delivery of mechanical parts from "Kogs," a new supplier. The parties discussed two key issues: price and delivery date. HomeStuff wanted to pay a low price and also wanted immediate delivery. Not surprisingly, Kogs wanted a high price and more time to deliver the goods.

Based on prevailing market rates, the parties agreed to a price of $17 million and a three-month delivery date. The supplier, however, voiced some anxiety about the delivery time frame: "This will be costly," he said, "but I'll manage."

The CEO of HomeStuff, aware that delaying delivery beyond three months would cost HomeStuff close to $1 million, offered to accept delayed delivery if Kogs would agree to cut the price by $1 million.

"I appreciate the offer," the supplier responded, "but I can't accept such a large price cut."

Normally, negotiations would end at this point. The CEO had tried to make both sides better off through logrolling and found this was not possible. Nonetheless, the CEO decided to pursue the matter further. "I'm surprised that a three-month deadline for delivery is creating such a problem for you," she said to the supplier. "I would have thought that you could easily manufacture the parts in a short amount of time. Would you mind telling me more about your production process so that I can better understand your constraints?"

"Actually, manufacturing is not the problem at all," the supplier said. "It's the shipping costs that are killing us. The freight rates that we have to pay at such short notice are extremely high."

When the CEO heard this, her eyes lit up. Had the problem been what she had assumed (no cheap way to *manufacture* in time), there was little to be done. But this problem (no cheap way to *transport* in time) was one that HomeStuff could solve for Kogs. HomeStuff had been involved in high-volume shipping for years and often had to ship products at short notice. As a result, the firm had negotiated very favorable terms for this kind of a delivery. Indeed, the CEO could have the parts shipped from the supplier in *less* than three months at a cost of only $500,000. In comparison, the supplier would have paid more than two times that much ($1.2 million).

The CEO made the following offer, which was immediately accepted:

- HomeStuff would have the parts delivered via its own shippers in 2.5 months.
- The supplier would pay the cost of shipping ($500,000).
- The supplier would lower the price from $17 million to $16.5 million, allowing both parties to share in the cost savings.

Another great result of this arrangement? The supplier now had a relationship with the low-cost shipper and could take advantage of the shipper's efficiency in the future.

As the HomeStuff story illustrates, when the other party's constraint destroys value, it is naive to view these constraints as "their problem." In this case, the supplier was constrained by the high costs of shipping, and this was destroying $700,000 in value for both parties. The HomeStuff CEO's genius lay in her desire to understand—and solve—the other side's problems; the CEO leveraged HomeStuff's cost advantage to fix the transportation dilemma. Similarly, in the UN negotiations, Ambassador Holbrooke was able to leverage his relationship with Ted Turner (who agreed to donate over $30 million to offset the one-year shortfall in UN dues) to solve the budget constraints faced by other member states. In both cases, a problem was solved not out of benevolence or altruism, but because the negotiators understood that an unconstrained "opponent" would have more to offer than would someone whose hands were tied.

PRINCIPLE 6: DON'T LET NEGOTIATIONS END WITH A REJECTION OF YOUR OFFER

How many times have you tried to make a sale, or tried to close a deal, only to have your final offer rejected? What do you do when this happens? If you are like most people, once the other side has said no to the best offer you could conceive, you feel there is little left for you to do. Often, you are correct. Sometimes, however, you are very wrong.

A few years ago, Linda, the CEO of a company that manufactures specialty gift items for many Fortune 500 clients, found herself at the receiving end of a rejection. A very big potential client, whom she had courted for months, had decided that they would purchase from her competitor. The final heartbreak came after both manufacturers had submitted their final offers and the client had picked Linda's competitor. Linda was surprised, but accepted the loss as a part of life. So she had no illusions of winning the deal when she decided to make one last call to the client. When the VP of purchasing came on the phone, Linda asked whether he would be willing to tell her why her final offer had not been sufficient to win the deal. "This information could help me improve my product and service offerings in the future," she explained.

Linda was quite surprised when the VP explained why the competitor had beaten her offer. As it turned out, Linda had been under the false assumption that the client cared mostly about price. In her final offer, Linda had done everything possible to reduce the cost to the client; in doing so, she had eliminated features of the product that the client valued significantly. Her competitor, on the other hand, was charging a much higher price, but included the key product features. After listening intently to the VP's explanation, Linda thanked him for his candor. She then explained that she had misunderstood the client's position. "Knowing what I know now," she said, "I'm confident that I can beat their offer." She then asked the VP whether he was still in a position to entertain a revised offer from her firm. The VP said that he was. One week later, Linda had won the client over—and signed the deal.

The key lesson of this story, one that Linda has applied ever since, is that negotiations should never end with a "no." Instead, they should either end with a "yes" or with an *explanation* as to "why not." You may discover that the other side has needs that you simply cannot meet, or that your competitor creates value in ways that you cannot. If so, you can confidently walk away from the negotiation knowing that no deal was possible. But you might instead discover that there were options you overlooked, needs you did not consider, or issues you did not explore carefully. The very least that an investigative negotiator will do after being rejected is to ask: "What would it have taken for us to reach an agreement?" Even if the answer confirms that you cannot win the deal, you may learn important information that will help you in your future negotiations with this or other potential customers.

In short, there is nothing wrong with "no deal" or with a rejection of your offer—as long as the reason for the "no deal" is that there is no ZOPA (i.e., no mutually agreeable outcome). If you are not the partner who helps the other side create the most value, then you do not deserve the deal. But if you can create the most value, and there is no deal because you were out-negotiated, then that is a tragic, value-destroying outcome. Investigative negotiators do not fear rejection, but they also don't let things end there; they investigate further to find out if there really is no scope for a deal. Investigative negotiators understand that "why not" is often as important a question as "why." And above all, investigative negotiators never stop learning—not even when the deal is lost and they have been asked to leave the room.

PRINCIPLE 7: UNDERSTAND THE DIFFERENCE BETWEEN "SELLING" AND "NEGOTIATING"

Imagine you're watching a salesperson at work. What do you see? What approach is the salesperson taking? What strategies is he employing? What does the salesperson focus on?

When asked to imagine a salesperson in action, most people envision someone making a "pitch"—arguing the merits of his case and trying to convince a potential target that they should buy what he has to offer.

Now imagine you're watching a negotiator at work. What do you see? What approach is the negotiator taking? What strategies is he employing? What does the negotiator focus on?

If you again envision someone making a pitch, you are failing to discern the crucial distinction between "selling" and "negotiating." Selling involves telling people about the virtues of the product or service you have to offer, focusing on the strengths of your case, and trying to induce agreement or compliance. Effective negotiating requires this kind of active selling, but it also entails focusing on the other side's interests, needs, priorities, constraints, and perspective. Negotiation geniuses—and all great salespeople—understand this difference. They also understand that their ability to structure a deal that maximizes value often hinges not on their ability to persuade, but on their ability to listen.

It is worth noting that most of the negotiated agreements we have considered in this chapter have not only satisfied each party's interests, but have also done so without requiring either party to make a substantive concession. In the 2000 presidential elections, the agreement between Gore and Nader supporters was designed for Gore to gain electoral votes and Nader to gain popular votes without either party having to give away anything of value. Similarly, in Chris's negotiation with the European supplier, Chris obtained protection against competitors, the supplier retained his right to sell to his cousin, and neither party had to make a substantive concession. In the cab ride negotiation, the driver made money, Shikha got a ride home, and no one made a concession. These negotiated agreements suggest that if you negotiate with an investigative approach, you may not have to "give a little to get a little," as the saying goes. Rather, you may be able to get everything you want by giving up nothing—except, perhaps, your mistaken assumption that one of you has to lose for the other to win.

FIVE STRATEGIES FOR ELICITING INFORMATION FROM RETICENT NEGOTIATORS

By now, you may have noticed that all of the principles we have outlined in this chapter, as well as all of the strategies for value creation presented in Chapter 2, assume that it is possible to discover the interests, priorities, and constraints of the other negotiator. For logrolling to occur, parties must understand who values an issue more. Similarly, to reconcile each party's interests, both parties must be willing to share private information. Unfortunately, negotiators often do not share such information. Typically, they keep their cards close to the vest for fear that if the other side knows what they value highly—or why they want or need something—they will be exploited.

How, then, can you elicit the information necessary to create value, resolve conflicts, and reach efficient agreements? Here are five strategies for dealing with reticent negotiators. The strategies build on each other; if the first one doesn't work, continue down the list. Of course, the better your relationship with the other side, the more likely it is that one of the earlier strategies will do the trick.

STRATEGY 1: BUILD TRUST AND SHARE INFORMATION

Negotiators are more willing to openly share information regarding their interests, constraints, and priorities when they trust one another. This fact is not surprising. What does surprise us is how rarely negotiators *invest* in trust building prior to, during, and after their negotiations. Negotiation geniuses do not simply leverage trust when it is present; they build trust when it is absent.

How can you build trust? First, understand that negotiation causes anxiety for everyone—even for that tough, poker-faced negotiator whom you hate to have across the table from you. This anxiety is rooted in the fear that the other party will exploit you if given the opportunity. If you can alleviate this fear, both sides will feel less anxious and will be able to share information more easily. Here are three powerful ways to alleviate fear and build trust:

Understand and speak their language. This advice is not only relevant in cross-cultural negotiations; executives from different firms and industries also speak different languages. In one case that we know of, a consulting firm lost its bid for a multimillion-dollar project because the firm's representative did not understand just *one* specific word of technical jargon that the client was using. That one brief moment of linguistic ignorance cost the firm millions in revenue. How could this have been avoided? The consulting firm could have taken the time to more thoroughly study the client's industry or could have picked as its representative someone with experience in the client's industry. When you speak the other side's language, you not only build a sense of kinship; you also signal that you care about their needs and are interested in building a long-term relationship.

Increase the ties that bind. If yours is a purely business or political relationship, the other side has every reason to believe that you will exploit them when it is in your economic or political interest to do so. Learning about the other side's family and their life, spending time with them in informal settings, sharing common friends, and living or working in the same community will facilitate trust. Even increasing your economic or political ties with the other side can facilitate trust. Imagine a firm that sells one service to a client under a one-year contract. Now imagine a firm that sells multiple services to the same client, with long-term contracts that expire at different times. Both of these firms will want to renew a contract when it expires. But which of these firms has a greater opportunity to cultivate the trust that is necessary for securing future business with the client?

Build trust when you're not negotiating. Your greatest opportunity to build trust comes when your cooperative, benevolent, or ethical behavior cannot be interpreted as self-serving. Anyone can be nice when they are trying to get the deal; smart negotiators maintain and strengthen relationships with others even when there is no obvious economic or political reason to do so. By keeping in touch with ex-clients, delivering a better product than promised, passing along unanticipated cost savings, and behaving ethically across the board, you can increase the likelihood that your next negotiation will be with someone who trusts you. This highlights another important point: the best way to build trust is to actually be trustworthy. Negotiators who strategize, economize, or cut corners when it comes to ethical behavior are typically not in a position to build the trust necessary for information exchange and value creation.

STRATEGY 2: ASK QUESTIONS—ESPECIALLY IF YOU ARE SURPRISED OR SKEPTICAL

Negotiators often do not bother to ask questions because they assume the other party will not answer them. This is a colossal mistake. While there is no guarantee that someone will answer your questions, one thing is certain: your questions are more likely to be answered if you ask them than if you don't. But asking the important questions is not enough; the real trick is in knowing *how* to ask them.

For example, if you want to know the other side's reservation value, it is usually futile to ask them for their bottom-line figures; they are unlikely to answer. But you can ask other questions that they *will* answer—and that will give you essentially the same information. Consider these less-threatening queries:

- "What do you plan to do with the products you're purchasing from us?"
- "Tell me about your customers."
- "What do you plan to do if we can't provide you with the services you need?"
- "How does this deal fit into your overall business strategy?"
- "Tell me more about your organization."

Unfortunately, many negotiators do not ask such indirect questions because they are too busy arguing the merits of their case.

As we've said previously, asking questions is especially important anytime you are surprised or skeptical. The negotiators in Chris's firm should not have needed him to fly to Europe and ask why the supplier was reluctant to allow exclusivity. The supplier's refusal—even after significant price concessions and minimum-purchase guarantees were offered—should have been a call to action—that is, a call to questioning. Similarly, in the *Moms.com* negotiation in Chapter 2, when Kim stated that the show's projected ratings were low, you should have taken this opportunity to ask a series of important questions: "What do those projections assume? How confident are you of those projections? What would happen if the projections were incorrect?" This line of questioning could lead to the structuring of a contingency contract.

STRATEGY 3: GIVE AWAY SOME INFORMATION

You have tried to build trust and share information. You have exhausted your list of questions. Yet the other party is still unwilling to give you the information you need. Now what?

Leverage the norm of reciprocity and be the first to give away some information. For example, you might say: "I know we have a lot to talk about. If you'd like, I can start by discussing some of the issues that are most important to me. Then you can do the same." This tactic helps reduce the other party's anxiety; if both parties are sharing information, both are mutually vulnerable. The key, then, is to share information incrementally, back and forth. In this way you can minimize your own risks: if the other party is still reluctant to discuss matters, you can decide to hold back as needed.

When using this strategy, it is critical for you to know what kinds of information to share and withhold. First, you should rarely give away your reservation value—and certainly not early in the negotiation. If you tell the other party that the lowest you can accept is $15,000, guess what they will offer you? On the other hand, it is generally safe to share information regarding your priorities across different issues. This advice often surprises people because they reason as follows: "If I tell them what I don't value, I won't be able to demand large concessions in return for giving it to them." The key is to share information about your *relative* priorities without minimizing the *absolute* importance of any one issue. Compare these two approaches:

> *What not to say:* "Of the five issues we are here to discuss, I only care about Issues 2 and 4. I don't really care what we decide about the other items."

> *How to say it:* "The five issues we are here to discuss are all critical because each has a significant impact on my bottom line. It may be difficult for me to offer concessions on any of the issues. But if I had to choose, I would say that Issues 2 and 4 may be the most critical—these are the issues on which I am least flexible."

Giving away such information provides two important benefits. First, if your counterpart is a skilled negotiator, she will start identifying trades that will allow you to logroll and create value. For example, she might suggest that she can give you what you need on Issue 2 in exchange for what she needs on Issue 1. Second, even if your counterpart is not a negotiation genius, she is still human—and humans tend to reciprocate behavior. When you lie to people, they often lie in return. When you apologize, they often express contrition or regret as well. And when you give them useful and credible information, they often respond by sharing information with you.

STRATEGY 4: NEGOTIATE MULTIPLE ISSUES SIMULTANEOUSLY

As we noted in Chapter 2, logrolling requires that you put all of the issues on the table at the same time and, instead of discussing them one by one, jump back and forth among them. Negotiating multiple issues simultaneously is also a great way to get information regarding the other party's relative preferences and priorities. If you discuss one issue at a time, the other party is likely to treat each issue as the most important one in the negotiation. To get a clear read on their true priorities, open up the discussion to include multiple issues and put them in a position where they must make an implicit choice about which issue or demand to emphasize. To determine which issues are most important to the other party, look for the following signs:

- Which issue does he want to return to constantly?
- Which issues make him the most emotional or tense?
- While discussing which issues is she most likely to talk rather than to listen?
- Which issues is she most obstinate about when you ask for a compromise?

STRATEGY 5: MAKE MULTIPLE OFFERS SIMULTANEOUSLY

Imagine that you have tried all of the strategies above and the other party is still reluctant to provide the information you need. What you need now is a tactic that elicits information without him even knowing that he is giving it. Try this: Next time you are preparing to make an offer, don't just make one. Instead, make *two* offers simultaneously. Specifically, make two offers that are of *equal value* to you, but that differ slightly from each other.

Consider the following negotiation with a real-estate agent you are hiring to sell your house. The two primary components of the agent's contract are commission (the percentage of the sale price that the agent will receive) and contract length (the length of time that the agent has exclusivity to sell the house). The agent wants a high commission (6 percent) and a long contract (six months). You want to give the agent a lower commission and keep the contract length to a minimum. How can you find out which issue the agent values more? First, calculate how these two issues trade off for *you* by creating a scoring system (see Chapter 2). Let's say that you discover that it would be equally valuable to you to reduce the commission by 1 percent or to reduce the contract length by one month. So, you make the following two offers to the agent:

Offer X: 2.5 percent commission, three-month contract
Offer Y: 3.5 percent commission, two-month contract

The agent responds that, while neither offer is entirely acceptable to her, she prefers Offer X to Offer Y. This gives you important information! Because these offers are equal in value to you, her choice reveals that (relative to commission rate) the agent values additional time (i.e., contract length) more than you do. Thus, if you try to structure a deal with a relatively low commission in exchange for a longer contract, you are likely to make both parties better off. The agent's stated preference might also tell you something else—something that should be of concern. Why does the agent value additional time so much? Is she very busy these days? Is she not a good salesperson? These are issues you can now investigate. This information may have been hard to obtain without the use of multiple simultaneous offers.

Keep in mind that the other party does not have to *accept* either of your two offers to signal her relative priorities. Indeed, the agent could respond to your offers by saying that both are entirely unacceptable because you have anchored too aggressively. This is not a problem. You can then ask: "Which offer is closer to something you could accept?" or "Which one is completely off the mark?" or "If I were to consider making some changes, which offer should I start working on?" Answers to any of these questions will give you the information you need to start logrolling.

Making multiple offers simultaneously is a great tactic for other reasons as well. Not only does it allow you to discover the interests of reticent negotiators, but it also allows you to anchor more strongly (with two offers rather than one) and to simultaneously come across as flexible. The fact that you are providing options signals that you are willing to be accommodating and are interested in understanding the other party's preferences and needs.

THE INFORMATION GAME

Negotiation is an information game. Those who know how to obtain information perform better than those who stick with what they know. In all of the examples presented in Part I of the book, we've seen that the decision to challenge assumptions and probe below the surface helped negotiators improve their options and structure more efficient deals. More generally, the investigative negotiation approach can help you transform competitive, zero-sum negotiations into ones that entail the possibility of cooperation, value creation, and mutual satisfaction.

It is not enough, however, to be equipped with a systematic approach for maximizing value creation and value claiming. In Part II of the book, we delve into the mind of the negotiator and expose some of the psychological traps that can derail the strategy of even the savviest of negotiators. Negotiation geniuses understand the workings—and the shortcomings—of the human mind, and are adept not only at overcoming their own psychological biases, but also confronting (and, when needed, leveraging) the biases of others.

PART II

THE PSYCHOLOGY OF NEGOTIATION

CHAPTER 4

When Rationality Fails:
Biases of the Mind

O n September 15, 2004, in the midst of a contentious labor dispute, the National Hockey League locked out its players. Five months and hundreds of canceled games later, the NHL officially called off the season. In doing so, it became the first major-league sport in U.S. history to lose an entire season to a labor dispute.

What went wrong?[1] Under the leadership of Commissioner Gary Bettman, the NHL expanded ambitiously throughout the 1990s, adding nine new U.S. teams, building new arenas, generating publicity, and increasing television time for the sport. But in its quest to ramp up its visibility and profits, NHL management allowed player salaries to reach unsustainable heights. By 2003, according to the league, salaries were 75 percent of NHL revenues—a 34 percent increase from the 1990–91 season.[2] By comparison, the National Football League paid its players 64 percent of revenues; the National Basketball Association paid 57 percent.

By 2004, the NHL could no longer ignore its growing financial dilemma. Nineteen of thirty franchises lost money during the 2003–04 season; the league claimed to have lost $225 million in this same period. The sale of television rights was also disappointing.[3] As a result, NHL management decided to take a hard line at the start of the 2004–05 season. The league sought a reduction in average player salary from $1.8 million to $1.3 million. In addition to salary rollbacks,

Commissioner Bettman demanded "cost certainty," a salary cap limiting payrolls to a maximum of 55 percent of team revenues.

On December 9, 2004, the NHL Players' Association (NHLPA) agreed to a 24 percent rollback of existing salaries but refused to link payroll to revenue. Bettman set a mid-February deadline for reaching agreement or canceling the season. On February 14, 2005, NHL owners proposed a salary cap that did not tie payroll to revenue. After further negotiation, the owners' salary cap offer stood at $42.5 million per team. The NHLPA came down from demanding a $52-million-per-team cap to $49 million, with certain exceptions.

"To be this close, they have to make a deal," Mighty Ducks player Mike Leclerc told the *Los Angeles Times* as Bettman's deadline approached. "It would be disgraceful to cancel the season."[4] Yet the deadline passed without agreement, and Bettman officially announced that the season had ended before it even began. Almost 400 of the NHL's 700-plus players defected to European teams for the season; older players found their careers suddenly cut short. Many felt betrayed by both their union and their team owners. Public sentiment was divided early on but quickly turned against the players, who were viewed as unrealistic and greedy.

On July 21, 2005, the NHL and the NHLPA finally ended the 310-day lockout and set the 2005–06 hockey season in motion by ratifying a collective-bargaining agreement. Backed by nearly 90 percent of NHL players, the agreement called for a $39-million-per-team salary cap—a $10 million decrease in the NHLPA's previous demands—and *lower* than what the league had offered five months earlier. Other cost-certainty measures were also included: payrolls would not exceed 54 percent of team revenues, all current player contracts were rolled back by 24 percent, and the arbitration clause was changed to make it less advantageous to the players.[5] The players received only nominal concessions in return (e.g., a guaranteed salary minimum per team). Major league hockey, a "gate-driven" sport that earns about three-fifths of its revenue from ticket sales, was now faced with the uphill challenge of luring fans back into stadiums in significant numbers.[6]

Why would the players' union reject an offer for $42.5 million in February only to accept $39 million in July? Why did they sacrifice a season's worth of revenues and goodwill to hold out for less? By most accounts, the deal that was eventually signed was achievable before the lockout. Why, then, did the two sides fail to avoid the loss of a season? Were the dispute, the lockout, and the cancellation of the 2004–05 season necessary and inevitable events? It is our view that the whims of fate are not to blame; rather, the negotiation failed in large part due to preventable negotiation mistakes.

WHEN REASON FAILS US

Daniel Kahneman received the 2002 Nobel Prize in Economics for his work with Amos Tversky on the systematic ways that the human mind deviates from rationality. This profound work has led to scientific revolutions in many fields, including economics, psychology, finance, law, medicine, and marketing. This work has also transformed the field of negotiation. Prior to the influence of what is known as *behavioral decision research,* negotiators were simply urged to approach problems from a rational perspective—in other words, they were told to take certain logical frameworks (e.g., very early versions of what we have developed in Chapters 1–3) and to "go be rational."

By contrast, behavioral decision research emphasizes that while advising negotiators to be rational is necessary, it is far from sufficient. Negotiators also need to be made aware of the mental habits and biases that might prevent them from following rational advice. Behavioral decision researchers have learned a great deal about the nature of the mistakes that we make in negotiations, how we can avoid such mistakes in our own thinking, and how we can anticipate and leverage them in the behavior of others. In this chapter and the next, we will help you develop the self-awareness and rationality that is often missing when negotiators are unprepared, caught off guard, or shoot from the hip. We will also assist you in anticipating the thoughts and moves of your negotiation opponents and partners.

Of course, it's not news that people are irrational and sometimes make mistakes. What *is* news is that, in the context of decision-making and negotiation, many of the mistakes people make are *systematic* and *predictable.* In fact, even the brightest of executives fall victim to four critical, systematic errors on a regular basis: the fixed-pie bias, the

vividness bias, nonrational escalation of commitment, and susceptibility to framing.

THE FIXED-PIE BIAS

Recall our story from Chapter 3, in which Chris was called in to break
an impasse over exclusivity terms between his company's team of negotiators and the European supplier. The U.S. negotiation team assumed that only one of the two companies could get what it wanted
on the issue of exclusivity: either exclusivity would be awarded or it
would not be awarded. Luckily, Chris's very simple question about
why the European firm would not allow exclusivity revealed that the
supplier only wanted to retain the right to provide small amounts of
the product to his cousin. Meanwhile, the U.S. firm did not mind if
the supplier sold a few hundred pounds to a local firm, as long as the
supplier could guarantee exclusivity otherwise. Thus, what appeared
to be one issue (exclusivity) was, in fact, two separate issues: exclusivity
over the first few hundred pounds of product and exclusivity over the
bulk of the supply. Despite appearances, one party did not have to lose
for the other to win.

Sometimes negotiation *is* about only one issue. As in the Hamilton
Real Estate case in Chapter 1, such negotiations are typically zero-sum
in nature: one party can gain only at the expense of the other (assuming they reach agreement). Such negotiations are said to have a "fixed
pie" of value or resources: the only thing negotiators can do is slice up
the pie and try to get a big piece of it.

In contrast, most negotiations involve more than one issue, including delivery, service, financing, bonuses, timing, and relationships. In
Chapters 2 and 3, we explained that the presence of multiple issues allows negotiators to create value by making wise trade-offs; we also offered concrete strategies for finding such trade-offs. Here, we add the
warning that negotiators often fail to create value because they *assume*
there is a *fixed pie* of value or resources even when it is possible to increase the size of the pie. In Chris's story, as in many successful negotiation stories, success required overcoming the fixed-pie bias and
moving toward a mutually beneficial trade.

The fixed-pie bias affects even the most seasoned negotiators, causing them to focus exclusively on capturing value for themselves and to ignore approaches that could create value. Congressman Floyd Spence (R-South Carolina) once analyzed a proposed agreement over nuclear disarmament between the United States and the Soviet Union and concluded, "I have had a philosophy for some time in regard to SALT [the proposed agreement], and it goes like this: the Russians will not accept a SALT treaty that is not in their best interest, and it seems to me that if it is in their best interest, it can't be in our best interest."[7] Spence's fixed-pie mind-set risked exposing the world to a higher probability of nuclear annihilation; he overlooked the possibility that both nations might benefit from disarmament activities.

One of Max's previous books, written with Jonathan Baron and Katherine Shonk, documented a multitude of ways in which the fixed-pie assumption leads to conflict between perceived opponents—and to value destruction for society.[8] Consider the story of Benjamin Cone, Jr., a forester who inherited 7,200 acres of land in North Carolina in 1982. Cone had tended to and preserved his land by planting fodder, conducting controlled burns, and keeping their timber sales low. Not surprisingly, songbirds, wild turkey, quail, and deer thrived on the property.

In 1991, a biologist hired by Cone informed him that approximately twenty-nine red-cockaded woodpeckers, members of an endangered species, were living in his woods. Responding to the 1973 Endangered Species Act (ESA), the U.S. Fish and Wildlife Service took control of the woodpeckers' habitat—which was 1,560 acres, or about 15 percent of Cone's property. Following the loss of this property, Cone drastically altered the way he forested the remaining 85 percent of his land. To keep the woodpeckers from taking over his entire property, he switched from the sustainable practices he had learned from his family and began clear-cutting (i.e., eliminating all trees and vegetation) 500 acres of forest every year. As he had hoped, clear-cutting prevented the woodpeckers from expanding their habitat—but this was a Pyrrhic victory. Cone had destroyed significant economic and environmental value in order to "win" the fight against woodpeckers and the ESA.

Cone's response was clearly not what the authors of the Endangered

Species Act had in mind when they wrote the legislation. But Cone decided to clear-cut his forest because he felt he had to choose between destroying his trees and donating them to the woodpeckers. Did this dispute between economic concerns (for Cone) and environmental concerns (for society) have to turn out so badly for both sides? In fact, Cone had alternatives to clear-cutting. At the time, the ESA allowed landowners to create a Habitat Conservation Plan (HCP), which gives private landowners permission to violate aspects of the ESA, as long as the landowners also take certain steps to preserve the endangered species. The HCP provided an opportunity to overcome the fixed-pie assumption by allowing landowners to seek out creative alternatives that serve the interests of both the endangered species and the landowners. Unfortunately, Cone rejected the idea of adopting an HCP; he assumed that if the plan was desirable to environmentalists, it must be bad for his business. His fixed-pie bias led him toward the adoption of a radically defensive, and ultimately self-defeating, strategy.

In another striking example of the power of the fixed-pie bias, researcher Leigh Thompson has shown that even when two sides want the exact same outcome, negotiators often settle for a different outcome because they assume that they must compromise to reach agreement. She developed a negotiation simulation that included two issues that were compatible; the parties had the exact same preference. From an objective standpoint, there was nothing to negotiate on these issues, as no real conflict existed. Yet 39 percent of negotiators did not agree on the mutually preferred outcome on at least one of the two compatible issues! Those who did reach an optimal agreement often did not realize that the other party had also benefited from the arrangement; they believed they had "out-negotiated" the other side on that issue.[9]

The fixed-pie bias not only makes value creation difficult, it can also lead to *reactive devaluation*: the tendency of negotiators to denigrate and devalue another party's concessions simply because these are being offered by an adversary. A study of how U.S. citizens responded to an arms-reduction proposal showed this tendency in action.[10] Researchers divided 137 study participants into two groups and then asked how favorable the proposal was to the United States and how favorable it was to the (now former) U.S.S.R. One group was correctly informed that the proposal was made by then–Communist Party secretary Gorbachev. The other group was falsely told that the proposal was made by then-president Reagan. Among those who believed the proposal originated with Gorbachev, 56 percent thought that the proposal favored the U.S.S.R. and only 16 percent felt that it favored the United States. The other 28 percent thought that it favored both sides equally. When participants were told that the proposal came from President Reagan, however, only 27 percent thought that it favored the U.S.S.R., another 27 percent thought it favored the United States, and 45 percent thought that it benefited both sides equally.

As this study demonstrates, even terms that appear mutually beneficial when you advance them may seem disadvantageous when proposed by the other party. Likewise, when the other party concedes on an issue, a negotiator may devalue the issue's worth: "If she's willing to make that concession, this issue must not be important." Or, when the other party seems happy, a negotiator may assume he got a bad deal: "If she is happy, we must have lost." These tendencies are all rooted in the fixed-pie bias, which mistakenly leads us to believe that "whatever is good for them is bad for us." The effect of this bias is also visible in the NHL dispute. Both parties focused on divisive issues related to salary, but ignored pie-enlarging issues such as salvaging the season, increasing revenues, and simply playing hockey. Moreover, the players eventually accepted an offer that was remarkably similar to—and perhaps worse than—what they could have received prior to the lockout. Unfortunately, because the offer came from the owners, the players immediately devalued it.

Chapters 2 and 3 outlined a number of strategies for value creation (e.g., negotiating multiple issues simultaneously, making multiple offers simultaneously, using contingency contracts, et cetera). Even before you attempt these strategies, however, it is important to be aware that your initial, automatic response in negotiation may be guided by a fixed-pie mentality and that you may need to adjust your thinking accordingly.

Bottom line: when approaching any important negotiation, enter the process with the goal of looking for areas in which you can create value. It is better to assume that you can enlarge the pie and later find out that you were wrong than to assume the pie is fixed and never find out you were wrong.

THE VIVIDNESS BIAS

Top MBA students from prestigious universities are in a strong position to negotiate with their employers for the issues critical to their career and personal happiness. These students are smart, well trained, and highly valued by the finest firms in the world. Thus, negotiating the right job package should be easy for this group. If this is the case, then why do so many MBA students change jobs very soon after accepting their first position? One important reason is that they are affected by the *vividness bias*. Specifically, they pay too much attention to vivid features of their offers and overlook less vivid features that could have a greater impact on their satisfaction. This is a potential trap even for seasoned negotiators.

At the Harvard Business School, MBA students spend a lot of time in a student center called Spangler. As recruiting season arrives, the most popular topic of conversation at Spangler revolves around interviews and job offers. Consider the statements that students might make in Spangler about different jobs:

- The medical benefits are very good.
- The company is located within ten miles of where I grew up.
- People seemed very happy during my visit to corporate headquarters.
- I would get to travel to Europe on a regular basis.
- The starting salary is $140,000.
- Employees have significant control over their work assignments.
- The office space is very nice.
- The offer is from McKinsey.
- I will not have to travel much.

Of these statements, which ones stand out? Which will travel fastest through the MBA student grapevine? Which statements convey the highest prestige? We believe that the answers to all of these questions are the *high salary* ($140,000) and the *offer from McKinsey* (a top consulting firm). These two items are not only the easiest to communicate quickly, but also the easiest for others to evaluate. Students who receive these offers will notice the impressed reactions of their peers when such information is shared, and these reactions will make the information more prominent in their mind. As conversation after conversation focuses on these two factors, other aspects of the offer will be overshadowed or entirely sidelined. One result: students accept—and soon quit—high-paying jobs with prestigious firms because they overweighted vivid or prestigious attributes of their offers and underweighted other issues that would affect their professional and personal satisfaction, such as office location, collegiality, and travel. (Notably, some research suggests that this error affects men more than women.)[11]

More generally, vivid information has a greater effect on negotiators than does dull (but equally valuable) information. Imagine a group of executives discussing where to allocate R&D dollars within their company. The CEO asks each executive in the room for his or her opinion, and each provides arguments that would channel more funds to his or her own division. Why? In part, it may be that the executives are self-interested and seeking to maximize their personal benefits. But on a less conscious level, each executive can vividly imagine how he or she would use the funds in his or her own unit. They will ignore possibilities that are less vivid (but no less valuable), such as how others will utilize the funds. Similarly, the CEO herself is likely to be most influenced by the option that is best on vivid features (e.g., projected sales, cost estimates, and return on investment) and to underweight other important considerations (e.g., time to completion, complexity of implementation, and opportunity costs).

The NHL players and team owners may have also fallen prey to the vividness bias. Certain vivid figures were clearly motivating the hardline approach of both parties—salaries as a percentage of revenues and salary cap chief among them. Other important considerations, such as daily loss of revenues, reputation effects, and changes to the game's rules that could increase the size of the pie, were overshadowed and seemingly under-weighted. The willingness of players to finally accept terms that were significantly lower than their earlier demands on these vivid issues seems to suggest that other (nonvivid) issues did eventually surface and helped the disputants to reach agreement. By this time, of course, a season had been lost.

What can you do to avoid overweighting vivid information in negotiations? In addition to anticipating the vividness bias, here are two strategies that will help you overcome it:

Create a scoring system. In Chapter 2, we described the process of creating a scoring system and explained how to use one to evaluate offers and structure appropriate counteroffers. A scoring system can also help defend against the vividness bias by keeping you focused on your true interests. If you cross-check your reactions and strategy against the content of your scoring system, you will avoid overweighting vivid issues in your decisions.

A colleague of ours, who now teaches negotiation at Carnegie Mellon University, took this advice to heart when he was looking for a faculty position some years ago. He began to list all of the aspects of an offer that would have some value to him. He ended up with a scoring system that had weights assigned to almost forty separate attributes, ranging from "what my wife likes" (weighted at 50 percent) to the distance to the closest national park and average rainfall. We believe that our friend went a little overboard. On the other hand, an MBA student who does not have at least five to ten issues ranked and weighted in her scoring system is probably not thinking rationally enough about all of the important issues in her job negotiations. Our colleague may have wasted an afternoon of his time; the MBA student may end up wasting a year of her life.

Separate information from influence. In Chapter 1, we introduced the importance of separating information from influence; we revisit this principle here, as it can help you overcome the vividness bias. Consider the fact that the same salesperson who convinces you of a car's reliability by showing you its rating in *Car and Driver* can also convince you to purchase an expensive extended warranty for the same car by vividly describing the horrors of high repair costs that were once incurred by someone just like you. Though contradictory, these two pieces of information can both influence you in ways that benefit the salesperson. Given that nearly 50 percent of new-car buyers purchase these (typically overpriced) extended warranties, it seems that many people do not try to reconcile the contradiction; instead, they fall prey to the power of vividness. When faced with a tough decision, negotiation geniuses remember to ask themselves these critical questions: Is this information valuable? Have I learned something new? Am I just being *influenced* to act in a certain way because of how this information was presented?

NONRATIONAL ESCALATION OF COMMITMENT

Imagine that you are attending an executive class on negotiation with many other experienced managers. The professor takes a $100 bill out of his pocket and announces the following:

> I am about to auction off this $100 bill. You are free to partici-
> pate or just watch the bidding of others. Bidding will start at
> $5, and people will be invited to call out bids in multiples of $5
> until no further bidding occurs, at which point the highest bid-
> der will pay the amount bid and win the $100. The only feature
> that distinguishes this auction from traditional auctions is a
> rule that the second-highest bidder must *also* pay the amount
> that he or she bids, although he or she will obviously *not* win
> the $100. For example, if Maria bids $15 and Jamaal bids $20,
> and the bidding stops, Jamaal will get $80 (the $100 he wins mi-
> nus the $20 he bid) and Maria, the second-highest bidder, will
> pay me $15 (the amount she bid).

Now, what would be your strategy? Would you bid in the auction?
Max has run this auction dozens of times, and previously ran similar $20 auctions hundreds of times. The typical outcome: Max wins
lots of money.

Here's how it happens. The bidding starts out enthusiastically. At around $60–$80, everyone except the two highest bidders usually drops out of the auction. The two bidders then begin to feel the tension. Suppose that one bidder has bid $70 and the other has bid $75. The $70 bidder must either bid $80 or stop bidding and suffer a sure loss of $70 (which he must pay as the second-highest bidder). The uncertainty associated with bidding further seems more attractive than the certain loss, so the $70 bidder bids $80, and the bids continue until they reach $95 and then $100. The room grows quiet as the class focuses on the $95 bidder, who must decide whether to accept a $95 loss or continue bidding past $100 in hopes that the other party will quit first. The class laughs as the $95 bidder inevitably bids $105. Bidding in this auction typically ends somewhere between $100 and $1,000.

Why do people start bidding in this auction? Clearly, it is because they are attracted by the possibility of winning and making money. But why do they continue to bid past $100? Because they are trapped—strategically *and* psychologically. Strategically, once an individual has entered the $100 auction and is among the final two bidders, it takes only a small additional bid to stay in the auction rather than quit—and it seems reasonable to do so. After all, one more bid may be all that is needed to get the other party to quit first. But if both bidders pursue this seemingly rational strategy, the bidding can increase to extremely high levels, with disastrous results for both parties.

Strategy is not the only pitfall in the $100 auction—nor in the countless other negotiations, disputes, and conflicts where individuals, firms, and nations escalate their commitment to a failing course of action. Research on the *nonrational escalation of commitment* reveals that negotiators have a strong psychological need to justify (to themselves and to others) their prior decisions and behaviors. It is often difficult for negotiators to admit that their initial strategy was ill conceived or that they may have made a mistake; to avoid acknowledging these facts, they will escalate their commitment even when it is extremely costly, and perhaps disastrous, to do so. Deepak and his colleagues have demonstrated that emotion can compound the escalation problem.[12] Their research on *competitive arousal* reveals that interactions that heighten feelings of rivalry can create in negotiators the desire to "win at any cost." Of course, as in the $100 auction, "winning" and "making money" may not be the same thing; if bidding continues past $100, even the "winner" loses!

Nonrational escalation of commitment occurs across a wide variety of real-world situations. Custody battles, labor strikes, joint-venture dissolutions, bidding wars, lawsuits, price wars, ethnic conflicts, and countless other disputes all have the potential of spiraling out of control. When all of the escalation forces—the hope of victory, the need to justify initial strategy, and the desire to beat the other side—come together, simple common sense often flies out the window. If disputants are unable to rein in their desire to escalate commitment, what may have seemed like a smart strategy initially (making a bid, threatening litigation, competing on price, et cetera) may lead to disastrous results. Escalation is all the more likely if negotiators believe they have "too much invested to quit now," if they have already incurred significant losses, if they dislike the other party and want to "win" at any cost, or if they have made a public commitment to their position. Think back to the NHL dispute. In that example, all of these factors were in play!

Imagine that you are a player in the NHL. The lockout was instituted almost five months ago, and the entire season is now in jeopardy. You do not want to see any more of the season (and its revenues) squandered; then again, you do not want to relinquish your demands, either. Will you be able to admit to yourself that your initial strategy has not worked? That you were wrong to have held out for a better deal for so long? That you now should agree to an offer that for months you have been saying is unfair? Will you be able to overcome your animosity toward the team owners and make the concessions they demand? Sounds difficult. Is there any way to avoid falling prey to the nonrational escalation of commitment?

In response to similar disputes in major league sports, Harvard Business School professors James Sebenius and Michael Wheeler devised a very useful strategy:[13] They advise disputants to end the strike or lockout and to resume the season immediately—but, important, they stipulate that the team owners should be prohibited from receiving any of the revenue and that the players should not receive any pay. Instead, the revenues and forgone pay are to be placed in an escrow account until a resolution to the conflict is reached. A critical provision of this arrangement is that a sizable portion of the escrow fund would be given to charity if the parties failed to reach agreement in a timely fashion. In other words, either you do whatever it takes to reach a deal, or the size of the pie shrinks! Sebenius and Wheeler argue that watching the funds pile up—and fearing that they could disappear—should provoke both sides to agree on a contract.

If the possibility of reaching such an agreement in the midst of intense conflict seems unrealistic, consider the 2005 dispute involving faulty brakes in the fast-speed ACELA trains on the East Coast of the United States. It became clear that the trains had unacceptable cracks in their brakes and that the brakes would need to be replaced. It was less clear who was responsible for the cracks and who should cover the costs incurred from closing down the ACELA for months. Three companies were potentially responsible: Amtrak, which had purchased the trains; Bombardier, the company that had made the trains; and Knorr, the German company that sold the brakes to Bombardier. Not surprisingly, the parties disagreed about who was to blame. Surprisingly, however, the three parties quickly agreed that they would first solve the brake problem and get ACELA running again as soon as possible; only then would they turn to the question of who would pay for the losses incurred by the failure and for the cost of repairs. The companies saved tens of millions of dollars by agreeing to focus first on common interests—and to avoid an escalation of the conflict.

In their negotiations during the 2004–05 season, why didn't the NHL and the NHLPA pursue a wise strategy such as the one outlined by Sebenius and Wheeler, or the one implemented by Amtrak, Bombardier, and Knorr? Largely because both parties—and perhaps especially the players—had fallen prey to the nonrational escalation of commitment: they became so locked in to pursuing their initial course of action that they ignored blatant signals that suggested a change in strategy was necessary.

How can you avoid escalating in the heat of battle? Here are three ideas to consider.

Start your negotiation with a preplanned exit strategy. In the $100 auction, since neither party knows when the other party will quit, it is difficult to conclude that bidding "just once more" is clearly a bad decision. Unfortunately, this is a slippery slope—whether for bidders participating in the $100 auction, disputants pursuing litigation, or nations whose presidents have committed them to war. This is why it is important to decide *in advance* the point at which you will cut your losses and stop bidding, litigating, or fighting, should the situation spiral out of control. Of course, this limit should be adjusted as events unfold *if* you obtain new information relevant to your strategy (e.g., if you learn that the other side has run out of money).

Assign and reward a "devil's advocate" whose job it is to criticize your decisions and find faults in your logic. Whom should you pick for this task? The person should have the following three characteristics: they should be trustworthy, they should not have invested in or helped to design the initial strategy, and they should have no conflict of interest regarding the final outcome. In negotiation, it is tempting to surround yourself with like-minded, supportive people who will be easy to deal with and who will boost your confidence. However, when it comes to dealing with the dangerous effects of escalation, you do not need confidence, but rather clarity of thought and good judgment. Since it is not always possible to keep your wits about you, it is a good idea to have someone close at hand whose unbiased judgment you trust.

Anticipate and prepare for the escalation forces you are likely to encounter. For example, if you are concerned about the need to justify your initial decisions to constituents, you might refrain from committing publicly to a specific course of action. Or if you think that personal animosity is likely to fuel your desire to escalate conflict, it may be better to let others in your team or organization (who are less personally invested) take over substantive negotiations when emotions are running high.

In the context of escalation, then, negotiation genius means a number of things: learning to identify competitive traps, understanding the causes and consequences of escalation, and preparing in advance to "de-escalate" or cut your losses as necessary. By understanding how escalation of commitment works, you will not only avoid expensive mistakes, but be better equipped to anticipate the potentially irrational behavior of your opponents.

SUSCEPTIBILITY TO FRAMING

Consider the choices presented in the "Asian Disease Problem," first discussed by Amos Tversky and Daniel Kahneman:[14]

> Imagine that the United States is preparing for the outbreak of an unusual Asian disease that is expected to kill six hundred people. Two alternative programs to combat the disease have been proposed. Assume that the exact scientific estimates of the consequences of the programs are as follows. Which of the two programs would you favor?
>
> Program A: If Program A is adopted, two hundred people will be saved.
>
> Program B: If Program B is adopted, there is a one-third probability that six hundred people will be saved and a two-thirds probability that no people will be saved.

Before reading further, choose whether you would prefer to implement Program A or B. Now, for the same problem, decide which of the following two options you would favor:

> Program C: If Program C is adopted, four hundred people will die.
>
> Program D: If Program D is adopted, there is a one-third probability that no one will die and a two-thirds probability that six hundred people will die.

If you read carefully, you will discover that Program A and Program C are identical: both result in two hundred lives saved and four hundred lives lost. Program B and Program D are also identical: both lead to a one-third probability of saving everyone and a two-thirds probability of losing everyone. In other words, if people prefer Program A to Program B, then they should also (obviously) prefer Program C to Program D. As it turns out, this is *not* how people respond. When different groups are given these two sets of options, Program A is favored over Program B (by 72 percent of respondents in

Tversky and Kahneman's initial research), but Program D is favored over Program C (by 78 percent of respondents). Why are people so inconsistent in their preferences?

It turns out that the critical factor is how the options are framed. The two sets of options are identical, but changing the description from "lives saved" to "lives lost" makes people think very differently. Even when the expected values are similar, we tend to be risk averse when thinking about potential gains and risk seeking when thinking about potential losses. In other words, we want the "sure thing" when we have something to gain, but want "all or nothing" when we have something to lose. This is why people choose the less risky program (saving two hundred people with certainty) when thinking about lives *saved* and the more risky program (saving six hundred people but with only one-third probability) when thinking about lives *lost*. This problem illustrates the power of framing.

Research on *framing effects* reveals that most of us will treat risks involving perceived gains (e.g., profits) differently from risks involving perceived losses (e.g., losing a court settlement). This way of thinking can powerfully affect our negotiation behavior. For example, we are much more likely to make concessions and try to compromise when we are negotiating over how to allocate gains (profits, rewards, bonuses, windfalls, et cetera), but more likely to be inflexible and risk reaching an impasse when we are negotiating over how to allocate losses (costs, penalties, and so on). We are also more likely to quit negotiating in favor of the risky path of litigation when involved in a dispute over who is responsible for assuming costs, losses, and liabilities than when the dispute concerns the share of profit that each side is entitled to receive.

Now imagine the following scenario. You have just arrived at a casino and are sitting down to play blackjack. How likely are you to make a $100 bet? Now imagine that you have been playing blackjack for an hour and are already down $600. How likely are you to make a $100 bet? It turns out that people are more willing to take a risk (gambling $100) when they are already in the domain of losses (down $600). Losing your first $100 is much more painful than losing the seventh or even the second $100. Once you are a "loser," you won't mind digging yourself into a bigger hole (i.e., losing even more) as long as there is some possibility of digging yourself out entirely.

Now imagine that you have already lost $600—but not at the casino. Instead, the stock market took a slight hit earlier in the week and your investment portfolio lost $600 in value. How will you behave that night at the blackjack table? It turns out you will *not* want to take the same risks that you took after losing $600 at the casino. In other words, the question is not whether or not you *are* a loser, but whether or not you *feel like* a loser in the current situation. Whether or not you feel like a loser depends on your *reference point*—the comparisons you make to other potential outcomes. If you are comparing your current situation to how much money you had in your pocket when you walked into the casino, you will behave differently than if your reference point is your overall wealth level.

This finding suggests some advice for gamblers: You will take less dangerous risks if you acquire the mental habit of constantly readjusting your reference point. When you're thinking about when to leave the casino and go home, recall your previously set gambling limit for the night. However, when you are deciding how much to stake on any given bet, think of your current bet as your first bet of the night; remind yourself that the money you lost earlier in the night will not (hopefully!) affect your overall wealth—so it's silly to think of yourself as being "in the hole."

The effect of reference points is even more critical for negotiators to understand. In a negotiation, you are not the only one who can manipulate reference points—the other side can, too. If you entered a negotiation imagining that you would extract millions of dollars from the deal, but now it looks as if the ZOPA is much smaller (and you stand to gain only thousands), you may find yourself adopting a loss frame that makes you risk seeking! You may become more aggressive, more likely to issue an ultimatum, and more willing to walk away from the deal. If, instead, you came in expecting to make very little, you will be pleasantly surprised and will adopt a gain frame that makes you risk averse. You will probably become more conciliatory, make less aggressive demands, and be less willing to risk an impasse. Clearly, the two frames lead to very different behaviors—but should they? The value of the deal hasn't changed across these situations. Your strategy shouldn't, either.

Understanding the effects of framing and reference points can help you anticipate their powerful consequences and strategize accordingly. In particular, we recommend the following steps:

1. Consider the various reference points that you could be using to evaluate the situation—including the status quo, your aspirations, your expectations, your feared outcome, and so on—and then pick the one that seems most appropriate.
2. Evaluate whether your strategy would still make sense if you were to use a different reference point.
3. Anytime you are considering the use of a risky strategy (such as making an ultimatum or pursuing litigation), think about whether this strategy still makes sense if you change the frame.

For example, note that in the NHL dispute, the owners were asking the players to accept losses in the form of reductions in their pay level. In effect, this made their previous salary the reference point for the players, putting them in a loss frame. But what if, instead, their reference point had been the percentage of revenue that NHL players receive compared with players in other sports leagues (such as the NBA or the NFL)? Thinking about how they would fare relative to players in other leagues, or how they would fare if they pursued their BATNA, might have resulted in a gain frame for NHL players, which in turn might have mitigated their willingness to risk losing the entire season.

BIASES OF THE MIND, BIASES OF THE HEART

As the behavioral decision research summarized in this chapter reveals, negotiators must contend not only with the tactics of the other party, but also with the predictable mental traps that can cloud their own judgment. In the next chapter, we reveal that cognitive biases are only half of the story; negotiator thought and behavior is also powerfully influenced by motivational biases—the mistakes in judgment that we make because of our strong desire to see ourselves and the world in a particular way. Fortunately, would-be negotiation geniuses can learn to appreciate and compensate for not only the peculiar workings of the mind, but also the powerful influences of the heart.

CHAPTER 5

When Rationality Fails: Biases of the Heart

A few years ago in Manhattan, a dispute arose between residents of one co-op apartment unit and the building's co-op board. The dispute was over $909. This is the amount that the unit's residents had spent to install window bars to childproof their apartment. The problem? It was unclear who should be responsible for footing the bill. The residents of the unit argued that the building as a whole should pay for the window bars because this was a safety and liability issue. The co-op board argued that, because the unit's residents were the only ones who wanted the window bars, they should cover the costs. The dispute escalated and eventually ended up in court.

One year later, the two sides' combined legal bills exceeded $1,000. This might have been a good time for them to end litigation and to negotiate instead. Yet the parties, both convinced that they would win, continued to litigate.

Another year passed. Now their combined legal bills exceeded $10,000—but the disputants were still unwilling to settle out of court. Their conflict was no longer about the money; it was about the justice that each side felt it deserved.

Finally, the co-op board won the court battle. The residents had to pay for the $909 window bars. Normally, this would be cause for the triumphant party to celebrate. Unfortunately, the ruling came after the litigants had spent close to $20,000 in combined legal costs.

That's bad. But it gets worse.

The unit's residents decided to appeal the ruling. The two sides then spent an *additional* $30,000 on litigation. Ultimately, the appellate court upheld the initial ruling. Now close to $50,000 had been spent on a dispute over $909.

That's *really* bad. But it gets worse yet.

The co-op board then sued the unit's residents to force them to pay the co-op board's legal fees. The ensuing litigation cost the two parties an *additional* $50,000. Finally, a judge threw the litigants out of court; the unit's residents were forced to pay some (but not most) of the co-op board's legal fees.

The final tally: the window bars dispute, which started with a $909 claim, lasted six years and cost more than $100,000 to resolve.

Not all negotiation errors result from the cognitive biases we discussed in the previous chapter. Emotions can be just as powerful in derailing agreements. Compounding the problem, we human beings are motivated to see ourselves as fairer, kinder, more competent, more generous, more deserving, and more likely to succeed than others. The result of these *motivational biases*? We tend to make judgments and decisions that are not optimal. In this chapter, we explore a number of motivational biases and their effects on negotiation strategy and outcomes: the problem of conflicting motivations, egocentrism, overconfidence, irrational optimism, the illusion of superiority, self-serving attributions, and regret aversion.

THE PROBLEM OF CONFLICTING MOTIVATIONS

In *The Odyssey*, Homer's epic poem, the hero, Ulysses, faced a difficult problem during his long sea voyage. He knew he would soon sail past the Sirens, female "enchanters" who used their beautiful and irresistible singing to lure men to their island—and to their subsequent deaths. No man had been able to listen to—and still resist—the Sirens, whose beach was "piled with boneheaps of men now rotted away."[1] To protect his crewmen, Ulysses had all of them put wax into their ears to block out the tempting voices of the Sirens. But, desperate to hear the

Sirens, Ulysses was unwilling to do this to himself. Then again, he also wanted to live. What to do? To solve this dilemma, Ulysses told his men to bind him to the ship with ropes and ordered them not to release him until after they had sailed safely past the Sirens, no matter how much he might beg. The crewmen complied and Ulysses was able to enjoy the Sirens' song without losing his life.

What is your Sirens' song? If you are angry with a negotiating counterpart, you may want to do or say something that you know will harm you in the long run. Your statements or actions might end the business relationship, destroy a personal friendship, or get you into trouble with your boss or even with the law. Still, in the heat of the moment, it can be difficult to resist the urge to lash out or retaliate. Similarly, if the other side makes you an attractive offer, you may be so excited that you are tempted to accept right away, though you know it would be smart to try to negotiate a better deal or find a better deal elsewhere. Note that you would not advise a friend to act rashly in either of these two situations—yet, at the time, you might find it hard to do otherwise.

Economist Thomas Schelling argued that each individual behaves like two people: "one who wants clear lungs and long life and another who adores tobacco, or one who wants a lean body and another who wants dessert."[2] People often face internal negotiations between doing what they *want* to do versus doing what they think they *should* do.[3] Usually the type of creative solution that Ulysses developed is unavailable, and negotiators must make a difficult choice. Too often, the *want-self* dominates the *should-self* in important real-world negotiations, leading to behavior and outcomes that you later regret. What can be done?

Many negotiation teachers, executives, and other professionals believe that you need to control your want-self in order to maximize your long-term benefits. According to this view, the should-self is more trustworthy than the want-self, and is better at gauging what is best for you.

There is a contrary view. Behavioral decision researcher George Loewenstein argues that gut-level impulsive responses—the responses of the want-self—are ignored at our peril. "Hunger signals the need for nutritional input," Loewenstein writes, "pain indicates the impingement of some type of potentially harmful environmental factors, and emotions serve a range of interrupting, prioritizing, and energizing functions."[4] Loewenstein argues that visceral reactions make us aware of issues that we care a great deal about, but that we tend to suppress these reactions because of the desire to be responsible, to be mature, or to otherwise conform to society.

These divergent perspectives simply highlight our dilemma: People who never control their want-selves engage in shortsighted behavior that often creates enormous long-term problems. Conversely, those who always listen to their should-selves ignore the potentially important signals being sent from their want-selves.

Our advice: it is critical for negotiators to anticipate and resolve the conflict between what they want to do versus what they think they should do *in advance* of an actual negotiation. You will find that your should-self and your want-self are in agreement both before and after the negotiation. The problem only arises *during* the negotiation; in the heat of the moment, you face strong emotional desires to satisfy your want-self in ways that are inconsistent with what you believe you should do.[5] Luckily, you can often predict the impulsive demands of your want-self and plan accordingly. For example, you might anticipate that the other side will make you angry, that you will want to say yes to an offer immediately, or that you will be tempted to behave shortsightedly. The better prepared you are for a negotiation, the less likely is it that you will act on emotional impulses in a way that scuttles your real interests. Thus, once again, we see that preparation is the key to negotiation success.

Think back to the co-op building's window-bars dispute. What could the disputants have done to resolve the conflict between their desire to "win" through litigation and their desire to minimize economic loss? One smart idea would have been for each disputant to decide, *in advance,* how much money and time each was willing to spend to try to win the case. If they reached the preset limit, they would end litigation and simply pay for the window bars on their own. It is unlikely that either side would have been willing to budget tens of thousands of dollars on this dispute before the conflict began to escalate. Thus, the pre-negotiation agreement between each side's want-self and should-self would have likely saved thousands of dollars.

The parties could have also agreed to a one-day arbitration session without attorneys (and to the provision that both sides would give up their rights to appeal the decision). This way, each side could be heard, and each could receive a decision from a neutral party—but without the costs and complexity of the courts.

Yet another way to cope with conflicting internal preferences would be for each party to hand over control of the negotiation process to someone who is less emotionally involved. For example, the co-op residents might have asked a relative to make key decisions regarding whether to hire lawyers, whether to appeal the decision, how much to spend on litigation, and so on. Similarly, the residents of the building would have been better served if non–board members (or board members who were not involved in the initial dispute) were asked to take control of the situation once it had spiraled out of control. This strategy is akin to that used by Ulysses: by giving up your *ability* to pursue what you want, you can ensure that you will do what you should. (This also explains why keeping little or no junk food in the house may be a good idea for some people who are trying to lose weight. Often, when temptation strikes, the only way to keep yourself from eating what you want is to make it unavailable.)

EGOCENTRISM

Consider these results of a survey conducted by *U.S. News & World Report:*[6]

- *Question:* "If someone sues you and you win the case, should he pay your legal costs?"
  ➢ Percentage of respondents who answered yes: 85 percent
- *Question:* "If you sue someone and lose the case, should you pay his costs?"
  ➢ Percentage of respondents who answered yes: 44 percent

What is going on here?

It is hard for any of us to escape *egocentrism*, or the tendency for our perceptions and expectations to be biased in our favor. Typically, negotiators first decide on a certain interpretation, belief, or outcome that would benefit them—or make them feel good—and then look for ways to justify this preference on the basis of fairness.[7] Thus, when faced with the possibility of having someone else pay for their court costs, people are likely to argue that this would be fair because such a policy discourages frivolous lawsuits and ensures that only the guilty party suffers. When the tables are turned, however, and people are confronted with the possibility of having to pay for someone else's court costs, they are likely to argue that the ruling could have gone either way, that it is unfair for one party to bear all the costs, and that such a policy discourages legitimate justice seeking. And there is every reason to believe that actual disputants would be even more biased than the survey respondents.

Egocentrism not only afflicts disputants, it abounds within organizations as well. Max once collaborated in the creation of a negotiation simulation that involved two departments of the same corporation.[8] The departments had different strengths: one had higher revenue, and the other had higher profitability. Participants in the simulation were asked to represent one of the departments and then were given either high or low resources from those in top management. What was the response? Participants viewed unequal allocations to be much fairer when their own department received the greater amount, regardless of whether their division was stronger on sales or profits.

As these examples suggest, there are many different ways to think about what is right and wrong (or fair and unfair), and people are resourceful enough to find the justification that best suits their purpose. As we all struggle to view ourselves in the best possible light, we downplay certain factors that should affect our judgments and heighten the importance of other factors; as a result, we can begin to see the exact same phenomenon quite differently from others. Consider the perceptions of Frederick Banting and John Macleod, cowinners of the 1923 Nobel Prize for the discovery of insulin. Both had a bit of an egocentrism problem. Banting contended that his partner, Macleod, had been more of a hindrance than an asset in their research. Meanwhile, in multiple speeches, Macleod forgot to mention that he even had a research partner.[9]

If you think this problem would go away if we liked and cared about the other side, consider this: If you ask a husband and wife to estimate the percentage of household work that they do, and then add up the two percentages, you will get a number that is significantly higher than 100 percent. Both are likely to believe that they do more than is actually the case.[10]

Of course, negative emotions tend to exacerbate the egocentrism bias. Case in point: divorcing couples who are dividing up their shared assets. Even if each spouse claims to want only what is "fair," it is quite likely that one will ask for 55 percent, while the other tries to claim 65 percent. Egocentrism causes all parties to believe that they deserve more of a shared resource than a neutral adviser would judge as fair; this discrepancy can easily start a conflict that escalates out of control. When someone demands more than you believe is fair, your reaction probably will not be "Gee, we must have different perceptions." More likely, you will decide that the other person is unethical and trying to cheat you.

Egocentrism is not only common, but also robust and resilient. It can also be extremely costly. We personally know of two companies that have been fighting over a series of legal issues for more than a decade. While both are highly respected in the market and in society, each views the other firm as truly "evil." Their legal battles have already cost literally hundreds of millions of dollars. At the center of the dispute is a poorly written contract that was drafted many years ago. Our assessment is that this ongoing dispute began with an ambiguous contract and escalated as a result of egocentric interpretations of its ambiguous clauses.

While many of us want to be fair, even well-intentioned people can act in seemingly unethical ways when we are motivated to claim more than we deserve. This doesn't make us bad, but merely human—and humans make biased judgments. By understanding the egocentrism bias and trying to correct it in our own behavior, we can move from *wanting* to be fair to actually *being* fair, and in doing so, make it less likely that we will initiate or escalate disputes and disagreements.

How might we overcome our egocentrism? Negotiation geniuses do so by following the advice of the philosopher John Rawls, who recommends that when you are trying to assess what is fair (regarding allocations, contributions, claiming value, et cetera), try doing so under the "veil of ignorance." That is, try to imagine what you would believe to be fair if you did not know your role in a given negotiation or dispute.[11] In other words, what would you believe or decide to be fair if you did not yet know whom you represented in the dispute? By overcoming our own egocentrism in this way, we eliminate a source of conflict in our negotiations. And by understanding the potential for this bias in the behavior of others, we can make more sympathetic and accurate attributions of their intentions.

OVERCONFIDENCE, IRRATIONAL OPTIMISM, AND THE ILLUSION OF SUPERIORITY

In her research, psychologist Shelley Taylor of UCLA has demonstrated that students have unrealistic expectations about their likelihood of graduating at the top of the class, getting a good job, obtaining a high salary, enjoying their first job, getting written up in the newspaper, and giving birth to a gifted child. They also assume that they are less likely than their classmates to become alcoholics, be fired, divorce, become depressed, or suffer physical problems.[12] Confidence in our negotiation ability tends to be similarly inflated: Rod Kramer of the Stanford Business School found that 68 percent of the MBA students in his negotiation class predicted that their bargaining outcomes would fall in the upper 25 percent of the class.[13] These MBA students also had positive, distorted expectations regarding their ability to learn more than their peers and add more to the class experience. More generally, *overconfidence* in our abilities and *irrational optimism* regarding our fate lead most of us to believe that our futures will be better and brighter than those of other people.

Why is this a problem? When a football team is running a play, it helps if the quarterback has as much confidence as possible. Similarly, when a salesperson is selling a product, it helps if she believes that the product is fantastic. Indeed, many social psychologists view *positive illusions* regarding our abilities and our future as evolutionarily adaptive.[14] According to this view, these illusions contribute to our psychological and material well-being by protecting our self-esteem and helping us persevere when faced with difficult tasks. In addition, overconfidence and irrational optimism can help us cope with negative life events. Undoubtedly, they also help to motivate the kind of risk-taking that creates entrepreneurs. Psychologist Martin Seligman goes as far as to recommend that firms base their selection of salespeople on the magnitude of their positive illusions—what he calls *learned optimism*.[15]

However, we take a contrarian position when it comes to negotiation. Overconfidence may help the quarterback execute a practiced play and the salesperson deliver a rehearsed pitch, but when you are making decisions, including decisions about your negotiation strategy, you need to take off the rose-tinted glasses. Unrealistic optimism can lead you to turn down the best job offer that you are likely to receive, reject an offer on your house when no better offer is forthcoming, and to hold out for contract terms that your counterpart is unlikely to accept. Overoptimistic negotiators are also likely to enter into negotiations with only one strategy for reaching agreement or resolving the dispute; they assume that their negotiation plan will work, and they devote all of their energy to developing and executing this one strategy. A more realistic negotiator realizes that an initial strategy may not work and is ready with a contingency plan.

We can also see the effects of overconfidence and irrational optimism away from the negotiating table. Too many people invest their life savings in new businesses that have little chance of success. Too many employees assume that they are indispensable to their organization, and are caught off guard when they are laid off or fired. Others apply for too few jobs because they believe falsely—and contrary to all available objective evidence—that they are great potential hires. And far too many people take their disputes to court, believing falsely that they have an airtight case—or at least a "very strong" case—a belief that many lawyers are more than happy to help you maintain. Would the litigants in the co-op dispute over window bars have been so willing to go to court if they had accurate, objective assessments of their likelihood of prevailing, of the costs associated with litigation, and of the time it would take to complete the process? Not likely.

Why, then, are positive illusions useful for quarterbacks and salespeople? Because, unlike negotiators, they are not *making* decisions so much as they are *implementing* decisions that have already been made. Overconfidence and irrational optimism may well provide them with the motivation and inspiration they need to improve their performance—at relatively low cost. But such illusions are extremely costly for negotiators, who must make decisions constantly—before, during, and after the negotiation.

Negotiators not only see their future *prospects* as better than they actually are, they also see *themselves* as better than a realistic assessment would suggest. This *illusion of superiority* leads people to view themselves as more flexible, competent, rational, honest, fair, and cooperative than their opponents.[16] One unfortunate result of this illusion of superiority is that far too many mediocre negotiators do not recognize the need to improve their inferior negotiation skills.

Interestingly, the illusion of superiority not only affects our self-judgments, but also our judgments regarding the groups to which we belong. We tend to view members of our group—whether our country, our firm, our department, or our family—as more honest, cooperative, trustworthy, diligent, and industrious than members of other groups.[17] If we believe that our fellow group members are above average, then how do we view our adversaries and opponents? In independent studies, management researchers Kristina Diekmann and Ann Tenbrunsel found that while MBA students rate themselves *above* the mean of their class on a variety of positive attributes, they rate their negotiation opponents *below* the mean.[18]

The tendency to denigrate our opponents and adversaries can be quite detrimental to negotiation success. If you view your opponent as uncooperative, unfair, or untrustworthy, you are less likely to share information with them—and hence less likely to create value. In addition, negotiators who think they are smarter, better prepared, or more honest than others often devalue or ignore the ideas and proposals of their counterparts. Doing so can decrease the likelihood of reaching efficient agreements and increase the likelihood of conflict.

SELF-SERVING ATTRIBUTIONS

Egocentrism, overconfidence, irrational optimism, and the illusion of superiority exist because we are motivated to see the world and ourselves in a positive light. But why do such biases *persist*? Why don't we learn from our experience and adjust our beliefs about our contributions, our abilities, and our likelihood of success? The answer is that, even as we try to learn from our experiences, we tend to evaluate the past in self-protective ways: the stories we tell ourselves, and the attributions that we make about ourselves and others, are the kind that will keep us feeling good about ourselves.

John F. Kennedy once said, "Victory has a thousand fathers, but defeat is an orphan."[19] This is certainly true of negotiators: we are quick to take credit for success and deny responsibility for failures. When negotiators are asked to explain their successful results, they usually give personalized internal reasons—e.g., the skill, perseverance, or creativity with which they handled the situation. In contrast, when asked about a failure, most negotiators cite external reasons: the difficult context in which they were negotiating, the incompetence of the other side, or plain bad luck.[20] One serious problem with this tendency is that external attributions for failure inhibit learning from experience.

Negotiators are even more likely to distort their beliefs regarding their shortcomings when their adversaries are more successful than they are.[21] For example, business school students who perform less well in negotiation simulations and exercises are more likely to attribute the success of other students to uncooperative and unethical bargaining tactics and to rate them as excessively competitive and self-interested.[22] What happens when we view successful others as unethical or hypercompetitive? First, we will not try to learn from them. Also, to the extent possible, we will avoid negotiating with them. Finally, when we have no choice but to negotiate with them, we will find it easy to justify our own unethical behavior.

This self-serving attitude can also be triggered when our "in-group" negotiates with an "out-group." For example, when two firms meet to negotiate the terms of a deal, both sides will inevitably need to make concessions. When our firm (the in-group) makes a concession, it is because we are being generous or because we are smart enough to understand the need for logrolling. When the other side (the out-group) makes a concession, it is because they have seen the wisdom of our argument or because they have no other choice!

Why is this problematic? Because when we attribute the cooperation of others to the constraints of the situation (e.g., their legal obligations or the mandates of a contract), rather than to their goodwill or integrity, it becomes difficult to build trust.[23] To build trust, negotiators need to see the cooperative actions of others as behaviors that they have chosen, not behaviors that they were unable to avoid. And, in the absence of trust, negotiators become reluctant to make concessions, share information, or take the risks inherent in building mutually rewarding relationships.

Negotiation geniuses understand the value of building trust with their negotiation partners, even in competitive or adversarial environments, and so seek to accurately gauge the reasons for others' behavior. Negotiation geniuses understand that mistaking a kind gesture for weakness is no more helpful than mistaking miscommunication for malice. And so they take the time necessary to understand the behavior of others before they react.

REGRET AVERSION

Imagine that you are an Olympic athlete. Which would you rather win: a silver medal or a bronze medal? Few people (if any) would prefer a bronze.

Now, which medal makes actual Olympic athletes happier, silver or bronze? As it turns out, Olympians are happier when they win bronze than when they win silver! Three clever psychologists, Vicki Medvec, Scott Madey, and Tom Gilovich demonstrated this phenomenon by having viewers watch video footage of various Olympic athletes as they received their medals.[24] The viewers were then asked to rate the facial expressions of the athletes. Because sound was eliminated from the footage and the medals were not shown, viewers could not know which medal had been presented. The result? Bronze-medal winners appeared much happier to the viewers than did silver-medal winners. Why might this be?

Once again, we see the power of reference points, or the comparisons we make to other potential outcomes that are salient to us. And what could be more salient than the "what-might-have-been" scenario? It seems that bronze-medal winners—who were close to winning no medal at all—are thrilled simply to be medal winners. Meanwhile, silver-medal winners—who were close to winning the gold—are disappointed not to have come in first. Objectively, they have achieved more, but they experience greater regret.

Because regret is such a painful psychological state, people try to avoid situations that might cause it. If you got a B+ in class and you could not change your grade through negotiation, would you really want to know how many points you were shy of receiving an A? If you were on a game show and failed to win the grand prize, would you really want to know what that prize would have been? If you were bidding in a sealed-bid auction, would you rather find out that you were the second-highest bidder (and *almost* won) or that you were the fifth-highest bidder (and were not close to winning)? In negotiation, would you want to accept an offer that you might later find out was not the best one you could have received? In fact, research shows that negotiators often contort their decisions to avoid facing any clear evidence that would cause regret.[25] Furthermore, we tend to feel greater regret about *acts of commission* (what we *did* do) than about *acts of omission* (what we *did not* do).[26]

This desire to avoid regretful decisions can induce negotiators to hold out longer—and for more—than they reasonably should. Again, consider the litigants in the co-op dispute. After having spent thousands of dollars, they would almost certainly view the decision to end litigation (and pay for the window bars) with a high degree of regret. "What might have happened if I'd persevered just a little longer?" they are likely to wonder. If "what might have been" will actually be revealed in the future, our decisions often become even more geared toward avoiding regret. For example, the seller of a house may reject reasonable offers in the belief that prices in the area could go up after the sale. Likewise, an investor may hold on to a seemingly weak stock too long out of fear that the stock price will go up shortly after he places his "sell" order.

Too many negotiators place too much emphasis on what might have been. The fact is, uncertainty is a fact of life; in hindsight, we will often see results that we could not have predicted in advance. While such hindsight can drive us crazy, the solution is *not* to ignore it. The way to leverage hindsight—without overemphasizing it—is to focus on what can be learned from the past about how to make better negotiation decisions in the future. If thinking about "what might have been" helps us improve our future negotiation behaviors, we should analyze the past carefully. If our regrets could only have been avoided with a crystal ball, then we should remind ourselves that if we make good decisions most of the time, our net outcomes in life will be good as well.

TOWARD DE-BIASING

As you've probably recognized, this chapter is as much about the human condition as it is about negotiation. It's important to remember that even highly educated, intelligent people who have a desire to be fair and objective are susceptible to psychological biases. We are biased because we are human, not because we are mean or stupid. This means that we need to be vigilant in our efforts to overcome our biases. It also means that we should be more understanding of the biases exhibited by others—and that we may even want to help others overcome them. The following chapter shows you how.

CHAPTER 6

Negotiating Rationally in an Irrational World

Biases of the heart and mind affect even the best and brightest. You may have superb people skills and great instincts for when to push and when to hold back, but your intuition will not protect you from the kind of systematic and predictable errors we have been documenting. Neither, surprisingly, will extensive experience. While experience can be valuable, experience without a clear understanding of potential negotiation pitfalls can be dangerous.

Our own experience teaching tens of thousands of executive students suggests that people trust their intuition and their experience. But learning from experience alone can be a disastrous mistake for executives.[1] The problem is that people who are extraordinarily successful—or lucky—tend to conclude from their "experience" that they are invulnerable. This belief leads them to insufficiently monitor or correct their own behavior and to overgeneralize their experience from one context to another. But consider the fact that many people are very good at negotiating in one domain but not in others. Someone may be great at negotiating sales contracts, but suffer from constant conflict in his personal life. A person may know how to negotiate mergers and strategic alliances but be lousy at negotiating her compensation package. Why? Because a negotiator can have significant experience in one domain, yet lack a thorough understanding of what she does well. As a result, she cannot generalize her experience—and success—to another context.

Our skeptical view of the value of experience grows out of extensive evidence that psychological biases afflict even highly trained and experienced professionals of all kinds, including investors, analysts, real-estate agents, medical doctors, politicians, and so on. Margaret Neale and Greg Northcraft, who are leading scholars of organizational behavior, argue that such biases *can* be overcome—not through the development of experience, but through the development of *expertise*.[2] According to Neale and Northcraft, individuals gain experience when they conduct a similar type of negotiation many times; by contrast, they develop expertise when they form a "strategic conceptualization" of what constitutes effective negotiation. This view of expertise is closely aligned with our view of negotiation genius. To overcome bias and negotiate effectively, you need a framework for thinking about, preparing for, and executing negotiations systematically and strategically. When it comes to biases, negotiation geniuses are aware of their limitations—and those of others—and work vigilantly to address them.

This chapter offers you the tools and framework you need to overcome your own biases and to effectively confront the biases of your negotiation counterparts. It is not enough to anticipate your own decision biases; you must also set up systems and processes that will help you overcome them. Similarly, you cannot always benefit from the mistakes your counterpart makes; sometimes, to improve your own outcomes, you need to help them overcome their own irrationality.

CONFRONTING YOUR OWN BIASES

Three powerful strategies can help you confront and manage your own biases in negotiation: using "System 2" thinking, applying analogical reasoning, and adopting the "outsider" lens.

STRATEGY 1: USE "SYSTEM 2" THINKING

What accounts for the difference between the times when we are susceptible to cognitive and motivational biases and the times when we think and behave rationally? One important answer lies in the distinction between "System 1" and "System 2" thinking, as proposed by researchers Keith Stanovich and R. F. West.[3] System 1, which corresponds to intuition, is typically fast, automatic, effortless, implicit, and emotional; we make most decisions in life using System 1 thinking. The biases described in Chapters 4 and 5 are also much more common when we are using System 1. By contrast, System 2 corresponds to reasoned thought and is slower, conscious, effortful, explicit, and logical.[4] When we are facing time pressures, we are more likely to use System 1. In other words, busy professionals are likely to rely on System 1 thinking most of the time—and more often than they should.[5]

This does not mean that a full System 2 process is necessary for every decision that you make. If you are buying groceries in the supermarket, responding to unimportant e-mails, or driving to work, System 1 will suit you fine. Ideally, however, System 2 thinking should influence your most important decisions and negotiations. (Of course, in the early stages of practicing to become a negotiation genius, it might be useful to stay in System 2 for even more mundane negotiations.) As a negotiator, you need to learn to identify situations in which you should move from the intuitively compelling System 1 to the more logical System 2. How can you do this?

The following negotiation techniques can help facilitate System 2 thinking in an otherwise System 1 world:

Make a System 2 list. At the beginning of each month or year, make a list of all of the upcoming negotiations that you think should be subject to System 2 thinking. These might be negotiations in which you are dealing with high stakes, complex issues, multiple parties, high-priority clients, or high degrees of uncertainty. Having planned in advance to be more prepared for and engaged in these negotiations will help you to allocate your time more appropriately. It will also help you think more carefully about when you should schedule these negotiations and will remind you to actively participate in the pre-negotiation discussions that will set the agenda for substantive negotiations; there is nothing worse than having a negotiation thrust upon you when you are not ready for it.

Avoid negotiating under time pressure. System 1 thinking takes over when we have little time and are feeling rushed. Smart negotiators anticipate this problem and avoid negotiating under time pressure, or at least recognize when the pressure is real versus when it is artificially created as a negotiation tactic. To avoid time pressure, instead of negotiating during a one-hour lunch, set aside an entire afternoon. If someone initiates substantive discussions with an unexpected phone call or visit, and you are unprepared, politely ask to reschedule the conversation for a later time or date. Some negotiators are extremely fond of forcing others to negotiate, make commitments, or respond to requests under immense time pressure. Unfortunately, many people fall prey to this tactic because they are worried about losing the deal or offending the other party. How *should* you respond to such tactics? In the vast majority of cases, there is little reason not to postpone your negotiation or decision—at least for a little while. Unless the other party has given you specific, credible information that time truly is of the essence, you should avoid giving in to their pressure tactics. This comes back to the principle (discussed in Chapter 1) of *separating information from influence.* For example, if a potential employer extends you a job offer and tells you that "we will need your answer by Friday"—and this does not give you enough time to make a wise decision—it is okay to probe a bit and find out whether this is a serious ultimatum. After articulating your gratitude and enthusiasm for the opportunity to work for the company, you might add a query such as one of these:

- "Is this a firm deadline?"
- "If, for personal reasons, I needed more time to make this decision, what would be the process for doing so?"

Partition the negotiation across multiple sessions. You do not have to complete an entire negotiation in one session. No matter how prepared you are, in most complex negotiations you will encounter information, issues, and tactics that you did not anticipate. If you want to avoid falling back on System 1 thinking at such times, you will need to structure a process that allows you to rethink or re-strategize as needed. For example, you might schedule breaks every hour or two so that you can spend time evaluating and organizing everything that you heard that was unexpected. Or you might negotiate over multiple days, such that you exchange preliminary information over e-mail on Day 1, have an initial telephone discussion on Day 2, and set aside time on Days 3 and 4 for substantive negotiations. This will give you the time you need to apply System 2 thinking throughout the negotiation process.

STRATEGY 2: LEARN THROUGH THE USE OF ANALOGIES

It is often said that we learn more from our mistakes and failures than we do from our successes. If this is true, then negotiators should be able to learn from the negative consequences of their decision biases and to adjust their subsequent behavior accordingly. However, it is often quite difficult for negotiators to learn from past mistakes; we tend to fall prey to the same biases time and time again.[6] Why? In the real world, where negotiation outcomes are determined by a host of factors, it can be difficult to assess whether a mistake was due to flawed strategy or to misfortune. Even if you acknowledge that your strategy was to blame, you may be uncertain which aspect of the strategy was flawed.

How, then, can negotiators maximize their learning from experience? People learn far more from an example, case study, exercise, or real-world experience when they are able to extract an abstract principle from it.[7] In other words, it does negotiators little good if they are told in retrospect how they *should have* behaved in a specific situation they recently encountered, but it is very useful for them to discover what *factors* to consider when facing similar situations in the future. Because no two situations are identical, negotiators are better off extracting the correct *principle* from past experience rather than the correct *answer*. The key is to figure out how to draw principles out of experiences and examples.

One way to do this is to apply *analogical reasoning*—the conscious comparison of different situations on dimensions that are similar. Extensive research has shown the power of this approach.

In studies by psychologists Jeffrey Loewenstein, Leigh Thompson, and Dedre Gentner, participants were provided with summaries of two complex negotiation problems that had the same underlying lesson (i.e., the same type of solution to the negotiator's problem). Half of the participants were asked to explain what lesson they had learned, one exercise at a time. The other half was asked how the two exercises were related and what lessons they had in common. Negotiators were much more able to draw out the critical lesson—and to overcome similar problems in their own subsequent negotiations—when they had been asked to compare the two exercises. In short, when we try to learn from one experience at a time, we too often focus on "surface" elements of the situation, whereas the process of comparing and contrasting different experiences helps us draw out similar "structural" elements.

Consider, for example, an executive who is reflecting on the recent dissolution of a business partnership. He might conclude that negotiating such dissolutions is very difficult and requires third-party mediation. Though intuitively appealing, this lesson may be minimally useful. It is also possible for partnerships to be dissolved without severe conflict, in which case the lesson is simply wrong. In contrast, another executive who reflects on multiple prior negotiations might conclude that, whatever the underlying situation, nonrational escalation of commitment is more likely when lawyers are involved and when emotions are running high. This executive might decide to bring in a third party to mediate whenever she encounters such conditions—a far more useful conclusion.

How can you use analogical reasoning to your advantage in negotiation? Try the following techniques:

Debrief multiple negotiations simultaneously. Negotiation geniuses make it a habit to review important negotiations after they are completed. Better yet, you should review multiple negotiations at the same time. As you are doing this, ask yourself how the negotiations were similar and how they were different. Having other members of your team or organization help you to think critically about your experiences, strategies, and outcomes may be especially useful, because they will be able to weigh in with their own experiences as well.

When firms hire us to train their employees in negotiation, we often conduct a "group-debrief" exercise, in which we set up groups of four to six people. Each employee is asked to discuss a recent or current negotiation situation, then all members of the group try to extract important lessons and insights from the various experiences. This exercise is extremely effective at promoting learning because it encourages negotiators to make comparisons across negotiations and form analogies.

Focus on the principles, not particulars. When reviewing past negotiations, try to understand the structural and conceptual aspects of what occurred. Rather than focusing on the uniqueness of the specific negotiation situation, dissect your recent experience into elements that map onto the negotiation concepts described in this book. While all negotiations are unique, they all have BATNAs, reservation values, ZOPAs, underlying interests, information exchange, and so on. Examining these concepts will help you better generalize learning from recently completed negotiations to the future.

STRATEGY 3: ADOPT THE OUTSIDER LENS

Why are we so overconfident in our own judgments and abilities, but more accurate in our assessments of the likely success of others? Daniel Kahneman and Dan Lovallo explain this inconsistency by arguing that people make decisions using two different perspectives, or "lenses": an *insider lens* and an *outsider lens*.[8] A negotiator usually adopts the insider lens when making judgments while immersed in the context or situation. By contrast, we usually adopt the outsider lens when removed or detached from the situation. The outsider lens is the cleaner lens. Obviously, it is better to use the cleaner lens than the dirty one; unfortunately, the outsider lens is typically not the default option when we are engaged in negotiation or embroiled in conflict. Thus, a negotiator might well be aware that the time it takes to go from an initial sales pitch to a signed contract is six to twelve weeks, yet still believe that he can close the deal within three weeks. More dangerously, the negotiator is likely to continue being overconfident despite having been proven wrong in the past. This is because the insider lens tends to focus on only the current situation, while the outsider lens is better at integrating information across multiple episodes.

Consider the case of homeowners negotiating with a contractor about building a new house. The homeowners know from their friends that such projects typically end up being 20–50 percent over budget and take much longer to complete than originally planned (the outsider view). Yet most homeowners believe that their experience will be different—that their home will be completed on time and close to the projected cost (the insider view). As a result of their poor planning, they end up needing to get last-minute financing for cost overruns, to give up features that they really wanted, and to scrounge for a place to live because the house is not yet ready for them to move in.

Nobel Laureate Kahneman tells his own story about the insider lens. Kahneman was working with a group of colleagues on defining a new curriculum and writing a book to encapsulate it.[9] The curriculum team estimated that the project would take eighteen to thirty months to complete. Kahneman approached a member of the team, a distinguished expert in curriculum design, and asked the following question: "We are surely not the only team to have tried to develop a curriculum for a new area of study. Please try to recall as many cases as you can. Think of them as they were in a stage comparable to ours at present. How long did it take them, from that point, to complete their project?" Having adopted the outsider perspective, the curriculum design expert said that the minimum completion time was seven years and that 40 percent of the projects were *never* completed. In fact, it ended up taking Kahneman's team *eight years* to finish the project!

Surely, would-be entrepreneurs should decide whether to go into business using the outsider lens—with a realistic understanding of the risks involved—rather than using the more tempting insider lens. Yet, in one study, more than 80 percent of entrepreneurs viewed their personal chances of success to be 70 percent or higher, and one-third of them described their success as *certain*.[10] This is clearly the insider speaking. The outsider can easily find out that the five-year survival rate for new businesses is only about 33 percent![11] Why would smart and motivated individuals be willing to stake large sums of money, their reputations, and years of their lives on a decision made using the biased insider lens? As we discussed in Chapter 5, people have a strong urge to see the world and themselves in a positive light, a tendency that can have powerful effects on decision-making.

The insider-outsider distinction leads us to another set of techniques that you can use to de-bias your judgment. Consider the following:

Bring in an outsider. When preparing for an important negotiation, bring an outsider to the preparation session. This may mean reaching out to experts within your firm, hiring a consultant with unique expertise, or talking to a friend. Remember that you are more likely to anticipate cost overruns when a friend is having her house built than when your own home is being built. When it comes to your own house, you anticipate that things will turn out better for you than a rational analysis would suggest. The same is true when you negotiate a deal. Others will see factors that you have ignored, weight negative information more appropriately than you do, and preserve an objective view of the situation in ways that are difficult for you to do.

Take the outsider perspective. It is often equally effective—and less costly—to ask yourself how you would assess a situation if you were not immersed in it. This might require you to think back to a time when someone else was faced with a similar situation or to collect data on what you can rationally expect in the current situation (e.g., data on industry averages). Or you might ask yourself this simple question: if someone I cared about asked me for advice in a negotiation such as this, what advice would I give?

Collectively, using System 2 thinking, applying analogical reasoning, and adopting the outsider lens are viable strategies for reducing the likelihood that decision biases will sabotage your next negotiation. If you are serious about becoming a negotiation genius, you must make the use of these strategies habitual. Too often, executives who attend negotiation courses (or read negotiation books) discover interesting ideas, but do not actually change their behavior. Gathering information is not enough. Real change requires you to "unfreeze" existing decision-making processes, understand the ideas and techniques that will help you make the desired change, and then "refreeze" the new ideas and techniques into your thoughts and behavior.[12] In other words, you must become aware of biases, consider how to avoid or overcome them, and work hard to integrate new and more effective strategies into your habitual approach to negotiation.

CONFRONTING THE BIASES OF OTHERS

The biases that others bring to the table can have serious implications for your negotiated outcomes. In the remainder of the chapter, we explore how to incorporate an understanding of the biases of others into your strategy, why and how to help others be less biased, why and how to adjust the information you receive from others, and how to respond to the other party's decision biases through contracting.

STRATEGY 1: INCORPORATE THE CONSEQUENCES OF THEIR BIASES IN YOUR STRATEGY

General managers of baseball teams spend a great deal of time deciding how to evaluate the talent they are considering acquiring and deciding with whom to negotiate a contract. Billy Beane, the general manager of the Oakland Athletics, found a way to do this better than anyone else—and succeeded in transforming his team from losers to winners. From 1999–2002, with a very limited budget, Beane led the Athletics to the second-best record in Major League Baseball (MLB). The team's players earned, on average, less than a third of the amount earned by the New York Yankees. Yet, during this four-year period, they still won more games than the Yankees.[13]

How did Beane accomplish this amazing feat? By studying the mistakes of other baseball managers and, with the help of a recent Harvard economics graduate, Paul DePodesta, using this knowledge to develop wiser negotiation strategies. In his book *Moneyball*, Michael

Lewis argues that other MLB managers were consistently guilty of three systematic mistakes that Beane and DePodesta were able to identify and exploit: 1) they overgeneralized from their personal experiences, 2) they were overly influenced by players' recent performances, and 3) they were overly influenced by what they had personally seen, even though players' multiyear records provided far better data. In other words, most baseball managers were relying on System 1 thinking.

Beane and DePodesta decided instead to look at the hard data. They found that players drafted out of high school were much less likely to succeed than players drafted out of college. Yet baseball executives systematically overvalued high-school players and systematically undervalued college players. Armed with this knowledge, Beane stopped drafting players out of high school. In addition, Beane and DePodesta learned that certain players had a dramatically higher tendency than others to be "walked," but that baseball professionals inappropriately undervalued this data.[14]

At the simplest level, the success of Beane and DePodesta's approach reveals that the use of systematic and rigorous analysis can be superior to the System 1 thinking on which many experienced negotiators rely. But much more was actually happening: Beane and DePodesta used their understanding of the decision biases of others to make trades with other teams. In doing so, they were able to get players who were more successful in exchange for players who would be less successful. Thus, they combined their System 2 thinking with an understanding of the consequences of the other side's System 1 thinking to make value-creating trades.

The lesson for negotiators? Use your System 2 thinking, but be ready to adapt to the other side's System 1 mistakes. If someone is obsessed with selling his company at a certain price point (perhaps because a broker mentioned a high number, or because a sibling sold her company for that amount), recognize the vividness of that number to him. Then, rather than fight it, see if you can creatively meet this vivid need. How? Offer the desired number in exchange for concessions on other issues that you value highly. For example, you might have him throw in related real estate or accept better financing terms. Indeed, too many negotiators focus excessively on salient dollar figures. If the other side will accept "not a penny less than $40 million," he may still accept $40 million paid to him over a very long period of time. When you start thinking about the decision biases of others, you can custom-design negotiation strategies that adapt to their errors.

STRATEGY 2: HELP OTHERS BE LESS BIASED

Our students often ask us, "Would you rather negotiate with a good negotiator or a bad negotiator?" Our answer is simple: we'd rather negotiate with good negotiators; bad negotiators will usually just get in the way of good deals. Unfortunately, many people falsely assume that bargaining with an incompetent or irrational (i.e., biased) partner gives them a valuable competitive advantage. While this is sometimes true (as the *Moneyball* example shows), biased negotiators also have tremendous potential for entirely derailing the negotiation. For example, if your counterpart is overconfident, she might wait for deals that you can never give her. If he irrationally escalates commitment to a course of action, he may become overly competitive and unwilling to compromise. If she is afflicted with the fixed-pie bias, she may refuse to share information and thus eliminate opportunities to create value. In these cases, the other party's biases hurt not only their own interests, but also yours.

For these reasons, it is often in your best interest to help your counterpart think more clearly. How can you promote careful, reasoned, and systematic thinking? Consider again that negotiators tend to be far more biased under time pressure than when they have time to think through a proposal or idea. Thus, when you have provided the other side with an offer that you believe to be better than your competitor's proposal, give him time to think it through rather than pushing for an immediate answer. Under pressure, negotiators who are overconfident in their ability to get a better deal often say no when they should say yes. If you are confident that you are offering more than he can get elsewhere, you'd be wise to encourage him to explore alternatives and get back to you after comparing your offer with others.

Most of us also assume that we want the other side to be less prepared. However, ill-prepared negotiators typically want to bargain over one issue at a time and to withhold information. They are also less able than prepared negotiators to evaluate or propose multi-issue (package) deals. All of these behaviors inhibit value creation. When dealing with an ill-prepared negotiator, encourage her to think through the relative importance of each issue to her. In addition, take the lead in negotiating multiple issues simultaneously and in making package offers—and encourage her to do the same. It is also important that you clarify for her that you value some issues more than others and that you are happy to jointly explore mutually beneficial trade-offs.

Finally, the best thing you can do to help an ill-prepared negotiator (and to help yourself) is to encourage her to be more prepared. If the negotiation is not going smoothly, you might suggest that both parties would benefit from thinking more about the issues that have surfaced during the recent discussion. You might then create a time line with the other party that includes milestones that encourage preparation and the sharing of information. For example, you might agree that, after one week, each of you will send an e-mail that lists your top priorities and concerns; after three more days, one of you will be responsible for making an initial package proposal; then, after the other party has a few days to consider this proposal, both parties will meet for further substantive discussions. While most people believe that giving the other party this much time to prepare is dangerous, a negotiation genius recognizes that your counterpart can only make wise trades, expand the pie, and accept your creative offers if she knows what she values—and that such knowledge requires preparation. So, the next time you run into a well-prepared negotiator, you should be encouraged about the potential to create an excellent agreement rather than nervous about being exploited or outperformed.

STRATEGY 3: CALIBRATE INFORMATION PROVIDED BY OTHERS

Imagine that you are moving to a new city and that you have interviewed a number of real-estate agents about selling your current home. While you want your agent to be a good salesperson, you also want him or her to provide an accurate estimate of your house's value. Unless you know how much your home will realistically sell for, you cannot be certain how expensive a home you can afford in your new location. Here is a dilemma that might arise. The agents know that you desire a high sales price and that providing you with a high estimate (within certain limits) will make you more likely to hire them. Unfortunately, the more inflated their estimates, the less accurate they could be, and the worse off you will be when assessing which new home to purchase.

How can you identify whether an agent is being overly optimistic and trying to pass on that optimism to you? Try this: instead of negotiating with one agent, ask four different agents for their opinions on the appropriate listing price. Then ask each agent to bring you computer printouts of the original *listing prices* of the last ten houses they sold as well as the final *selling price* of each of these ten homes. This is information that is readily available to them. (To verify the accuracy of the data they provide, you can even ask the agents to cross-check each other.) Armed with the agents' recommendations for your home, and also the data on historic differences between their listing prices and sales prices, you are in a far better position to estimate the true worth of your own house. You also have the data you need to hire the best agent of the bunch—the one who is not only selling high, but also is more realistic (or more truthful).

Undoubtedly, you'd choose different data in other types of negotiations. Imagine that you are an executive of a retail organization and that a group of regional managers reports to you. Each regional manager is in charge of roughly one-eighth of the country. You are meeting to negotiate the region-specific advertising budgets for the coming year. As the meeting begins, the managers of last year's two most successful regions suggest to you that the available resources should be allocated in proportion to last year's sales. They argue that last year's sales are the best predictor of next year's sales, and that sales are a good indicator of where advertising will be most effective. What is wrong with this logic?

First, some regions will have higher sales than other regions regardless of advertising (for example, you will sell more snow shovels in the northern than in the southern United States). Thus, the managers may be choosing the "appropriate measure of success" self-servingly. If so, perhaps you should ask each manager instead to report on an analysis of the marginal impact of advertising dollars on increases in sales over the past ten years. A second problem with their logic is that it fails to account for the fact that many outcomes "regress to the mean" over time.[15] Fantastic students frequently have less successful younger siblings. Extremely tall parents tend to have children that are shorter than them. Spectacular rookies tend to have mediocre second years (the "sophomore jinx"). And regions that have just had a fantastic year will tend to perform less well the next year. Why? Because every successful outcome is due in part to the factor you suspect (skill, advertising dollars, genetics, et cetera) and in part due to chance (or unknown factors). Furthermore, *extremely* successful outcomes are likely to be high on both of these factors. Unfortunately, you cannot count on chance to work strongly in your favor every year. Thus, you need to adjust your estimates downward. Regression to the mean does not mean that the past has no predictability for the future. Rather, it means that the past may predict the future less reliably than we assume.

Armed with an understanding of these biases, the executive is better prepared to negotiate with the regional managers—and to expect that the two high-performing regions from last year may continue to perform above the mean, but not necessarily by the same amount as the previous year. The key lesson: thinking about the decision biases of others allows you to calibrate, quantitatively and qualitatively, the information, data, and arguments that you hear from them.

STRATEGY 4: USE CONTINGENCY CONTRACTS TO RESOLVE CONFLICTS STEMMING FROM BIASES

"Curing" your negotiation counterpart's biases is not always the answer. Your opponent may be extremely confident about his view of the future, while you are confident that he is wrong. Rather than arguing the point, it sometimes pays to leverage the other side's biased expectations. How? Using a contingency contract. In Chapters 1 and 2, we discussed the use of contingency contracts, which allow both sides in a negotiation to bet on their beliefs about the future. When you know that the other side is biased, you can draft a contract that allows him to bet on the information that you believe to be inaccurate. In doing so, you make a bet that you expect to be favorable to you and costly to your counterpart.

Suppose that a salesperson claims that her product is measurably better than that of her competitor. You are fairly sure that her claim doesn't apply to your intended use of the product, and you don't want to run the risk of being disappointed if the product performs at less than her expectations. Instead of calling the salesperson a liar or trying to disprove her claim, propose a contingency contract instead. Specifically, offer to pay her asking price if the product performs at the level she promises, but insist upon a very large discount if it fails to meet her targeted performance level. If she has been overselling intentionally, she will back away from your proposal. But if she is simply overconfident, she'll say yes, and you'll get a very good deal. Of course, if it turns out that she is right, you will end up paying more—but for a better product than you expected. You will also find out that she is better informed and more credible than you believed.

MOVING FORWARD

Many smart people are faced with situations in which they are suspicious of another negotiator's decision-making process but lack the vocabulary to articulate the flaws in the other side's logic. In Chapters 4–6, we've summarized clearly defined and rigorously researched concepts to help you recognize and understand the biases you confront. If you would like to practice spotting others' biases, you need simply to read the newspaper or watch a sporting event on television. Journalists, politicians, sportscasters, and other "expert" information providers constantly make statements that exemplify the biased decision-making processes that we have outlined. But they are not the only ones who are biased. The worst mistake you can make right now is to think that you have just read three chapters that explain to you how *others* are biased.

Negotiation geniuses do not assume that they are immune from bias. Rather, they accept the fact that their intuition, like that of other smart people, is fundamentally flawed. They attempt to reduce the degree to which they are affected by biases and, when necessary, adopt more systematic decision processes to avoid bias. In addition, rather than expecting rationality from their counterparts, negotiation geniuses anticipate bias in others and use the strategies we have highlighted to respond to these biases.

Taken together, Parts I and II of this book (Chapters 1–6) should provide you with the tools you need to negotiate more effectively in the wide variety of negotiation contexts that you will encounter. In Part III, we will build on this knowledge and equip you to handle even the most difficult and complex negotiations.

PART III

NEGOTIATING IN THE REAL WORLD

CHAPTER 7

Strategies of Influence

Throughout the earlier chapters of this book, we have empha-
sized the need to understand the other side's perspective. For example, the principles and strategies of investigative negotiation are
critical because discovering the hidden interests, priorities, and constraints of the other side allows you to create and claim value more effectively. One of our fundamental messages is that negotiation success is
typically more a function of how well we listen than how well we talk.

But that is not the whole story. When you are making a pitch, asking for concessions, or trying to amass support for your proposal,
success also depends on your ability to "sell" your ideas, persuade
reluctant opponents, and convince others regarding the merits of
your case. These skills not only help you claim value for yourself, but
also create value for both parties. One of the most common complaints of seasoned negotiators is that defensive, untrusting, or incompetent people can stymie even mutually beneficial ideas and
proposals. Thus, would-be negotiation geniuses must find ways to
overcome not only the reasonable objections of others, but also their
close-mindedness.

In this chapter, we leverage some of the most fascinating current
research on the psychology of influence and persuasion—including
the pioneering work of renowned social psychologist Robert
Cialdini[1]—to develop strategies that will help you convince others to
comply with your requests, proposals, and ideas. Note that these influence strategies are *not* designed to help you improve the merits of

your proposal. Rather, they will increase the likelihood that others will say yes to your proposals without the *need* for you to improve them. Of course, you can also expect to be the *target* of influence tactics originating from the other side. This chapter provides numerous "defense strategies" for resisting their ploys, as well as a host of factors to consider before you say yes.

STRATEGY 1: HIGHLIGHT THEIR POTENTIAL LOSSES RATHER THAN THEIR POTENTIAL GAINS

A representative from your local power company comes to your neighborhood offering free energy audits to homeowners. You agree to the audit, after which the representative advises you to invest in products and services that will help insulate your home and lower your energy costs. Will you say yes? As researchers at the University of Santa Cruz discovered, your answer probably depends on exactly how the pitch is made. In the Santa Cruz study, the representative told half of the homeowners the following: "If you insulate your home, you will save X cents per day." (The value of X was determined by the audit.) For the other half of homeowners, the pitch was reversed: "If you *fail* to insulate your home, you will *lose* X cents per day." Notice that the information content of these two statements is identical. However, those who were told how much they stood to *lose* by not complying with the recommendation were significantly more likely to purchase the insulation![2]

As this study illustrates, people are more motivated to avoid losses than they are to accrue gains, consistent with the principle of *loss aversion*.[3] In other words, decision makers weigh information about potential losses more heavily than they do information about potential gains—even when the gains and losses are of equal magnitude. As a result, when you frame the exact same set of information as a loss, it will be more influential in negotiation than when you frame it as a gain.

Consider the following ways to leverage the power of loss aversion in negotiation:

- State your proposal in terms of what potential gains the other side stands to forgo if your idea or proposal is rejected, rather than on what he or she stands to gain by accepting.

- When holding an auction, tell bidders "you will miss out on the opportunity to have X if you do not increase your bid" rather than "you will have the opportunity to get X if you increase your bid."
- Point out that "the offer from our competitor does not give you X, Y, or Z," instead of pointing out that "our offer gives you X, Y, and Z."

In each of these cases, the *information* content of the proposal remains unchanged when you adopt a loss frame rather than a gain frame. The *influence* content, however, changes dramatically.

Once you are aware of the principle of loss aversion, you will start to notice how often the tactic crops up, not only in negotiations, but also in your life as a manager, consumer, and citizen. For example, when a consultant or a task-force representative tells you that "failure to implement these changes will result in a revenue loss of 1.5 percent," you are at the receiving end of an influence strategy. Loss aversion is also one reason why negative political ads are so effective, even though everyone professes to hate them: when candidates warn you about the dangers associated with electing their opponent (rather than touting their own merits), they are leveraging this strategy.

The principle of loss aversion can also be aimed toward benevolent ends. In a study conducted at a medical clinic in a U.S. city, women were shown videos designed to promote HIV testing. In one version of the video (the "control" condition), information was framed in terms of the benefits associated with getting tested. In another version (the "loss-frame" condition), the information was framed in terms of the costs and risks associated with not getting tested (e.g., "By not getting tested a woman is putting herself, the people she loves, and her unborn children if she becomes pregnant at risk"). Sixty-three percent of women who were shown the loss-frame video chose to be tested for HIV within two weeks. Among those who were shown the gain-frame video, only 23 percent chose to be tested.[4] In similar research, loss frames were also more effective in persuading people to obtain skin cancer detection exams[5] and in increasing the likelihood that women would conduct breast self-examinations.[6]

Despite its power to motivate compliance with demands and pro-posals, we have one important caveat on the use of this strategy: an overreliance on loss frames can sour relationships. Those who focus only on risks, costs, losses, and downsides may be perceived as hostile, threatening, or simply unpleasant. These attributions can create bar-riers to negotiation if they induce the other party to retaliate in kind. Thus, your use of loss frames should be strategic and targeted, not pervasive. It may be best to reserve the use of loss frames for summa-rizing your argument, or making your "final pitch" statement, and to avoid negativity earlier in your presentation or discussion.

STRATEGY 2: DISAGGREGATE THEIR GAINS AND AGGREGATE THEIR LOSSES

Which of these two situations would likely make you happier?

Scenario 1: You are walking down the street and find a $20 bill.
Scenario 2: You are walking down the street and find a $10 bill. The next day, as you are walking on a different street, you find an-other $10 bill.

Notice that the two scenarios have identical payoffs: both result in a $20 gain. However, the vast majority of people believe that they would be happier in Scenario 2. Why? Before we try to answer this, let's consider another two scenarios.

Which of the following would make you unhappier?

Scenario X: You open your wallet and discover you have lost a $20 bill.
Scenario Y: You open your wallet and discover you have lost a $10 bill. The following day you lose another $10 bill.

Again, the scenarios are identical with regard to financial outcome. However, this time the vast majority of people claim that Scenario Y would make them *unhappier.*

As these two exercises demonstrate, people seem to prefer *finding* money in installments but *losing* money in one lump sum.[7] In order to maximize pleasure, then, you should separate the total gain into lots of small wins (rather than one big win). Meanwhile, to minimize pain, you should put all of the losses together—this gives you only one loss to absorb.

Here are the implications of this finding for negotiators:

Disaggregate Their Gains:

- If you have the ability to make concessions, do not make them all at once. For example, if you can increase your offer by $100, break up this concession into smaller concessions that add up to $100 and distribute the smaller concessions individually. Your counterpart will evaluate this string of concessions more positively than one lump-sum concession.
- If you have good news to share, try to parcel the information into smaller "gems" that will give the other party more occasions to smile. For example, if you have completed a project under budget and also earlier than scheduled, do not share all of this good news with your client all at once. You will make your client happier if, one day, you tell her you have completed the project early, and on another day, you tell her you were also under budget.
- If you have benefits or rewards to offer, separate them into installments that you can make over time. For example, if you have been authorized to give an unsuspecting employee both a raise and a promotion, you will make the employee happier if you tell them about the raise today and about the promotion tomorrow.

Aggregate Their Losses:

- If you are requesting or demanding that the other side make concessions, make one comprehensive demand rather than several partial demands.
- If you have bad news to share, share it all at once.
- If you have costs or burdens to impose, combine them into one.

STRATEGY 3: EMPLOY THE "DOOR IN THE FACE" TECHNIQUE

Many salespeople swear by this old rule of thumb: "Keep them saying yes!" The theory behind this approach is that, as the seller in a negotiation, you should strive to keep the buyer in a positive, agreeable, and accommodating mood. After all, the longer she agrees with you, the more likely she is to believe that your interests are compatible with hers. There is also the issue of momentum to consider: you want to build momentum toward final acceptance of your demands—not ultimate rejection.

Like so many rules of thumb, this one is only partially true. In fact, one way to get the "yes" you want is to allow (or provoke) the other party to say "no" first. Consider some fascinating research conducted by Professor Robert Cialdini of Arizona State University. Cialdini's research assistants went around the city posing as workers from the county juvenile detention center. They stopped people on the street at random and asked them for a favor: "Would you be willing to chaperone a group of juvenile delinquents on a day trip to the zoo?" As you might imagine, most people were taken aback by the extreme request, and only 17 percent said yes. The researchers then tried a different approach. This time when they stopped a person, they asked for an even greater favor: "Would you be willing to serve as a counselor at the juvenile detention center? This will require two hours of your time each week for three years." Not surprisingly, *everyone* turned down this request. Without skipping a beat, the researchers then went on to ask: "Well, if you can't do that, would you be willing to chaperone a group of juvenile delinquents on a day trip to the zoo?" The response was staggering. Now, 50 percent of those asked to chaperone agreed to comply! When the exact same proposal—a request to chaperone—was preceded by an extreme demand that was sure to be rejected, three times as many people said yes.

Why does compliance increase after an initial rejection? Because, according to Cialdini, when the person making the request moderates his demands (and asks for something less extreme), the other side views this as a concession that must be reciprocated.[8] In other words, because the rejected party has "compromised" by asking for less, it is incumbent on the other side to "meet them halfway." Another factor is the *contrast effect*—our tendency to judge the size of something based on the context in which it is situated. Placed next to the request for a three-year investment of time, chaperoning a zoo trip does not seem like much to ask! Cialdini refers to this extreme-then-moderate approach as the "door in the face" (DITF) strategy, referring to the image of a salesperson having the door slammed in his face when he makes an outrageous request. Of course, in this case, the salesperson does not walk away after the door is slammed; instead, she makes a second, less outrageous request.

The negotiation implications of Cialdini's study are obvious, and we've already covered some of them in our discussion of first offers and anchors in Chapter 1. Simply put, if you want something, ask for more than you want (or expect), and be prepared to make concessions. Unfortunately, negotiators often censor themselves, assuming that too aggressive an offer will be rejected—but as Cialdini's research demonstrates, rejection is not necessarily a bad thing. There are, of course, some risks associated with making outrageous demands. Your counterpart might consider your request to be ignorant, crazy, or plain offensive (though the zoo-trip study suggests that you can sometimes get away with some fairly outrageous requests!). In Strategy 5, we will consider one powerful way to mitigate the possibility of offending the other party when you have made an extreme demand.

STRATEGY 4: EMPLOY THE "FOOT IN THE DOOR" TECHNIQUE

Consider the results of the following experiment.[9] In a study conducted near a college campus, the bartender at a local bar identified a set of regular patrons and asked half of them to sign a petition against drunk driving. They all did so. The bartender did not approach the other half of the group with this request. Over the next six weeks, the bartender noted when any of the identified patrons became intoxicated. Then, as the inebriated patron prepared to leave the bar, the bartender made a second request: "May I call a taxi to take you home?" Among those who had *not* been asked to sign a petition, only 10 percent agreed to wait for the taxi. In contrast, 58 percent of those who had signed were willing to wait.

Why did more people agree to the more onerous request (wait for a taxi) after they had first complied with a less burdensome request (sign a petition)? Research suggests that once someone has agreed to an initial request, they are more psychologically committed to seeing the process through to its end. Thus, willingness to agree with one request leads to an increased commitment to agree with additional re-quests *that naturally follow from the initial request.* The critical factor here is the motivation that people have to justify past decisions and to preserve consistency between their statements and actions. Once someone has said yes to the bartender's initial request, she is psycho-logically committed. She begins to see herself as someone who takes a stand against drunk driving. When confronted with the bartender's second request, she may feel she has no choice but to comply; if she does not, it becomes difficult to justify her willingness to sign the pe-tition in the first place.[10]

This approach, which has been referred to as the "foot in the door" (FITD) strategy, may appear to contradict Cialdini's "door in the face" strategy in which the more extreme request is made *initially.* However, these strategies have different underlying mechanisms and objectives. DITF (aim for rejection, then moderate your demand) is appropriate (as in the zoo-trip study) when your goal is to make your key demand seem reasonable. The FITD (aim for compliance with a simple request, then increase your demands) is appropriate when you are in need of building commitment toward your key demand.

For example, a car salesman may employ the DITF technique by showing a potential buyer a more expensive car first, even though he has already determined that the buyer is only considering the cheaper model. Because of the contrast effect, seeing the more expensive car first will make the price of the cheaper car seem reasonable. Later, dur-ing the same interaction, the salesman might *also* use the FITD tech-nique. He can do this by asking the buyer to take the *cheaper* car for a test drive (a moderate request). Once the test drive is over, and the buyer has increased his commitment to the cheaper car, the salesman is in a better position to ask the buyer to purchase it (the more ex-treme request).

There is another important distinction between using the DITF and FITD strategies: When applying the DITF (extreme-then-moderate) strategy, try to make the moderate request very soon after the other side rejects your extreme request. Otherwise, the contrast effect di-minishes and the moderate request is perceived not as a concession, but as an entirely different demand. The FITD (moderate-then-extreme) approach, in contrast, seems to work better when the extreme request is made after some time has passed since the moderate request was accepted (assuming the earlier agreement has not been forgotten). If the second demand is made too soon, there is less time for feelings of commitment to be processed; also, making a second demand right after the first may be seen as overly aggressive, pushy, or blatantly strategic.

STRATEGY 5: LEVERAGE THE POWER OF JUSTIFICATION

Harvard psychologist Ellen Langer and her colleagues set the stage for another fascinating study when they asked the university librarian to shut down all but one of the copy machines in the library. As a result of this conspiracy, long lines began to form at the one remaining copy machine. The researchers were interested in finding out what would convince people who were in line to let others cut in front of them. In some instances, a researcher simply said, "Excuse me, I have five pages. May I use the Xerox machine?" Sixty percent of those approached this way allowed the researcher to cut in front of them. Other people were approached with a slightly different request: "Excuse me, I have five pages. May I use the Xerox machine *because I have to make some copies?*" As you can see, the second approach added an entirely inane justification (obviously, the reason for wanting to cut in line at a copy machine is to make copies!). What was the response this time? Ninety-three percent of those approached with this request allowed the researcher to cut in front of them![11]

As these results suggest, even entirely frivolous justifications have the power to induce compliance. Why? Because human beings are "hardwired" to accommodate the (seemingly) legitimate demands and impositions of others because doing so allows us to build mutually rewarding relationships with them. In other words, we are willing to go the extra mile in order to help those who will become obligated to us, but not to help those who feel they can simply impose their will upon us and who may not ever reciprocate. And so, even though people tend to resist the demands you impose upon them, they are willing to lower their resistance and consider your demands if they feel that *at least you* think the demands are justified. To make these judgments, according to Langer and her colleagues, humans use heuristics, or simple "rules of thumb," and even a simple signal such as the word "because" is often sufficient to win compliance. In the copy machine experiment, for example, the lack of substantive information following the "because" was less relevant than the word itself.

How can negotiators use this insight? Here is one critical piece of advice, which we first shared in Chapter 1: refrain from making demands (especially aggressive offers) that will not fit into a sentence with approximately the following structure: "I am asking for X because ..." In other words, if you can find some way to justify your position, that justification will probably increase the odds of compliance—or, at the very least, mitigate the risk that your demand will be perceived as illegitimate, unfounded, crazy, or offensive. Even if your goal is not to "sell" an extreme demand (as in the DITF technique), adding a justification can strengthen your case and make it less likely that the other side will simply walk away.

What are some potential justifications for your demands? Typically, many *potential* justifications exist, and negotiators must choose the one that best suits the desired outcome. The seller of a piece of real estate might try to maximize bids by citing the high sale prices of recent properties in the area, the above-average condition of the property being sold, or the optimistic projections of analysts regarding real-estate prices in the region. Meanwhile, a buyer might justify her low offer on the *same* piece of property based on the low recent valuation, the risk that current prices are inflated due to a nationwide real-estate bubble, or the low price of another property that she saw earlier that day.

As another example, consider the difference among the following three scripts that an employee might use in her attempt to negotiate a higher salary.

> *Offer A:* "You had asked how much of a salary increase I feel that I deserve. I have thought about it, and I believe that a 10 percent raise would be fair."
>
> *Offer B:* "You had asked how much of a salary increase I feel that I deserve. I have thought about it, and I believe that a 10 percent raise would be fair because my performance over the last year has been exceptional."
>
> *Offer C:* "You had asked how much of a salary increase I feel that I deserve. I have thought about it, and I believe that a

10 percent raise would be fair because my performance over the last year has been exceptional. Here is some data on the revenues I have generated that support my claim."

Offer B is clearly superior to Offer A because it provides a justification for the demand (a 10 percent increase in salary). However, Offer C represents the best approach: it provides a justification *and* follows that up with evidence to support this justification. There are potentially many ways to measure work performance, but by taking control of the discussion early on, you have an opportunity to *define* what is the appropriate measure. Offer C, then, includes a justification for the demand, but also frames the negotiation in a way that helps maximize the power of the justification. More generally, in negotiation, don't let your offer "speak for itself"; provide a justification for your demand and then tell a story that legitimizes your justification.

STRATEGY 6: LEVERAGE THE POWER OF SOCIAL PROOF

In recent years, "infomercials"—long advertisements that provide extensive information regarding the benefits, application, or celebrity use of a product—have become a hallmark of late-night television in the United States. At various points during the typical thirty-minute infomercial, the host will ask viewers to "call the number on the screen" to purchase the advertised product at discounted prices. Many of us have wondered what in the world would persuade someone to actually pick up the phone in the middle of the night to buy something like a self-cleaning oven mitt. Apparently, an infomercial writer named Colleen Szot spent a lot of time wondering the exact same thing. At one point, she decided to change the standard request that appeared in virtually all infomercials: "Operators are standing by, please call now." She simply changed three words in the statement: "If operators are busy, please call again." What was the result? The number of calls skyrocketed![12]

Why? On the surface, both statements seem to convey identical information, and neither says anything about the *product*. But what message does each statement convey about the behavior of *other viewers*? The old message seems to suggest that very few (if any) people are calling and that the operators are simply waiting for the phone to ring. The second message, in contrast, suggests that the phones are ringing off the hook and that you may have to try calling multiple times *because other people are buying this product.* Psychologists refer to this phenomenon as the power of *social proof.*[13] As every teenager knows, whenever there is uncertainty or ambiguity regarding the appropriate course of action, you should look to the behavior of similar others for guidance ("But, Mom, everybody's doing it!"). As it turns out, teenagers are not the only ones who think this way. This is why bars and nightclubs maintain long lines outside the entrance even when the interior is almost empty (you would think they would prefer to sell alcohol to these people). It is also why television sitcoms use "laugh tracks": we think a joke is funnier when we hear other people laughing at it.

How can the principle of social proof improve your negotiation outcomes? Consider the following tactics:

- The seller of a house limits the open-house viewing of the property to only one hour so that all potential buyers will be present at the same time.
- When a potential client asks her to provide a list of dates on which to schedule an initial meeting, the consultant (who is secretly desperate for work) provides very few available dates in the following week.
- A sales representative begins his pitch by listing his firm's many other clients. (Or a business school fills its brochures with the names and photographs of famous alumni.)

STRATEGY 7: MAKE TOKEN UNILATERAL CONCESSIONS

Some years ago, a national trade association for construction subcontractors determined that it needed to survey its membership. They were aware, however, of one of the key barriers to such market research: target audiences are notoriously reluctant to respond to surveys and questionnaires. In the hopes of learning how best to increase response rates, they decided to test the power of providing a financial incentive for filling out the survey. One randomly chosen subgroup of members was sent the questionnaire with no financial incentive. Of this subgroup, 20.7 percent returned a completed questionnaire. Another randomly chosen subgroup of members was promised a $50 payment for completing and returning the questionnaire. Unfortunately, the $50 incentive did not significantly change behavior; this time, 23.3 percent of members responded. Why such a weak effect? One plausible theory is that the incentive was not large enough; perhaps the association should have promised $100 or $200. However, consider what happened with a third group of members. This group was sent the questionnaire and, along with it, a single $1 bill. This time, 40.7 percent of members returned a completed questionnaire![14]

Standard economic theories fail to explain the behavior of these survey respondents. Not only was the $1 incentive considerably smaller than the $50 incentive, but the $1 incentive was not really an "incentive" at all—it was guaranteed payment *regardless* of whether the member complied with the request. While economic theorists rush to create a model that explains this behavior, the rest of us might note that it is precisely *because* the $1 was not an incentive, but rather a unilateral concession—or gift—that the recipients felt obliged to reciprocate. What is striking, nonetheless, is the fact that such a small concession would be so effective. Research on trust and reciprocity suggests that recipients of gifts and concessions are often insensitive to the degree of cost incurred by the giver;[15] thus, even a low-cost (i.e., "token") concession may be sufficient to induce reciprocity, compliance, or agreement.

For example, consider some token concessions that you might make in your next negotiation:

- You agree to meet at a time—or at a location—that is more convenient for the other side than it is for you.
- On the way to the negotiation, you purchase doughnuts and coffee to share with your negotiation counterpart.
- You begin substantive discussions by agreeing to one of the smaller requests that the other side had made.

In each case, the more salient your concession is to the other side (e.g., the other side knows that you have agreed to the location despite its inconvenience for you), the more likely it is that they will be compelled to reciprocate in substantive ways.

STRATEGY 8: USE REFERENCE POINTS TO MAKE YOUR OFFERS AND DEMANDS SEEM REASONABLE

In a recent negotiation training session for executives, we presented the following scenario (adapted from the work of Daniel Kahneman and Amos Tversky[16]) to half of the participants:

> *Scenario A:* Imagine that you are about to purchase a calculator for $50. The calculator salesperson informs you that this calculator is on sale at the store's other branch, located a twenty-minute drive away from where you are now. Assuming that you cannot negotiate the price at your current location, what is the minimum discount you would need at the other location to make it worth the twenty-minute trip?

Before you read further, take a moment to write down your own response to Scenario A. Then consider the next scenario, which was presented to the other half of the participants in the session.

> *Scenario B:* Imagine that you are about to purchase a laptop computer for $2,000. The computer salesperson informs you that this computer is on sale at the store's other branch, located a twenty-minute drive from where you are now. Assuming that you cannot negotiate the price at your current location, what is the minimum discount you would need at the other location to make it worth the twenty-minute trip?

If you look closely, you will notice that both scenarios are asking the *same* question: how much is twenty minutes of your time worth? But consider how differently executives valued twenty minutes of their time, depending on whether they read Scenario A or Scenario B. Those who read Scenario A said that they would need, on average, a discount of $20 for it to be worth driving across town. Those who read Scenario B said that they would need, on average, a discount of almost $200 for it to be worth the same trip!

As this experiment suggests, the way in which people value their own interests (in this case, their time) is open to influence. Going across town to save $20 may seem foolish when we are purchasing a big-ticket item (such as a computer or an automobile). But if there was a $20 discount on something relatively cheap (such as a calculator or a $60 sweater), we might feel compelled to make the trip. In other words, people do not objectively evaluate the cost of an item or an issue; rather, they evaluate costs in comparison with salient reference points (e.g., the total amount they are spending that day). This is exactly why car salespeople get away with selling so many add-ons. When you are already paying $30,000 for the car, paying an additional $200–$500 for floor mats or scratch proofing does not seem like a big deal. On the other hand, if you already owned the car and someone came to your door selling floor mats or scratch proofing at the same prices, you would probably slam the door in their face!

There is another reason why the executives in our training session were willing to chase a $20 discount on a calculator but not on a computer: people care not only about the value of the item they are purchasing, but also about getting a "good deal." The desire to get a good or "fair" deal makes negotiators susceptible to influence.[17] For example, shoppers will be more likely to pay $500 for an item when they discover that it was originally priced at $750, regardless of how much the item is truly worth to them. Likewise, in a study conducted by economist Richard Thaler, people were willing to pay significantly more for a beer purchased from a "fancy resort hotel" than from a "run-down grocery store," even though they would consume the beer at the beach in both cases. In other words, even when the value of the deal is identical, negotiators are likely to find it more or less attractive depending on how it is presented, what it is compared with, and how much of a "steal" it represents.

DEFENDING YOURSELF AGAINST STRATEGIES OF INFLUENCE

All of the strategies we have described are grounded not only in scientific research, but also in the experience of practitioners who make their living by inducing you to concur, consent, or comply with their wishes and demands. As a negotiator, you will likely be confronted by many skilled wielders of influence. Unfortunately, simply learning about the strategies is unlikely to protect you from their powerful effects. To protect yourself, you must make a conscious effort to anticipate and mitigate them.[18] Here, we review a number of defense strategies that you can employ in your own negotiations.

DEFENSE STRATEGY 1: PREPARE SYSTEMATICALLY

One of the best ways to defend against influence strategies is to prepare systematically and comprehensively for negotiations. This entails a rigorous BATNA analysis, a careful evaluation of the ZOPA, and a thorough investigation of all the issues. Negotiators who have carefully evaluated their interests and priorities prior to entering talks are unlikely to accept an unfavorable offer simply because of the way in which it is presented.

DEFENSE STRATEGY 2: CREATE A SCORING SYSTEM

As described in Chapter 2, a scoring system allows you to objectively evaluate the total value of a stated offer by comparing it with the total value of alternative offers, to the value of your BATNA, or to the degree of your aspirations. Influence strategies are less likely to persuade a negotiator who can objectively evaluate every proposal that is made.

DEFENSE STRATEGY 3: EXPLICITLY SEPARATE INFORMATION FROM INFLUENCE

As explained in Chapter 1, negotiation geniuses understand that everything that the other side says is part information and part influence. Your task is to explicitly separate the two before reacting or responding. When the other side makes a seemingly compelling statement, effective negotiators ask themselves questions such as these: "Did I learn something new here? If so, what did I learn? How should I evaluate what she said in the context of my interests and my priorities?" Here is another line of questioning that can help separate influence from information: "Would I be willing to do this for anyone else? Would I have been willing to do this yesterday—or even an hour ago? Can I defend my decision to critical others?"

DEFENSE STRATEGY 4: REPHRASE THEIR OFFER IN OTHER TERMS

You can also mitigate the impact of influence strategies by taking time to rephrase substantive statements that the other party makes. You might rephrase their loss-frame statement (to yourself) using a gain frame—and then see how tempting their proposal seems. For example, if the other side says, "If you do not increase your bid, you will lose the opportunity to win this deal," you may be tempted to submit a higher bid. Before you do, take a moment and rephrase their statement as follows: "If I want to have a chance at winning this deal, I will have to increase my bid." Are you just as tempted to bid higher? The key is to identify whether your reaction to their proposal stems from its merits or from their presentation.

DEFENSE STRATEGY 5: APPOINT A DEVIL'S ADVOCATE

As suggested in Chapter 4, a useful negotiation strategy is to appoint someone on your side to play the role of devil's advocate. This person's role is to question your beliefs regarding everything that is relevant to the negotiation. Your devil's advocate need not be present during the negotiation; you might find it more appropriate to structure a process that allows you to "call in" every so often to confer with her.

DEFENSE STRATEGY 6: IF POSSIBLE, DO NOT NEGOTIATE UNDER TIME PRESSURE

Influence tactics are more likely to have an effect when their target must respond quickly. This suggests that negotiators should try to set aside ample time to negotiate, be willing to wait a day or more before making important decisions, and be comfortable asking other parties to allow time for consideration of the offer or proposal. For example, it is likely that many of those approached in the zoo-trip study would have rejected the request to chaperone juvenile delinquents if given the chance to sleep on it.

Of course, these defense strategies are not mutually exclusive. Negotiation geniuses rely simultaneously on many or all of them. Furthermore, these strategies are not simply useful for countering influence tactics; all of them are sound negotiation advice in any situation.

THE LIMITS OF INFLUENCE

The influence strategies that we have described will not help you improve your ideas or offers; rather, they simplify the task of selling what you have to offer. And, while these strategies are a powerful means of persuading others to accept your offers and comply with your demands, negotiators who rely exclusively on influence strategies are likely to achieve only limited success, for two reasons. First, as highlighted in Chapter 3, those who focus exclusively on "selling" rather than on "negotiating" will forgo opportunities to learn about the other side's interests, and as a consequence, to create value. Second, if you are up against a tough negotiator—or embroiled in a bitter dispute—your ability to get the other side to comply, concur, or consent may be seriously limited. If all you have to fall back on are the "soft" strategies of influence, you will be seriously outgunned. Not all negotiations go smoothly, and not all negotiators are amicable. Negotiation geniuses anticipate this, and they know what to do when times get tough. In the following chapters (and especially in Chapter 12, which focuses on strategies for handling difficult negotiators), we will share their secrets.

CHAPTER 8

Blind Spots in Negotiation

On December 15, 2004, Johnson & Johnson (J&J) agreed to buy medical products manufacturer Guidant for $25.4 billion.[1] Initially, this appeared to be good news for both Guidant stockholders and for J&J, as the market believed the acquisition had synergy—that is, Guidant appeared to be worth more to J&J than as a stand-alone company.

On May 24, 2005, well before J&J and Guidant could close the deal, a *New York Times* article disclosed that, for three years, Guidant had failed to tell doctors that its implantable defibrillator contained a flaw that had caused twenty-six of them to short-circuit and malfunction. The unit was implanted in 24,000 patients. The FDA opened an investigation into Guidant; a few weeks later, on June 17, Guidant announced a product recall of its defibrillator.

On October 18, J&J indicated that it wanted to renegotiate the terms of its deal with Guidant, and on November 2, J&J released a statement saying that it believed the federal investigation and recall had affected Guidant's "short-term results and long-term outlook."[2] On the same day, New York attorney general Eliot Spitzer announced a lawsuit against Guidant, and the FTC conditionally approved the J&J/Guidant merger. Under the terms of the agreement, J&J had forty-eight hours to execute and finalize the deal after the FTC had approved it. If J&J were to let the deadline expire, possibly citing a "material adverse change" in Guidant's business, Guidant could sue J&J to force completion of the acquisition. J&J chose not to execute the deal within forty-eight hours. On November 7, Guidant sued J&J.[3] Nine days later, as negative press surrounding Guidant continued to mount,[4] J&J proposed a revised bid for Guidant of $21.5 billion.

Meanwhile, virtually unmentioned throughout the initial reporting on the Guidant acquisition was another firm, Boston Scientific, which would be put at a strategic disadvantage if J&J were to acquire Guidant. Boston Scientific was a key competitor of J&J in the medical-care industry, which was now being reshaped by J&J's bid for Guidant. Between December 14, 2004 (the day before J&J's offer), and April 28 (the day after Guidant shareholders approved the offer), the stock price of Boston Scientific had fallen from $35.88 to $29.46 per share.

By the time J&J proposed its revised bid of $21.5 billion, Boston Scientific's stock price had fallen to $25 per share. On December 5, unable to stomach J&J's acquisition of Guidant, Boston Scientific offered $24.7 billion for Guidant. Meanwhile, Guidant's legal and public image problems continued to worsen; on December 27, the FDA made public a warning letter that it had sent to Guidant about problems with its products.[5]

Negotiations involving these three companies continued into 2006. Preferring the structure of J&J's deal over Boston Scientific's higher-priced deal, Guidant tentatively accepted J&J's raised offer of $23.2 billion on January 11. The next day, Boston Scientific raised its bid to $25 billion. The following day, Guidant tentatively accepted J&J's newly revised bid of $24.2 billion. On the seventeenth, Boston Scientific offered to buy Guidant for $27 billion, well above the amount J&J had been willing to pay even prior to Guidant's legal troubles.[6] J&J decided against reraising its bid and made that decision public the next morning, on January 25.[7] That day, Guidant accepted Boston Scientific's bid of $27 billion.[8] Boston Scientific had won the battle. But who had won the war?

The day after having its bid accepted, Boston Scientific's share price fell to $23.15—almost $2 lower than it had been prior to the company's first bid for Guidant. Notably, J&J's share price had fallen every time it announced a bid on Guidant; it had fallen 4.4 percent between the time that Boston Scientific first entered the bidding war and the day Guidant accepted Boston Scientific's $27 billion offer.

Months later, in June 2006, Boston Scientific was forced to recall 23,000 pacemakers from the Guidant division and to advise 27,000 patients with Guidant devices to consult their doctors. By now, Boston Scientific's share price had fallen below $17 per share. *Fortune* magazine would later describe Boston Scientific's acquisition of Guidant as "arguably the second-worst ever, trailing only the spectacular AOL Time Warner debacle."[9]

Why did Boston Scientific make decisions that caused its stock price to plummet by more than 50 percent? Why did Boston Scientific aggressively pursue the takeover of a company that had obvious technological, legal, financial, and public-image liabilities? Why did J&J initiate a process (via its initial bid for Guidant) that would lead to such a significant drop in its share price? Could J&J and Boston Scientific have foreseen and avoided what eventually transpired? We think so. Many organizations and individuals make poor decisions in competitive environments due to their failure to consider all of the relevant information. Very often, this information is both available and highly critical, yet a negotiator overlooks it because it is located in what we refer to as the negotiator's "blind spot." According to a phenomenon that Max and his colleague Dolly Chugh call *bounded awareness,* negotiators tend to focus narrowly on the decisions they must make and thus often ignore information that is relevant but outside the scope of their narrow focus.[10]

In this chapter, we will identify the systematic ways in which negotiators make this common decision-making mistake. Specifically, we will reveal how negotiators often overlook the following factors:

- the role of parties that are not at the bargaining table;
- the ways in which other parties are likely to make decisions;
- the role of information asymmetries;
- the strength of competitors;
- information that is not immediately relevant but that will be critical in the future.

In each situation, we will also provide you with strategies for seeing more clearly the information that falls in your blind spot.

WHEN PARTIES AWAY FROM THE TABLE ARE IN YOUR BLIND SPOT

As we seek to clarify the flaws behind J&J and Boston Scientific's costly pursuit of Guidant, consider this more abstract problem:

> Two companies, A and B, are the leading players in their industry. Company C, which falls in the next tier in the same industry, is worth $1 billion as a stand-alone company, and its management has announced that it would be interested in being acquired at a favorable price. Analysts have identified A and B as the obvious bidders, since the acquisition of C by either A or B would make either company the dominant player in the industry. Both A and B have analyzed the possible acquisition of C and both have concluded that C would be worth $1.2 billion if managed by A or B. This means that if A or B could acquire C for under $1.2 billion, it would be a profitable acquisition, but anything above $1.2 billion would create a net loss and would lead to a drop in the acquirer's stock price. However, if A were to acquire C, B would be at a catastrophic disadvantage and would lose $0.5 billion. Similarly, if B were to acquire C, A would also lose $0.5 billion. Finally, if either A or B makes an offer for C, the other company will learn of the offer. So, as the CEO of Company A, what should you do?

When we present this problem in our executive education classrooms, our students often suggest that A should offer C $1.1 billion. This offer, if accepted, would create a $100 million net benefit for A and a $100 million net benefit for C. Clearly, the $1.1 billion offer is in the ZOPA.

But what about B? When you think about B's position, it becomes clear that C will not have to accept A's $1.1 billion offer. Once A has made this offer, B stands to lose $0.5 billion unless B outbids A. Rather than suffering a $0.5 billion loss, B is likely to offer $1.2 billion to break even.

But what about A? Unless A bids again, A will now lose $0.5 billion. Thus, A will offer $1.3 billion, and the problem reverts to B.

The pattern is now clear: each party is better off bidding again rather than losing $0.5 billion. As a result, we can easily predict that the auction will escalate until it reaches $1.7 billion, at which point it will end. One of the two competitors (A or B) will lose $0.5 billion because it has lost the deal, and the other will lose $0.5 billion because it has "won" the deal by overpaying by $0.5 billion for C. Unfortunately, as soon as the first bid is made, neither party can quit without suffering a $0.5 billion loss.

What is the key to winning in this auction? First, you must recognize that *any* bid for the target (C) will lead to dysfunctional competition. Second, you should develop a (legal) strategy to discourage your competitor from initiating the value-destroying escalation process.

Why do most of our executive students miss these solutions and instead propose that A make a bid for C? This strategy (A should bid $1.1 billion for C) results from an overly narrow definition of the scope of this negotiation. Specifically, the offer emerges when A views the negotiation as involving only A and C. If the world were that simple, A need only consider whether there is a ZOPA—i.e., whether C is worth more to A than as a stand-alone entity. But this analysis ignores two key elements: 1) the effect of A's behavior on *B's* outcomes, and 2) the rules that allow C to bring B into the game after it gets an offer from A.

More broadly, the ABC story illustrates what happens when negotiators fail to consider the perspective of parties who are not at the bargaining table. Negotiation geniuses, in contrast, learn to broaden their focus to consider the impact of their actions on others and to think through the competitive dynamics that will result from their strategy.

The ABC problem is based on a real case: a mid-1990s negotiation involving American Airlines, United Airlines, and USAir. Like Company C, USAir made public the fact that it was for sale at the right price. Business journalists quickly speculated that the two industry leaders, United and American Airlines, would end up in a bidding war for USAir, because the value of USAir was higher to an acquirer

(United or American) than as a stand-alone company. The stakes for both potential acquirers were enormous: the sale of USAir to American would be a major setback for United; the sale of USAir to United would be a similarly damaging blow to American. In other words, American and United faced the same dilemma as companies A and B in the ABC problem. So, what did they do?

Soon after USAir's revelation that it was for sale, Robert Crandall, the CEO of American Airlines, wrote an open letter to American's 118,000 employees that stated:[11]

> We continue to believe, as we always have, that the best way for American to increase its size and reach is by internal growth— not by consolidation.... So we will not be the first to make a bid for USAir. On the other hand, if United seeks to acquire USAir, we will be prepared to respond with a bid, or by other means as necessary, to protect American's competitive position.

While the letter was nominally addressed to American Airlines employees, it is quite possible that the message was actually intended for United. In other words, Crandall's message to United was "Keep things as they are, or we will both end up losing a lot of money." What was the result? No offers were made on USAir in the mid-1990s, and this became one of the few instances in which the U.S. airline industry avoided dysfunctional competition. As he considered the scope of a possible negotiation for USAir, Crandall clearly broadened his focus to include the dilemma United would face if American made a bid and the likely outcome of the bidding war that would ensue if either side made an offer.

The USAir story is not unique; many other acquisition wars have a similar structure. Whenever two companies know that the loser of a bidding war will incur a loss of market value once the bidding begins, each has an incentive to continue bidding beyond the value of the target. In such battles, as in the $100 auction described in Chapter 4, it is easier to stay out of the bidding altogether than it is to get out safely once you have entered. From all appearances, even such market leaders as J&J and Boston Scientific are capable of falling into this trap.

WHEN THE OTHER SIDE'S DECISION RULES ARE IN YOUR BLIND SPOT

Imagine that your company, under your leadership, is considering making an offer to acquire a small firm that has invented a great new product that fits your company's needs. You believe that your firm can uniquely add value to the smaller firm's product. Your assessment is that the firm currently could be worth as little as $5 million or as much as $10 million in the marketplace, depending on valuation assumptions. But, due to the unique synergies that your firm could create, you value the smaller firm at roughly $14 million. You know that the other firm's three founders own the entire firm in equal shares and they may have different opinions about the worth of their firm. How much will you offer to buy the company?

Wait a minute! Suppose you learn that the three founders have an agreement that they will only sell the firm if all three agree to accept an offer. Does this new information change your offer? If so, what is your new offer?

Now let's try one more variation. Imagine instead that you learn that the founders have an agreement that, if they ever receive an offer, any one of the three can force the sale of the firm (unless the other two buy her shares at an equivalent price, which you are fairly certain the others cannot afford to do). Does this information change your offer? If so, what is your new offer?

Once you realize that each of the founders is likely to have a different reservation value (i.e., a different minimum price that they require before they will sell), it becomes obvious that you need to consider what type of arrangement the three founders have regarding how and when to sell. In other words, you need to focus on their decision rules. What may be your best strategy when any one founder can ratify a sale is probably not the best strategy when every founder must agree to the sale.

Imagine that each of the three founders has a different reservation value for selling the firm: Founder A's reservation value is $6 million, Founder B's reservation value is $7 million, and Founder C's reservation value is $9 million. Clearly, if one founder can force the sale, you can successfully offer a much lower price—just above $6 million—because Founder A will accept this price and force the sale. If, however, all three founders must be in agreement, Founder C is the critical player, and you will have to offer more than $9 million to secure the deal. (And if majority rule was the arrangement, you would have to satisfy Founders A and B and offer more than $7 million.)

Once we have analyzed this problem carefully, it becomes clear that we need to think through the decision rules, constraints, and politics of the other side. However, when we present this scenario to executives, they often fail to see the importance of considering the decision rights of the three founders. Moreover, they tell us that they do not typically focus on such issues in the real world. Instead, in situations such as the one we just described, many executives will focus entirely on financial and accounting issues, such as calculating revenue multiples, projecting financial synergies, et cetera. These calculations are clearly necessary, as they provide an objective valuation for the company and help you to understand the highest you should be willing to pay for your acquisition. But focusing only on these issues and overlooking the other side's decision-making dynamics can lead you to pay more than is necessary.

For most negotiators, the decision rules of other parties lie outside the bounds of awareness. In contrast, negotiation geniuses understand that they need to consider not only the interests of the other side, but also how the other side will evaluate and make their decisions.

WHEN THE OTHER SIDE'S INFORMATION ADVANTAGE IS IN YOUR BLIND SPOT

Read the following exercise and write down your response before reading further.

ACQUIRING A COMPANY

You represent Company A (the acquirer), and you are planning to make a tender offer, in cash, for 100 percent of Company T's (the target) shares. The main complication is this: The value of

Company T depends directly on the outcome of a major oil exploration project that it is currently undertaking. If the project fails, Company T under current management will be worth nothing (i.e., $0 per share). But if the project succeeds, the value of the company under current management could be as high as $100 per share. All share values between $0 and $100 are considered equally likely.

By all estimates, the company will be worth 50 percent more in the hands of Company A than under current management. If the project fails, the company is worth $0 per share under either management. If the exploration project generates a $50 per share value under current management, the value under Company A will be $75 per share. Similarly, a $100 per share value under Company T implies a $150 per share value under Company A, and so on.

One last detail: Your offer must be made now, before the outcome of the drilling project is known. Company T will accept your price per share if it is greater than the value under current management. However, Company T will delay its decision on your bid until the results of the project are known and then accept or reject your offer. Thus, you (Company A) will not know the results of the exploration project when submitting your offer, but Company T will know the results when deciding whether or not to accept your offer. No other firms are involved; the target will be acquired by you or by no one.

As the representative of Company A, you are deliberating over price offers ranging from $0 per share (which is tantamount to making no offer at all) to $150 per share. What price per share offer would you tender for Company T's stock?

Your response: "My tender price is $_____ per share."

What should you, as the acquirer, offer for the target? The problem appears simple and straightforward, but it is in fact analytically complex for many people. The range of responses from the thousands of auditing partners, investment bankers, CEOs, and other executives who have participated in our executive programs is typically between $50 and $75 per share. This common—but dangerously incorrect—

response is based on the logic that "on average, the firm will be worth $50 to the target and $75 to the acquirer; consequently, a sale price in this range will, on average, be profitable to both parties." Put another way, the ZOPA (on average) ranges from $50–$75; thus, an offer in this range makes strategic sense.

But let's see what actually happens when we work through the logic of whether to make an offer in this range. Imagine, for instance, that you offer $60 per share:

> The $60 offer will be accepted 60 percent of the time—that is, whenever the firm is worth between $0 and $60 to the target. Since all values between $0 and $60 are equally likely, the firm will, on average, be worth $30 per share to the target. This means, it will be worth (on average) $45 per share to the acquirer. Because the offer is for $60 per share, the acquirer will *lose* (on average) $15 per share. Consequently, a $60 per share offer is unwise.

If you work through the logic, a similar analysis applies to *any* positive offer. On average, for an offer to be accepted at all, the acquirer will get a company worth 25 percent less than the price paid. This is because, for any offer that is accepted, the value of the company (after exploration) will fall anywhere between $0 and the amount offered, with all values equally likely. Thus, on average, the firm will be worth half of the offered value to the target and three-fourths of the offered value to the acquirer. As a result, all offers above $0 per share are more likely to lose money than to make money. This means you should have offered $0 per share.

The key to this paradox is the target firm's information advantage. Specifically, because the target will accept the acquirer's offer only after the exploration project is complete, the target will sell the firm sometimes when it is profitable for the acquirer, but very often when it is of extremely low value—that is, when it is a "lemon."

George Akerlof won the Nobel Prize in Economics for research demonstrating that the selective acceptance of offers can lead to market distortions.[12] For instance, Akerlof noted, the average used car on the market is not an average-*quality* used car, since car owners tend to hold on to good cars or sell them to relatives or friends. The worse the car, the more likely it is to enter the general marketplace. Knowing this, buyers should reasonably become wary; the result is a lowering of the value that you can get for your used car, even when you are trying to sell a good product.

Akerlof's analysis highlights the danger of being the less-informed party in a negotiation—a common situation for buyers. But why don't smart people foresee this problem and avoid making an offer in the "Acquiring a Company" exercise? Because we have a tendency to systematically exclude critical information regarding what the other side knows in our analysis. Specifically, we fail to recognize that the benefit to us of making an offer depends on the offer being accepted by the other party, and that acceptance is most likely to occur when we have offered too much! This phenomenon is the embodiment of the *winner's curse* problem.

The winner's curse describes situations in which a bidder gets a prize, but only by paying more than the item is worth, due to his or her failure to consider the information advantage of the other party. The winner's curse is a specific form of a blind spot in which the key is the informational advantage of the other side. Groucho Marx appeared to grasp the intuition behind the "winner's curse" when he quipped that he didn't want to belong to any club that would have him as a member. If a club's standards were so low as to accept *him*, he didn't want any part of it.

Many people believe that experience is the key to avoiding the winner's curse. In this case, however, experience is not the solution. Max and his colleagues Sheryl Ball and John Carroll tested the ability of bright MBA students to learn to avoid the winner's curse.[13] These students played twenty trials of the Acquiring a Company exercise, where they earned real money based on the profitability of their decisions. Participants received full feedback immediately after each trial, based on a randomly selected value of the firm; in addition, we let them observe changes (which were overwhelmingly decreases) in their asset balance. Despite the mounting evidence that bidding above $0 was poor strategy, and despite the accumulation of financial losses, across the twenty trials, participants failed to learn the correct response; the mean bid continued to hover above $50 per share. In fact, *only five out of seventy-two* participants from a leading MBA program learned to make a bid of zero over the course of the trials. In more recent research, these errors were shown to persist even after one hundred trials.[14]

How, then, can you avoid becoming a victim of the winner's curse?

1. Imagine how you will feel if your offer is immediately accepted. Before making an offer, imagine that the other side *will* immediately accept the offer that you plan to make (for the car, the house, or the company). Now ask yourself, "Does her acceptance tell me anything about the value of the commodity? Does she know something that I don't know, and does that reason explain her acceptance?" The winner's curse results not from an inability to think about the decisions of other parties, but from our failure to consider the effect of their information advantage.

2. Seek out objective, expert advice. Another strategy for your most important negotiations is to obtain the help of an expert, such as a mechanic's unbiased evaluation of a used car, a professional inspector's assessment of a house, or a high-quality, independent valuation of a target firm.

3. Make your offer on a contingency basis. More generally, whenever you are dealing with a better-informed counterpart in the midst of an important transaction, you should seek to lessen the impact of the other side's information advantage. Consider the following way in which an acquirer in the Acquiring a Company exercise could profitably offer a value above $0. Instead of offering a precise dollar value per share, the acquirer could agree to pay a fixed *percentage* above the firm's value after exploration. For example, if the agreement was to pay 25 percent above value per share to Company T, both companies would stand to benefit from the eventual sale. Contingency clauses are in fact common features of acquisition agreements.

WHEN THE STRENGTH OF THE COMPETITION IS IN YOUR BLIND SPOT

Imagine that your company is in a patent race against four other firms. The first company to complete the scientific research needed for the patent will earn an enormous market advantage, but the research is very expensive. The four firms that lose the patent race will lose their entire R&D investment.

You ask your chief scientist for an assessment of the likelihood that your company will win the patent race. "This is not a difficult engineering problem for us," he tells you. "We have a 40 percent chance of winning."

Should you trust that assessment? How could you get a more accurate estimate?

Here is another situation where recent psychological research can help you. Researcher Don Moore has shown that people are much more willing to bet on their likelihood of winning a competition against others when they are asked to perform a familiar or objectively easy task than when they are asked to perform an objectively difficult task.[15] Of course, what people often fail to realize is that if the task is easy for you, it is likely to be easy for your competitor as well; the same is true for difficult tasks. In other words, if the challenge is adding up two-digit numbers, which you consider easy, you may be overconfident about winning. But if you're hesitant about entering a juggling competition for amateurs, you may have lost sight of how hard it is for the other contestants as well. The same principle can operate in a complex R&D decision.

Research on *reference group neglect*[16] follows a similar pattern. Decision researchers Colin Camerer and Dan Lovallo show that companies tend to focus on their unique skills, products, distribution system, and so on, while the quality of their competition stays out of focus. For example, competitors often fail to assess the strength of their competition when deciding whether to enter a market—an extremely costly mistake.

The good news is that it is possible to fix this problem by explicitly focusing on the unique capabilities of the competition.[17] When we focus on our competitors individually, we are able to more accurately assess the other side's likelihood of success (and by extension, our own likelihood of failure).

Returning to the patent forecast, how should you interpret your chief scientist's response? At the very least, you should ask yourself the following questions:

1) Has she considered the fact that this is an easy engineering problem for us but overlooked the fact that it may also be easy for our competitors?
2) Has she focused on our firm's unique skills and overlooked the advantages and threats posed by our competitors?
3) Has she considered, individually, each competing firm's likelihood of winning, or has she lumped all "others" into one combined threat?

Having considered these possibilities, you might discover that, while the 40 percent estimate may be a good indication of how well your R&D is developing ("Things are going great!"), it may not capture the threat posed by your competitors (things may be going great for them as well).

WHEN THE FUTURE IS IN
YOUR BLIND SPOT

Max recently developed and taught (as part of a team) a course for the most senior executives of one of the twenty largest firms in the world. This firm often creates long-term contracts and makes significant investments in nations that are in flux and where business relations do not always follow Western expectations. They wanted the very best corporate diplomacy training possible.

One negotiation case we presented was set in a country where many of the executives had negotiated or would soon be negotiating. The case itself was based on a recent episode involving the firm. We also invited high-level former diplomats to sit in on the classes. These diplomats had worked in the country where our case occurred, and we could call on them to provide insight into local customs, changing political circumstances, and business norms. They provided this knowledge, and also much more.

The key insight offered by these diplomats was that effective negotiators must begin to think more broadly about what it means to collect "relevant" information. Often, it is not obvious what is—or might one day become—relevant, or perhaps even crucial. Because most negotiators are too focused on the "current" opportunity, problem, or crisis, they do a poor job of asking the questions and collecting the information that they will need in the future.

Here are some of the important questions that the diplomats posed:

- How will changing laws affect the wisdom of the transaction?
- What precedent are you creating for future deals?
- How can you gain information about the key personnel of an organization with which you plan to pursue a joint venture?
- How will the partner firm's competitors react to the joint venture?
- How much power do these competitors have? What is the source of their power?
- What assumptions are you making when you estimate the long-term success of this strategy?

As the discussion continued, it became clear that the executives involved in the actual case had not asked the questions that the diplomats were now identifying; if they had done so, the corporation's business development activities would have been more successful.

This "diplomat's perspective" is shared by many negotiators and dealmakers who have had the experience of negotiating in contexts that are culturally distinct from their own or in dynamic environments. In 2002, the Program on Negotiation at the Harvard Law School presented United Nations ambassador Lakhdar Brahimi with its annual "Great Negotiator" award. The award recognized Brahimi's many diplomatic accomplishments, chief among them his role in mediating the political negotiations that followed the overthrow of the Taliban government as the UN secretary general's special envoy to Afghanistan in 2002. Brahimi had also headed UN troubleshooting missions to Yemen, Liberia, Sudan, Nigeria, South Africa, and other nations in crisis. During a panel discussion, Brahimi was asked how he prepared for the difficult and complex negotiation in Afghanistan. Brahimi recalled the advice an "old British diplomat" had once given him: "You go somewhere and you try and understand that country *because one day you may need to negotiate with that country.*"[18]

Negotiation geniuses—in business, in politics, and in everyday life—do not begin to focus on a situation only after it erupts into a crisis. Rather, they prepare for eventualities well in advance. They are able to do so because they understand the difference between focusing narrowly on information that seems relevant to the present concern and focusing globally on information that may one day make the difference between success and failure.

WHEN WHAT IS RIGHT IN FRONT OF YOUR EYES IS IN YOUR BLIND SPOT

In the 1970s, Ulric Neisser, a psychologist at Cornell University, created a now-famous video that showed two superimposed groups of students passing basketballs to each other.[19] In the video, one group wore white shirts and passed a basketball to one another, and the other group wore dark shirts, and passed a different basketball to one another. We have often shown this video to our executive and MBA students and asked them to count the number of times the members of the white-shirt group pass the ball. Because the two groups were filmed separately and then superimposed, the pass-counting task is difficult; the viewers have to pay close attention to avoid confusing the two different basketballs.

Many of our students are able to accurately count the total number of passes: eleven. Yet most of them miss something. After the players in the white shirts make their fourth pass, a person holding an open umbrella walks from one end of the screen to the other, passing right in front of the two groups of students. Anyone watching this video who has *not* been asked to count passes immediately spots the person with the umbrella. However, among viewers who are busy counting passes, typically only between 5–20 percent see the person carrying an umbrella! Full disclosure: neither Deepak nor Max saw it the first time they saw the video. Neisser referred to this phenomenon as *inattentional blindness.*[20] This blindness is not due to a flaw in our vision; rather, it is a natural consequence of the human mind's limited ability to focus on multiple tasks simultaneously.

If it is this easy to miss an image that is (literally) right in front of your eyes, imagine how much easier it is to miss issues, interests, and perspectives that are important to the other party, but which are not in plain sight because they are less critical to you.

EXPANDING YOUR AWARENESS

Certainly, the ability to focus narrowly on a problem is a critical skill that allows us to complete many tasks effectively and efficiently. But the research on bounded awareness should cause you to wonder what you may have missed during periods of intense focus in negotiation. When you are busy estimating the other side's maximum willingness to pay, are you ignoring the effect that this deal will have on your competitors? When you are focusing on the potential for synergy with your acquisition target, are you overlooking the possibility that influential and self-interested decision makers could derail the negotiation? When you are busy explaining to the customer how many of their problems your product or service will solve, are you ignoring other interests and concerns that could push them toward your competitors? When, as a new player in the industry, you are doing everything possible to increase your firm's revenue, are you ignoring future difficulties you could face when you want to transition into a high-margin business model?

If these problems sound familiar, you probably want to know how to have the best of both worlds in negotiation: focusing intently when necessary and expanding your awareness to include elements that are typically in your blind spot. How can you accomplish these seemingly contradictory tasks? First, the content of this chapter should help you predict which factors will typically fall in your blind spot. You should be extra vigilant in seeking out such commonly "invisible" information. Furthermore, the more important and complex the negotiation, the more necessary it is for you to seek out information that tends to fall in your blind spot.

Another strategy is to take time to reflect on your most important past negotiations. Did you miss any important opportunities? Did you fail to explore information that may have helped you? How would you have found that information? The answers to these questions may provide hints as to how you can improve information gathering and strategy development in your current and upcoming negotiations.

Finally, you can simplify the task of gathering and synthesizing information from diverse sources by enlisting the help of others in your organization. For your most important negotiations, assemble a team whose purpose is to expose blind spots. Define the roles of your team members by putting each person in charge of a particular blind spot. For instance, one person could be in charge of assessing and monitoring parties that are not at the table, another person could be in charge of evaluating the strength of competitors, and so on. Then, set aside time (e.g., during your weekly meeting) for each person to update the group and for the team to revise its strategy accordingly. Just as "many hands make light work," the many eyes of your team can lighten the task of expanding your awareness.

WHY NEGOTIATION GENIUSES HAVE FEW BLIND SPOTS

Does it seem as if we have identified too many areas for you to focus on while negotiating? If so, you can make easier the task of increasing your awareness by adopting the investigative negotiation perspective outlined in Chapter 3. If you approach every negotiation as a mystery to be solved and make it a point to carefully identify your assumptions, you will naturally gravitate toward the sources of information that many negotiators ignore. It is when we overestimate the value of what we know and underestimate the value of what others know that we fall victim to those elements of negotiation that lurk in our blind spot. By adopting an investigative mind-set, negotiation geniuses avoid this fate. Genius, then, is sometimes nothing more than taking the time to see that to which others have turned a blind eye.

CHAPTER 9

Confronting Lies and Deception

When we've asked groups of executives or MBA students whether they have ever lied in a negotiation, most of them admit that they have. When we've asked the same group whether they have ever been *lied to* in a negotiation, *all* of them claim that they have been. Indeed, many of our students and clients tell us that deception is simply part of negotiating in their industry. In other words, as much as we may wish otherwise, every negotiator has to deal with lies and deception. Fortunately, there is a lot you can do to prepare for this.

Consider the following three stories. How many of them ring true to you? How often have you found yourself in a similar situation?

STORY 1: THE OBVIOUS LIE

Rafael, the founder and president of a small firm that manufactures lighting equipment, was negotiating the sale of a large order with a potential customer. After Rafael quoted his price, which he felt was in line with prevailing market rates, the customer asked for some time to consider the offer. Two days later, the customer called back and told Rafael that he had another offer that was 5 percent lower than the one Rafael had made. If Rafael could beat this other offer, the customer was ready to make the purchase. Rafael was not sure what to do. On the one hand, he seriously doubted that another firm would have beaten his price by 5 percent. On the other hand, he could not simply call the customer a liar. Furthermore, even if Rafael was sure that the customer did not have a better offer, if he refused to lower his price, the customer would have to walk away in order to save face—to accept Rafael's price would make it obvious that there was no other offer and that the customer had been lying. Caught in this dilemma, and quite confident that he was being lied to, Rafael lowered his price and made the sale.

STORY 2: THE DECEPTION YOU DISCOVERED TOO LATE

Stacy, who had twenty years of industry experience, was a highly successful executive at a Fortune 500 company. When she decided to switch jobs, she had a number of lucrative job offers from some of the most prestigious firms in the country. But Stacy was particularly attracted to an offer made by the CEO of a small start-up company to whom she was introduced through a mutual acquaintance. The compensation package was not particularly stellar—she would make much more money at a larger firm—but she would have the opportunity to try something different and to make a big impact in a fledgling niche of the industry. More than anything else, Stacy was sold on the breadth of decision-making authority she would have in shaping and growing the business. Stacy accepted the job. Less than a year later, Stacy left the firm disappointed, disgruntled, and in disbelief. It turned out that the CEO had not been straightforward with her regarding the role she would play and the authority she would have. Instead, he had simply wanted to hire a high-profile executive with contacts in the industry; once hired, Stacy had been relegated to the role of salesperson. Stacy felt that she had been lied to from the beginning.

STORY 3: THE DECEPTION YOU NEVER DISCOVERED

Thomas, the purchasing agent for a manufacturing firm, was in negotiations with a supplier. Typically, when purchasing components from outside vendors, Thomas's firm would hold an auction and buy from the lowest-price supplier. Because of the unique nature of this particular component, however, Thomas found himself in the uncomfortable position of having to negotiate with the one and only supplier that could meet the firm's specifications by the required deadline. To make matters worse, the supplier knew that no other supplier could meet Thomas's current needs. After much discussion, the supplier quoted Thomas a price. It was higher than Thomas had expected, and higher than his firm had budgeted for the component. Hoping to get at least a slight concession from the supplier, Thomas asked, "My firm is making a big purchase, and we are likely to make purchases from you in the future. Is this really the lowest price at which you can sell this component to us?" The supplier looked Thomas straight in the eye and responded, "I appreciate your business now, and I would appreciate it in the future, but this is the lowest price at which we have ever sold this component." Still somewhat disappointed with the price, but satisfied with the supplier's response, Thomas accepted the deal. He had no idea that the supplier could have lowered the price by another 20–25 percent.

As these stories demonstrate, deception can take many different forms. Sometimes your counterpart will tell you something that she knows is untrue (a lie); sometimes she will craft technically correct statements that are designed to mislead and misinform you. Sometimes the deception is big, sometimes it is small; sometimes it is obvious, sometimes it is difficult to discover; sometimes it is expected, and sometimes it catches you completely by surprise.

Before we go further, it is worth noting that the *reasons* people lie in negotiation can also vary. People might tell "benevolent" lies to make others feel good ("You look great today!"), to help others save face ("I'm glad you accepted our offer, since I couldn't have moved another inch"), or to avoid unnecessary conflict ("You represented us well in that negotiation"). More often, however, lies and deception are designed to fulfill entirely self-serving ends: to make more money and to get a better deal.

While no one can ever be entirely safe from the lies and deceptions of others, negotiation geniuses understand what it takes to tackle and diffuse a wide variety of nefarious tactics. In this chapter, we will confront the darker side of negotiation head-on and present the following strategies:

- how to make it less likely that people will lie to you;
- how to detect when someone is lying to you;
- what to do when you catch someone in a lie;
- how to eliminate your own desire—and need—to lie.

Many of our students and clients have complained to us that they would like to be more ethical in their dealings with others, but admit that sometimes the temptation to lie is irresistible. They would be willing to be truthful—as long as honesty would not cost them thousands or millions of dollars. This chapter will also help you understand how you can be ethical without losing your shirt at the bargaining table.

PRE-EMPTING LIES AND DECEPTION

The best defense against lies and deception is to eliminate your counterpart's temptation to lie. Typically, the other side has certain motivations to lie—for example, they may get a better deal by lying. But the other side also has certain motivations *not to* lie—if the lie is discovered, they risk losing the deal or damaging their reputation. To eliminate their motivations to lie, you need to make salient to them the reasons they should not lie to you. This can be done in a number of ways.

DEFENSE STRATEGY 1: LOOK PREPARED

Throughout this book, we have exalted the merits of preparation—the more prepared you are, the better you will negotiate. But that is not the whole story. It not only pays to *be* more prepared, it also pays to *look* more prepared! Put simply, the more prepared you seem, the less people will want to lie to you. Why? Because if you look prepared, it makes them think that you might be able to detect when they are lying—thus making it risky for them to lie to you.

Consider Story 1, in which the customer came to Rafael with "a better offer" from a competitor. Imagine what would have happened if, in their earlier discussions, Rafael had (truthfully) mentioned to the customer that he knows, on a personal level, most of his competitors, or that his firm keeps an eye on the rates competitors are charging. Either of those statements would have made the customer reconsider the strategy of coming to Rafael with a fake offer from an alleged competitor.

It is easy to see why it helps to look prepared when it comes to issues related to price. But negotiators often overlook the value of appearing prepared more generally. Consider these other ways in which Rafael—or you—could signal to the other side that you have done your homework and are prepared:

- Arriving on time for all meetings and negotiations.
- Being well prepared to discuss details regarding the myriad of issues that are involved.
- Being well organized and efficient.
- Speaking intelligently on issues related to their business and the industry—including issues that are not directly relevant to the current negotiation.
- Remembering the finer details of prior discussions with the other side and/or referring explicitly to notes you made during an earlier meeting.
- Responding expeditiously to requests for information or to the other side's offers.

All of these tactics will not only help you to negotiate more effectively, but also make it less likely that others will lie to you. If you present yourself as someone who is always prepared and who is systematic in her approach to negotiations, you will garner respect and discourage deception at the same time.

DEFENSE STRATEGY 2: SIGNAL YOUR ABILITY TO OBTAIN INFORMATION

Imagine that you have no idea whether the other side is lying—and he knows that you are clueless. Does this mean that you are in serious jeopardy? Not necessarily. You may not know whether he is lying right now, but what if you could discover his deception tomorrow? If you can signal that you have the ability to discover (in the future) whether someone lied to you, you may dissuade him from lying in the first place.

How might this work? Think about Thomas (from Story 3), to whom the supplier suggested that it was impossible to obtain a lower price on the component. How would the supplier have responded if Thomas had stated his request for a concession differently? Consider these two variations:

> *Original script:* "My firm is making a big purchase, and we are likely to make purchases from you in the future. Is this really the lowest price at which you can sell this component to us?"

> *Revised script:* "My firm is making a big purchase, and we are likely to make purchases in the future. As you know, we need the supplies quickly this time around, which puts you in a unique position to fill the order. But, as you also know, other vendors have the resources to fulfill our need for future orders. As such, I will be meeting with them to discuss how low a price they will charge for these components in the future. Perhaps they will not be able to beat your price. But I would like to know from you before I talk to them: Is this really the lowest price at which you can sell this component to us? Can you find a way to lower the price, or should I assume that if the other vendors can beat this price we should go with them in the future?"

DEFENSE STRATEGY 3: ASK LESS THREATENING, INDIRECT QUESTIONS

What do you suppose will happen if you ask someone to reveal her reservation value? Unless considerable trust exists between you and her, she will either refuse to tell you her reservation value—or she will lie about it. This should come as no surprise, yet negotiators often ask questions that are almost guaranteed to motivate the other side to lie. There is a better way to get essentially the same information: ask *less threatening, indirect* questions.

Imagine that you are interested in finding out the production costs of a vendor with whom you are dealing. If you ask her directly to reveal her company's costs, you are inviting her to lie to you because she knows that as soon as you know these costs, you are in a position to make an offer just above cost. Here are some alternative questions she would be more likely to answer truthfully:

- Can you please give me some information regarding your production process?
- Can you explain to me how your supply chain operates?
- Do you purchase your materials domestically?
- Who are your primary suppliers?
- What are the characteristics of your typical buyer?
- Can you provide me with a list of some of your other customers?
- How much would I need to increase the size of my order to qualify for a price concession?

While no one of these questions gives you all of the information you need to calculate their costs, if you know your industry well, the combined responses should help you make a very accurate estimate.

DEFENSE STRATEGY 4: DON'T LIE

If we asked you to never again lie to anyone during a negotiation, would you agree to be truthful forevermore? If not, why not? If you're like most people we've asked, one reason is that you do not want to be the only sucker at the bargaining table. You'd love to be entirely honest, you might say, but, unfortunately, you live in a world where other people lie. Being the only truthful person would put you at a disadvantage. Sounds reasonable.

But there's a problem with this perspective: what if everyone else is justifying their own lies using the same logic? What if most people would love to live in a world without deception, but each is stuck telling lies in self-defense? Unfortunately, many of us face this vicious cycle in negotiation. We are face-to-face with other negotiators who might prefer to be honest, but who do not trust us enough to risk it. In response, we, too, become more willing to lie.

Fortunately, this logic also yields a potential solution: we can make it easier for others to be truthful if *we* make it a point not to lie. This strategy will not dissuade those who want to exploit your honesty, but it will dissuade those who are lying out of self-defense. As time goes on, and your counterpart discovers that you have been honest with him, he will find it easier to be more honest with you.

How can you signal your desire for this kind of relationship? By revealing information that makes you somewhat vulnerable. In other words, reveal something that the other side recognizes is somewhat costly to you. What kind of message would this move send? It is possible that your counterpart will view you as naive or unprepared, but it is also highly likely that she will appreciate the trusting gesture and reciprocate in kind. You can help your cause by making your intentions explicit: "I know that there is a lot at stake in this relationship and that this is likely to make everyone more guarded and skeptical. But I also know that the more open and honest we are with each other from the start, the easier it will be for us to develop a mutually rewarding long-term relationship. With that in mind, I would like to share with you some information related to our cost structure." Someone must take the first step, and it may as well be the one who is aspiring to become a negotiation genius.

LIE DETECTION

Do you think you can tell when someone is lying to you? Many people believe they can. Unfortunately, most of these people are wrong. Too many of us trust our intuition when our intuition is not trustworthy. To make matters worse, many "experts" tell us that we should trust our intuition (for example, Malcolm Gladwell in his popular book *Blink*), when the evidence suggests serious limitations in our intuitive judgments.[1] Psychologist Paul Ekman, who has spent decades measuring the ability of people to distinguish truth from lies, has concluded that the average person is actually a very bad lie detector.[2] Ekman has also developed expert techniques for lie detection; his research suggests that negotiators should focus on telltale signs such as pupil dilation, changes in voice pitch, and facial "micro-expressions."

We take a different approach. Unlike participants in Ekman's laboratory experiments, negotiators find themselves in complex, dynamic environments where it is difficult to focus on the subtle telltale signs of lying. You would not be well advised to ask your negotiation counterpart to repeat what he just said so that you can lean forward and peer into his eye sockets in hopes of seeing his pupils dilate. Instead, we recommend the following tactics:

DETECTION STRATEGY 1: GATHER INFORMATION FROM MULTIPLE SOURCES

The first thing to remember is that deception depends upon *information asymmetry*. Inevitably in negotiation, there will be some facts and data that the other side knows that you don't—and can't—know. This information asymmetry makes you vulnerable to deception. But there are also many facts and pieces of data that you don't know, but which you can *learn* about—from your counterpart, or from others. To reduce your vulnerability, you must rely on your preparation.

Negotiation geniuses exhaust all sources of information prior to, during, and after negotiation. The more information you have, the easier it will be for you to detect lies. For example, Stacy (from Story 2) did not know that the CEO who hired her was planning to sideline her on issues of substance and to use her only for the purposes of networking. It may have been possible for her to learn this, however. For starters, she could have spoken with the last person who held her position in the firm. She could also have tried to gather information about the CEO's management style from other employees of the firm. Finally, she could have asked the person who introduced her to the CEO what he knew about the CEO's interests in hiring her. None of these conversations would guarantee that Stacy would detect the CEO's deception, but each would increase her odds of diagnosing the CEO's dishonesty.

DETECTION STRATEGY 2: SET A TRAP

Some seasoned negotiators tell us that they have a very simple way of testing the honesty of the other party: they ask a question to which they already know the answer, and then evaluate the response. Of course, for the trap to work, the question must concern an issue about which the other side has an incentive to lie.

For example, a student of ours who worked as a buyer in the textile industry once asked a seller whether the price he had quoted was the lowest price at which the particular material could be sold. The seller, who was aware that the buyer was new to the industry, swore that he had never sold the material to anyone for a lower price. Unfortunately for the seller, the buyer had come prepared; she had spoken with a friend in the industry who had recently purchased the material for a lower price from the same seller. As a result of that initial interaction, the buyer decided never to work with that seller again.

DETECTION STRATEGY 3: TRIANGULATE ON THE TRUTH

Centuries ago, when ships were the primary means of travel, navigators had to rely on star charts and basic trigonometry to determine their position on the open seas. By considering their ship to be the third point in a triangle whose other two points were stars that maintained a constant distance, the navigators were able to "triangulate" their way to discovering the ship's location.

What does this have to do with lie detection in negotiation? The point is that you may never discover a lie if you ask only one question (especially if you don't know the answer to it). Instead, you need to ask many questions and "triangulate" on the truth. The more questions you ask, the more difficult it becomes for the other party to come up with consistent answers—unless they are telling the truth. To find out whether his customer truly had another offer from a competitor, Rafael (in Story 1) could have triangulated on the truth by asking questions such as these:

- When did you receive this offer?
- What exactly did my competitor offer?
- Did he provide you with specific product information?
- What was that information?
- Did my competitor give this offer to you in writing?
- If not, why do you think that is? Did you ask for it in writing?
- If you did get it in writing, may I see it?

What if your customer is unwilling to answer any such questions? This should make you at least a little suspicious. He may not wish to reveal his reservation value to you, but if he is completely tight-lipped about the most straightforward questions regarding his alternatives—and if he has no reasonable explanation for his secrecy—then you should proceed as if he has been bluffing.

DETECTION STRATEGY 4: LOOK OUT FOR RESPONSES THAT DO NOT ANSWER THE QUESTION YOU ASKED

Our most useful advice regarding lie detection stems from this critical insight: *most people do not like to lie, but they are usually very comfortable with you being deceived.* In other words, people will often go to great lengths to avoid saying something that is technically untrue (i.e., a lie), but they will be happy to mislead you indirectly with their response. Let's consider a classic example.

Recall the dialogue (from Story 3) between Thomas and the supplier:

> *Thomas:* "My firm is making a big purchase, and we are likely to make purchases from you in the future. Is this really the lowest price at which you can sell this component to us?"

> *Supplier:* "I appreciate your business now, and I would appreciate it in the future, but this is the lowest price at which we have ever sold this component."

If you read carefully, you will realize that the supplier *never answered* Thomas's question! He had asked whether this was the lowest price at which the supplier *could* sell. The supplier responded that he had *never before* sold the component at a lower price. That *sounds* like an answer to Thomas's question (it implies that "we can't sell any cheaper"), but it clearly is not. It is quite possible that the supplier has never sold the specific component to someone else at a lower price—technically, the supplier may have told the truth—but that is quite irrelevant.

If Thomas had been more perceptive, he would have spotted the nonresponse and questioned the relevance of prior sale prices in the current situation. He could reiterate, for example, that he is making a large purchase (perhaps the largest that the supplier has ever received for this component) and that he will be a repeat customer. Furthermore, it is possible that even though the supplier has not sold the exact same component at a lower price, he may have sold similar components more cheaply. Facing this more intense scrutiny, the supplier would have found it much more difficult to justify his position.

As it is, the supplier is unlikely to feel any guilt about this transaction. In addition to the host of self-serving justifications he could give for his behavior, he could also remind himself that he "never lied." That's the key. Instead of lying outright, people tend to make sure that they have *technically* told the truth—while at the same time trying to mislead you. This maneuver is a boon to would-be lie detectors. Negotiation geniuses ask clear, focused questions that make it incumbent upon the other party to respond transparently. Since people are more likely to deceive indirectly than to explicitly lie, negotiation geniuses who listen carefully to the answers provided (and to the answers that are *not* provided) are in a great position to catch "nonlying deceivers" in the act.

DETECTION STRATEGY 5: USE CONTINGENCY CONTRACTS

One of the authors has a large consulting client in the retail business. When the retailer buys goods overseas, it often purchases in very large quantities. For one key agreement that we heard about, the contract was so specific that it included the name of the ship that would bring the goods to the United States. After the contract was signed, but before the boat was loaded in the foreign country, the retailer learned that the United States government had created an embargo against this particular group of goods that was to go into effect at approximately the same date the goods would reach the United States. The ship might arrive by the embargo deadline, or it might not.

The U.S. retailer told the foreign manufacturer about the embargo, asked for the goods to be sent by air, and asked the manufacturer to pay for the greatly increased costs of shipping by air. The manufacturer told the retailer to relax, assured them that the ship would arrive before the embargo, and suggested that the Americans were being unnecessarily nervous. The retailer responded that if the goods were not sent by air, there would be no deal. The manufacturer pointed out that they would have been happy to accommodate the retailer if there was some actual risk that the goods would not reach the United States in time; however, as things stood, there was no risk—but there *was* a signed contract—and they would be happy to fax the retailer a copy of it. The negotiation was becoming quite heated, and the time pressure was mounting.

Then the retailer had a stroke of (negotiation) genius. He proposed to the manufacturer that the goods be sent by air and that the extra shipping costs be borne by the party whose claim turned out to be wrong. Although the ship would be carrying no goods of interest to either party (because the goods would be shipped by air), both parties would track when it actually reached the United States. If the ship beat the embargo, the retailer would pay the entire excess shipping costs of sending the goods by air; if the ship was late, the manufacturer would bear the costs. The retailer thought this was a wonderful contingency contract. Both sides could stand by their assessments, the goods would get to the United States on time, and, given current technology, both sides could check the Web daily to see how they were doing on the "bet." The arrangement seemed perfect— until the manufacturer's representative called to say that they would not accept the contingency contract. "This is getting way too complicated," the manufacturer's rep said. "Why don't we just split the extra costs 50–50?"

What did the retailer learn from this response? That the manufacturer never believed its claims! If it had, it would have jumped at the opportunity to accept a clause that allowed it to avoid additional shipping costs. As we discussed in Chapters 1 and 2, when the other side makes a dubious claim regarding some future prospect, you do not have to take their word for it, nor do you have to argue about who is right. Instead, ask them to "put their money where their mouth is" by proposing a contingency contract. Contingency contracts are an excellent device for allowing honest people to stake financial outcomes on their differences in expectations (see Chapter 2). They are also an excellent device for diagnosing when the other side is lying about their beliefs and expectations. If they are unwilling to agree to a contingency contract, you can be more certain that they do not believe their own claims.

You may be curious about what happened next in our client's

negotiation with the manufacturer: The retailer needed the goods badly and agreed to the 50–50 split. The boat arrived one day late!

YOU CAUGHT THEM IN
A LIE . . . NOW WHAT?

It's hard to detect lies. It's not much easier to know what to do after you have detected a lie. For one thing, you are likely to experience a range of emotions: anger, anxiety, disappointment, and surprise. In addition, you likely will have multiple conflicting motivations: Should you take revenge or try to salvage the relationship? Should you walk away from the deal or try to maximize your value from it? Should you tell the other party to stop lying or wait to see what they will say next? Should you call him a liar and stay true to your principles or hide your outrage and focus on your profits?

While there is no single right answer to any of these questions, there are systematic ways to think about how to resolve these conflicts. The first thing to do in such a situation is to stay calm and treat the deception like any other negotiation problem—something that needs to be better understood and carefully resolved. Then, answer the following three questions, which will help you make the best decision for you.

QUESTION 1: WAS IT REALLY A LIE?

Is it possible that your counterpart does not even know that what she said was untrue? In other words, she may not have intended to lie, but was simply uninformed. In most negotiations, it is best to give the other side the benefit of the doubt—but to also be more careful as you move forward. If you think you were lied to, but aren't sure, investigate using the strategies outlined above. But unless you are certain that the other side lied, you will likely gain little by calling her a liar. Almost certainly, she will deny the allegation, and you will find yourself in an escalating conflict.

In addition, keep in mind that what sounds like a lie to you may not sound like a lie to your counterpart. In Story 3, Thomas and the supplier are likely to characterize the supplier's remarks very differently.

If Thomas discovers that a lower price was possible, he will think that the supplier lied. The supplier will certainly think otherwise. Similarly, when our executive and MBA students engage in negotiation simulations, it is common for one student to claim that her counterpart lied during the negotiation, and for the counterpart to strongly deny the accusation. Typically, the "liar" never actually uttered an untrue statement, but *did* allow the other side to be deceived. What should you do in such a situation? Don't call your counterpart a liar, but explain that you feel you were misled or deceived, then discuss whether the deception was intentional or not.

Finally, note that not all lies are considered "unethical" in all contexts and cultures. If you are haggling for a piece of art with a street vendor in India, you can be certain that you will hear lots of prices, justifications, and stories that are based in fiction. Few people would consider these claims unethical; rather, that is the "language" in which the vendor's business is conducted. Similar behavior in other contexts would be highly unethical, however. Before labeling your negotiation counterpart dishonest, audit your cultural assumptions. Was it a lie? Or are you negotiating in a context where you do not understand the norms?

QUESTION 2: DO I WANT TO CONTINUE WITH THIS NEGOTIATION?

If and when you are certain that someone has deliberately lied, you must decide whether to simply walk away from the negotiation or whether you have too much to lose by doing so. If you are willing to walk away on principle, your task is easy. You will decide whether or not to confront the liar and give voice to your emotions; then you will revert to your BATNA. Often, however, it is not easy to walk away.

QUESTION 3: DO I NEED TO WARN THEM OR CONFRONT THEM?

If you would like to continue the negotiation, you probably should not scream "Liar!" Instead, you need a strategy that allows you to signal that you are aware of the lie, while also giving the other side the opportunity to save face. There are two ways of doing so; the strategy you choose depends on what you are trying to accomplish. If you are not particularly upset about the lie, but want to discourage your counterpart from lying in the future, you should use a "warn" script.

If the lie was more egregious, and you want to extract an apology or concession in exchange for your willingness to continue negotiations, you should use a "confront" script. Here is how each of these strategies sounds:

Warn Script: "You mentioned that the cost of these materials is $1.05 per unit. I think that you may need to check your data. We have strong ties with a number of suppliers and are certain that the cost is $0.90. Perhaps you are working with old data or were misinformed along the way. In any case, let's try to be more careful about facts and figures as we go forward with this deal."

Confront Script: "You mentioned that the cost of these materials is $1.05 per unit. I feel the need to point out to you that, unlike some of your other customers, we have strong ties with a number of suppliers. Because of this, we know when someone is inflating costs. For example, the cost of the materials in question is actually $0.90. We have been negotiating in good faith with you and are taking part in this negotiation to create value for both sides. But we are now a little uneasy about the way in which you have negotiated with us. Perhaps there is a simple explanation for the discrepancy in our numbers; perhaps you were misinformed. But I would just like to make you aware that we are disappointed with this exchange. Can you help us understand your perspective and suggest some way for us to overcome the anxiety we are now feeling?"

As you will notice, the second script contains much stronger language and also implies the need for an apology or concession. In some instances, it may even be appropriate for you to ask for a specific concession as reparation. You will also notice that *both* scripts provide an opportunity for the other side to save face. This is critical if you have already decided that you wish to continue the negotiation or the relationship.

It is often tempting—but not always judicious—to retaliate quickly when you feel you have been deceived. Negotiation geniuses take the time to evaluate whether the other side might have been misinformed or had considered their behavior to be appropriate to the context. They also keep an eye on their own interests, which may require a response that is powerful enough to fix the problem but controlled enough to allow the other side some room to navigate.

SMART ALTERNATIVES TO LYING

Lies and deception do not simply emanate from those sitting on the other side of the table. How often do we say things in negotiations (and in everyday life) that we know are not the most precise versions of the truth? How often do we say things that are ambiguous, and that we hope will conceal the truth to our benefit? Obviously, ethical questions surround this issue—and most people we know wish that they were more honest and ethical. If you are one of these people, the strategies that follow will help you. But even if you have no interest in being more ethical, there are reasons for you to heed this advice. For lies are not only potentially unethical; they are also, very often, poor strategy.

Most negotiators have at some point felt the pain of being trapped by their own lies. Consider what happens if you are willing to pay up to $15,000 for a purchase, but during the negotiation, you strenuously argue that you "cannot pay a dollar more than $13,000." As negotiations continue, you eventually discover that the other side will accept nothing less than $14,000. In other words, your "final offer" does not fall in the ZOPA. What will you do now? Unfortunately, you must either walk away from the deal (which could have been consummated at a price between $14,000 and $15,000) or admit that you were lying about your reservation value. Or consider what happens when, during a negotiation, you pretend that you value an issue greatly, when in fact you place very little value on it. Your hope is that by overstating its value to you, you will be able to extract greater concessions in return for giving it up. But what if the other side gives in *to you* on that issue? You may end up with something you do not really value, while the other side waits for you to reciprocate on other issues.

Whether your motivation is to improve your own character or to reduce the costs associated with ill-conceived lies, the strategies that follow will help you negotiate more honestly without putting you at a disadvantage against others who are dishonest, corrupt, or—more likely—complex individuals with virtues and vices just like you.[3]

STRATEGY 1: INCORPORATE REPUTATION AND RELATIONSHIP COSTS IN YOUR CALCULUS

When we ask our MBA students whether it is acceptable to lie in negotiations to get what you want, a disappointingly large minority says that it is. When we ask our executive students the same question, very few (if any) say that lying is acceptable. In large part, this difference in perspective is attributable to the fact that our executive students have many more years of negotiation experience than our MBA students. They have witnessed and experienced the consequences of negotiating in bad faith. Whether they have learned from their own experiences or those of others in their organizations and industry, they have discovered how easy it is to destroy a relationship or a reputation—and how hard it is to build these up again.

Unfortunately, most negotiators are myopic; they do not see past the current deal or the current relationship. Those who do adopt a more long-term perspective find it much easier to be truthful and honest—even if this costs money in the short run—because the long-term payoff is worth it.

STRATEGY 2: PREPARE TO ANSWER DIFFICULT QUESTIONS

One of the biggest reasons people lie in negotiation is that they do not know how to answer tough questions. Caught off guard, and worried that they will say something that puts them at a disadvantage, they opt to lie. You can learn to avoid this reaction. Those who anticipate the tough, probing questions the other side will ask can prepare truthful responses that will not hurt them. Consider these two responses to the question that a potential employer might ask a candidate who has no other job offers: "Do you have any other job offers?"

Unprepared Response: "Yes, I do. I have a few other offers that I am considering."

Prepared Response: "No, this is the only offer that I currently have. But I only recently sent out my resumes, and I have many interviews scheduled."

A job candidate is more likely to resort to the first response (a lie) when he or she is unprepared. When someone asks you about your other job offers, your likely immediate reaction is to worry that having none makes you seem desperate; the most obvious way to avoid this perception is to lie. But such lies are very risky. If the employer probes further about these other offers, your lie may be discovered. The prepared response not only avoids the lie, but also mitigates the perception that you are desperate.

STRATEGY 3: TRY NOT TO NEGOTIATE OR RESPOND TO QUESTIONS WHILE UNDER TIME PRESSURE

Regardless of how prepared you are, there will be times when a question catches you off guard. What to do? To the extent possible, avoid answering the question until you have had an opportunity to think more carefully about your response. This is not as difficult or awkward as it sounds. There is usually nothing wrong with making one of the following statements:

- "I don't have that information with me, but I'm sure I can get it for you later today."
- "That's an interesting question. I'll have to think about the answer and get back to you."
- "I've never been asked that before. I could try to give you a partial answer right now. But if it's okay with you, I'd like to take some time to find out our company's stance on that issue and give you a more complete response later."

Another way to avoid answering tough questions under time pressure is to structure your negotiation differently. For example, you may have some preliminary discussions aimed at raising difficult questions over e-mail; this will give you the opportunity to respond at your own pace. Similarly, instead of negotiating by phone (which may make you feel compelled to answer questions immediately), you could set up an informal lunch meeting where you would feel less pressure to answer every question as soon as it is "your turn" to speak.

STRATEGY 4: REFUSE TO ANSWER CERTAIN QUESTIONS

You do not need to answer every question that your counterpart asks. If he asks you to reveal your reservation value, for example, you should not feel compelled to answer. Suppose that the other party asks, "What's the lowest price you will accept for this shipment?" One way to respond, and to defuse the awkward moment with humor, is to say: "I think you already know the answer—it happens to be the most you are willing to pay for it!" More generally, it is often acceptable to respond to a question that you do not wish to answer with one of the following remarks:

- "This is a discussion that we can have later on, once we have both committed to the deal. I don't feel comfortable divulging this information at the moment."
- "As you undoubtedly understand, we cannot share that information for strategic reasons."
- "The answer to your question depends on many other factors that we need to discuss."

STRATEGY 5: OFFER TO ANSWER A DIFFERENT QUESTION

If you feel uncomfortable about refusing to answer a direct question, you can mitigate your unease by offering to answer a different, related question. Here, the idea is to be up front about your inability or unwillingness to respond to the specific question, then to offer a concession by providing other useful information. For example, if someone asks you to tell them the production cost of the goods you are selling, and you are tempted to lie in order to secure a higher margin, you can instead say the following: "Unfortunately, I'm not at liberty to divulge specific cost information, but I can appreciate why you're asking for it. You want to make sure that you're getting a high-value product for the price you're paying. Well, let me provide you with some information that will give you that confidence. I can share a lot of specific information regarding our production process and some information regarding our pricing model."

By providing information that the other side values, and which does not put you at a disadvantage, you serve multiple purposes simultaneously: you avoid lying, you give them information that is of value to them, you appear reasonable and forthcoming, and you make it more likely that a deal will be consummated.

STRATEGY 6: CHANGE REALITY TO MAKE THE TRUTH MORE BEARABLE

Why, fundamentally, are human beings tempted to lie? We often lie because reality is not what we want it to be. Returning to our job interview story, the candidate is tempted to lie because reality (having no offers) differs from what he desires (having multiple offers). We earlier resolved this dilemma with the following "prepared response":

> *Prepared Response:* "No, this is the only offer that I currently have. But I only recently sent out my resumes, and I have many interviews scheduled."

But what if the candidate does not even have any interviews scheduled? Worse yet, what if all of the resumes he sent out have already been rejected? Must he now reveal his desperation by telling the truth? Is "No, this is the only offer that I currently have" the only truthful response?

Not quite. If the candidate can *change the reality* of the situation before he is asked the tough question, he has another option. For example, the day before his one-and-only interview, the candidate might send out *another* dozen resumes to another set of companies. Then, during his interview, he can truthfully respond to the employer's question as follows:

> *Changed-Reality Response:* "No, this is the only offer that I currently have. But I only recently sent out a dozen resumes and am looking forward to hearing back from those companies in the next few weeks."

With this response, the candidate is able to be truthful because he has made lying unnecessary. More generally, when you are tempted to lie or to deceive, take some time to think about why you feel the need to portray a false reality. Is it because you are embarrassed or ashamed of your situation? If so, can you do something to change your reality instead of lying about it?

STRATEGY 7: ELIMINATE CONSTRAINTS THAT TEMPT YOU TO LIE

Dan, a manager at a large consumer-products firm, was asked by his VP to submit a detailed annual budget request for his department. Unfortunately, Dan had an incentive to overstate anticipated costs; in the event of cost overruns, it would be useful to have a little surplus to fall back on. His department's projected costs for the coming year were close to $14 million, but Dan instead submitted a report with cost estimates totaling $16 million. Of course, the managers of other departments in the firm had similar incentives to lie about (or "inflate") their cost estimates. As a result, the company's total budget exceeded the amount earmarked for departmental budgets. Without an accurate understanding of who needed how much money, the VP did his best to apportion the funds efficiently. Not surprisingly, some departments received less than they needed and others ended up with much more. Those that got the most (including Dan's department) felt compelled to spend the surplus money frivolously in order to justify their initial demands.

Consider a possible solution to this problem. Dan's least predictable costs each year were related to the hiring of subcontractors. The budget request was due in February, but many of the subcontractors could not be hired until March. If Dan had asked the VP to be allowed to submit a second, revised budget a month later, and if the VP had agreed, he would not have had to lie in the first place. Instead, Dan could have used the extra time to gather more precise cost estimates, thereby eliminating the need to inflate his figures.

Often, our own honesty (and that of others whom we label unethical) is constrained by rules, policies, time pressures, and incentive systems. It is fine to argue that a "truly" ethical person would be honest despite these constraints. Nonetheless, it behooves us—and our organizations—to try to create the kinds of environments that encourage rather than discourage truthful and honest behavior.

DO NEGOTIATION GENIUSES EVER LIE?

We have both been asked (often!) whether it is okay to lie in negotiation—or, in a variant of the same question, *when* is it okay to lie in negotiation? Our answer is very simple. Don't do it. Don't ever lie. Lying is not worth the costs. Instead, spend your time and energy honing your skills as an effective negotiator. It is our belief that negotiation geniuses do not feel the need to lie. Of course, a philosophical question remains: is it okay to lie if the lie would help others, save lives, or make someone feel good? In our experience, you do not need help answering this question. If your motives are genuinely benevolent—and are not in the least self-serving—your answer to the question will be at least as good as ours.

CHAPTER 10

Recognizing and Resolving Ethical Dilemmas

- "Sure, I will benefit if you buy our product, but I wouldn't try to sell it to you if I didn't believe it was the best product for you and your company."
- "When you work for us, you know you're working for a company that treats all of its employees equally, regardless of race or gender."
- "Our agreement creates value for everyone—we're expanding the pie and also benefiting society."
- "My sales team deserves 70 percent of the credit for the company's success over the last two years."

Imagine that you are negotiating with a person who has made one of these statements. In addition, assume that you do not believe that the facts that they report are true. What is your first reaction? If you are like most people, you will probably conclude that your counterpart is unethical and is lying to gain the upper hand in the negotiation.

But there is an alternative explanation, one that you should consider the next time you think (or know) that a statement made by the other party is false: most people—and negotiators are no exception—

make incorrect, self-serving statements on a fairly regular basis without even being aware that they are engaging in unethical behavior. When you treat such negotiators as liars, they are likely to be highly offended, as they believe—and can often justify—every word they said. In addition, treating them like liars may well start an escalatory path that destroys the relationship. How, then, can you deal with this problem?

THE PROBLEM OF BOUNDED ETHICALITY

Many (and perhaps most) of the unethical behaviors in which people engage during negotiations result from ordinary, unintentional psychological processes, not from deliberate—or even conscious—deception. In Chapter 8, we used the term "bounded awareness" to refer to the systematic failure of negotiators to see readily available and important information in their environment. In his work with Mahzarin Banaji and Dolly Chugh, Max also uses the term "bounded ethicality"[1] to refer to the systematic and predictable psychological processes that lead people, including negotiators, to engage in ethically questionable behaviors that are inconsistent with even their *own* preferred ethics. Bounded ethicality comes into play when a negotiator acts in a manner that harms others and that clashes with his or her own conscious beliefs about right and wrong.

The first step in understanding the power of bounded ethicality is to discard the common assumption that the seemingly unethical behavior you observe suggests that the other party lacks your high ethical standards, or that they have consciously chosen self-rewarding behavior over what they believe to be right. In recent years, research in social psychology has thoroughly debunked the notion that all human behavior is intentional and has underscored the powerful impact of the unconscious mind on our actions.

The second critical step is to understand that the problem of bounded ethicality does not only affect others. You, too, are vulnerable. If behaving ethically is genuinely one of your objectives, you need to understand the ways in which an honest person such as yourself might act unethically without conscious awareness. You may think that you are doing nothing wrong, while at the same time acting in ways that fall short of your own ethical standards. Because your morality isn't the problem, your moral compass will not help you at such times. Rather, the solution is to increase your awareness of the psychological pitfalls that bedevil even the most well-intentioned and ethical negotiators. In this chapter, we will show you how various factors can lead you and your negotiating partners to behave unethically—without conscious awareness—and how you can correct such behavior.

CONFLICTS OF INTEREST

When people talk about conflicts of interest, they usually assume that professionals consciously consider these opposing forces (what's good for them versus their professional obligations). Take, for example, the old lawyer joke, "It's not whether you win or lose, it's how *long* you play the game," which implies that attorneys are primarily motivated to maximize their billable hours. However, when lawyers are paid by the hour, they may truly come to believe that their clients are best served by a thorough, time-intensive process, whereas lawyers whose clients pay them a percentage of a settlement may be more likely to believe that their clients are best served by a quick agreement. These beliefs are not conscious or deliberately unethical, but they are biased by circumstance. Or as Upton Sinclair once stated, "It is difficult to get a man to understand something when his salary depends upon his not understanding it."

In buyer-seller negotiations, it is common for the seller to believe that she is selling a higher-quality product than the buyer thinks he is buying. In fact, buyers often believe that the goods offered by different sellers are indistinguishable from each other, while the sellers view their own products as significantly better than those of other providers. Thus, when a salesperson says, "Sure, I will benefit if you buy our product, but I wouldn't try to sell it to you if I didn't believe it was the best product for you and your company," she may well believe this statement. Yet substantial research tells us that the seller's conflict of interest (being honest versus making the sale) can lead her to unconsciously view the world through a biased lens and to believe that her product is the very best option for you—even when that is not the case. When a seller claims that his products are the best on the market, and a prospective buyer believes that the products are indistinguishable from those of the competition, the buyer is likely to make sinister attributions about the seller's ethics. When the discussion is over, the buyer assumes that the seller's statements were indicative of unethical behavior when, in fact, the seller was falling prey to the psychological trap that Sinclair predicted.

THE PROBLEM OF AGENTS

Conflicts of interest often become most problematic when agents are involved—whether the agents are investment bankers, lawyers, literary agents, real-estate agents, or some other type of third party with a stake in the negotiation's outcome. Consider what happens when a real-estate agent advises you, the buyer, to raise your bid on a house even though your current bid is consistent with a rational assessment of the property's value. Is the agent thinking only of her own commission? We would argue that she is probably not intentionally corrupt, but simply human, and therefore implicitly motivated to see the world in a way that maximizes her own returns from the deal. The agent can quickly think of past situations in which a buyer preferred to overpay rather than risk losing a house, or bitterly regretted not heeding the agent's advice to overpay. On the other hand, it will be much harder for her to recall times when this was the wrong advice, even though this happened more frequently.

When you are planning to buy or sell a house, your agent will undoubtedly tell you that she is working in your best interest.[2] But when we look at the situation objectively, it becomes clear that the agent is a third party in the transaction, one whose interests do not perfectly match those of her principal (the buyer or seller). The buyer who wishes to pay as little as possible and who is in no hurry to buy may have to deal with a well-intentioned agent who is paid more when the selling price is high and who would love to close the deal as soon as possible. Similarly, a seller may be in no rush to sell, yet her agent devotes considerable energy to persuading her that it is best to make a sale before the market cools down. What can be done about this problem?

Due to the failure of agents to act professionally in many domains, including auditing, investment banking, and real estate, both federal and state governments have stepped in to remedy the situation. The most popular solution has been to implement rules mandating disclosure. The reasoning is that, if consumers understand that their advisers and agents have a conflict of interest, they can take the steps necessary to protect themselves. Are such remedies effective? Perhaps not. Consider that, in most states, real-estate agents for buyers and sellers are required to have their customers sign a disclosure statement clarifying that the agent will earn a percentage of any sales transaction. Most people sign the disclosure form and then never again consider the actual conflict of interest between buyer and agent. Instead, they truly believe that their agent is providing objective advice.

Furthermore, research suggests that disclosure could actually *increase* the problems that result from conflicts of interest.[3] In a study conducted by decision researchers Daylian Cain, Don Moore, and George Loewenstein, participants playing the role of "adviser" were (in some cases) required to tell a participant playing the role of "client" that he had a vested stake in having the client believe that a commodity had a high value. As it turns out, this disclosure led "advisers" to feel *more* comfortable exaggerating their estimates; after all, "I already told them I was biased." At the same time, the "clients" often believed that their advisers were *more* trustworthy if they had disclosed their conflict of interest. In other words, advisers would have been more honest, and clients would have been more cautious, if there had been *no* disclosure!

If disclosure will not help resolve this ethical dilemma, what are we to do? First, to the extent possible, try to solicit advice and expertise from people who do not have a stake in the outcome and who do not profit from manipulating your behavior or decisions. When this is not possible, try to collect additional information from outside sources that can serve as a reality check on the advice you have been given. For example, if the real-estate agent tells you that a particular property or region is worth investing in, solicit an outsider's opinion by asking a different real-estate agent (a friend, an acquaintance, or a stranger whom you have not hired) whether this advice seems sound. Finally, be willing to ask your agent to justify her analysis. Instead of taking her "expert opinion" at face value, try to discover what objective criteria or procedure she employed before making her claims. She may trust her "intuition," but there is no reason that you should.

A final note: most of us view conflicts of interest as a genuine societal problem that must be remedied. We understand that conflicts of interest can contort people's judgments. Yet we have trouble believing that they affect our *own* judgments. The truth is that none of us is immune. There is no good reason to believe that you will behave any differently from the agent, the auditor, the buyer, or the seller when you have conflicting motivations and interests. To avoid such unintended unethical behaviors, the first step is to recognize your own fallibility.

IMPLICIT ASSOCIATIONS AND STEREOTYPES

Steve Barrett, the purchasing agent for his firm, had to choose between two landscaping companies to maintain the grounds of five different buildings. Company A had a long history in the area and offered fairly traditional services. Company B was newer and offered many more contemporary and innovative ideas. Company A was owned and represented in meetings by a white male; Company B was owned and represented by a Hispanic female. Barrett weighed the proven reliability of Company A against the contemporary image that his firm wished to convey. Almost every discussion and analysis led Barrett to believe that he should move into final negotiations with Company B. In the end, however, Barrett decided to go with his gut. He hired the older, more traditional firm.

A month later, Barrett was filling out some paperwork that asked him to report on diversity in the firm's supplier relationships. Barrett didn't mind filling out the forms, as he was a strong supporter of his firm's view that women- and minority-owned companies should be seriously considered as contractors. As he checked the "Caucasian" and "male" boxes to indicate the ethnicity and gender of the owner of Company A, Barrett scanned the race and ethnicity of the finalists for his past dozen supply contracts. He noticed that women- and minority-owned companies were often finalists in his searches, but rarely got the contract. As he thought back, Barrett began to feel a bit guilty. In the end, however, he concluded that these suppliers were not yet fully competitive, though he hoped they would be in the near future. Barrett remained proud of his continued (and often vocal) support of equity and fairness in society and of his company's aggressive affirmative-action policies.

Soon after the landscaping contract was signed, Barrett watched a segment of the TV show *Dateline NBC* featuring Harvard psychologist Mahzarin Banaji that disturbed him. The segment was about the Implicit Association Test (IAT) on Harvard University's website (http://implicit.harvard.edu).[4] (We encourage readers to visit the website before reading further and to try one or two of the "tests.") This website provides a set of exercises designed to identify unconscious racial and gender biases. With the landscaping episode on his mind, Barrett decided to take one of the tests to prove to himself that his decision had been unbiased.

The first set of items on the test that Barrett selected asked him to categorize photographs of Hispanics and European-Americans as quickly as possible. Using computer keys as described on the site, Barrett identified faces as either "Hispanic" or "white." In the next test, he was asked to identify words that appeared on the screen as positive (i.e., "good") or negative (i.e., "bad"). Barrett had no trouble classifying words such as "nice," "love," and "peace" as "good" and classifying words such as "death," "devil," and "bomb" as "bad."

In the next stage, these two tests were merged. Now Barrett was asked to hit one key if a Hispanic face *or* a "good" word appeared on the screen. He was to hit a different key if a white face *or* a "bad" word appeared. This task proved to be more complicated; Barrett found himself making a few errors and responding considerably slower than he had in previous tasks.

After thirty words or photos had appeared, the task changed. Now Barrett was asked to use one key to identify either a Hispanic face or a "bad" word and to hit a different key to identify either a white face or a "good" word. Barrett was pleased that he was able to complete this task very accurately and quickly.

As he had expected, the computer confirmed that Barrett's responses for the second combined set of words and faces were much faster than his responses for the first combined set. It appears that Barrett processed information and completed tasks more quickly when white faces were associated with "good" and Hispanic faces were associated with "bad" than when Hispanic was associated with "good" and white with "bad." As a result, the computer suggested to Barrett that he showed an implicit association between "Hispanic" and "bad" and between "white" and "good." Although he didn't consciously endorse such a preference, Barrett's implicit attitudes seemed to favor whites over Hispanics. Were these implicit associations connected to his landscaping decision? If the company owned by the white male had been the one that was newer but more innovative, would Barrett have concluded that innovation was a more critical factor than experience? Would he have found a way to justify hiring the white male anyway? Barrett was unsettled by the results of the study and what they might imply.

Most of us, including those who perceive ourselves to be liberal and non-discriminating on the basis of race and gender, may be unaware of our implicit associations. Typically, people are not only unaware of their implicit processes, but are also reluctant to believe that there can exist thought processes (which affect behavior!) that are inaccessible to them. So, consider what it could mean when a potential employer says in a negotiation, "When you work for us, you know you're working for a company that treats all employees equally, regardless of race or gender." One likely possibility is that the employer believes her statement, but that she and other members of her firm nonetheless discriminate through their implicit thought processes.

Humans tend to stereotype people from groups other than our own, often without conscious awareness. *Stereotyping* consists of identifying a key feature that is perceived to describe some members of a group, applying these descriptions to all members of the group, and failing to notice the uniqueness of specific group members. Clearly, a major drawback of stereotyping is that it can lead people to become prejudiced and to behave unkindly toward members of other groups. It can also lead us to overlook important information about the individual, causing us to behave in ways that are inappropriate, uninformed, or irrational given what the other person is *really* like. One result of stereotyping is that our own negotiated outcomes tend to suffer. Dolly Chugh, of the Stern School of Business at NYU, refers to this as the *stereotype tax*, the price we pay for not overcoming our stereotypes of others.[5] In other words, our stereotypes not only hurt other people, they can also hurt us.

Unfortunately, many negotiation texts encourage you to stereotype your negotiation opponent. Such books promote stereotypic and overly simplistic advice on how to negotiate with the Chinese, the Japanese, South Americans, Israelis, and so on. While it is critically important that you learn as much as possible about cultural norms before you enter into cross-cultural negotiations, it is dangerous to negotiate with "them" as if they are all the same. We readily identify variation in the way that people from our own culture behave, but we too easily accept stereotypes about people from other countries and cultures. Too often, these stereotypes lead negotiators to act as if they already know a great deal about the other side, when they could learn much more by entering the negotiation with an open mind and searching for individuating information—or, better yet, by preparing in advance, by asking questions, and by trying to learn about the perspective, personality, and diverse interests of the other party.

We most commonly think about stereotyping based on obvious differences such as race, gender, nationality, and so on. Yet it's also possible to form stereotypes about specific companies and their negotiating styles that lead us to snap judgments about how a particular company "thinks." Of course, companies don't think; people do, and individuals within a specific company differ. When negotiating with different members of the same organization, we, too, often treat these individuals as a single actor—even as we recognize the diversity of thought and opinion within our own organization. Have you ever started a conversation with a representative of a phone company—or an airline—in a heated manner because you had a previous conversation with a representative of that company who was unhelpful and rude? How did that work out for you? Probably not well.

So, when Steve Barrett chose to hire a traditional landscaping company owned by a white male rather than an innovative firm owned by a Hispanic female, was he aware of his implicit attitudes and the degree to which he was showing a preference for those who were a lot like him? Probably not. Becoming a more ethical, effective negotiator requires that we not only confront our intentional biases, but also seek to understand our implicit preferences. Negotiation geniuses are not unbiased people. Rather, they are people who confront their biases and do as much as they can to overcome or offset them.

PARASITIC VALUE CREATION

Pharmaceutical Firm X manufactures a beneficial drug and is selling 100 million pills per year at a price of $4.05 per pill. The manufacturing cost is $0.05 per pill, so the drug is earning Firm X $400 million per year. After a period of time, Pharmaceutical Firm Y introduces a drug that treats the same ailment. Best estimates suggest that this competition from Y will lead X to reduce the price of its drug by about $1, to $3.05. Furthermore, Y is expected to capture 40 percent of the market by charging an even lower price of $2.55 per pill. In other words, X is expected to sell 60 million pills for a $180 million profit per year, and Y is expected to sell 40 million pills for a $100 million profit per year. After Y's entry into the market, X's and Y's combined profitability ($280 million) will be significantly less than the $400 million that X was earning as a monopolist.

Fortunately, the chief negotiator for Firm X has taken a course on negotiation and value creation and has mastered the ideas presented in Chapters 2 and 3 of this book. He approaches Y's chief negotiator with the following offer: What if X were to pay Y $125 million annually to stay out of the market? Because $125 million is more than the $100 million that Y expects to earn, Y would be better off financially if it did not compete with X in this market. X would also be better off, since its current $400 million profit minus a $125 million payment to Y would exceed the $180 million profit it expects if Y enters the marketplace.

This solution seems perfect, doesn't it? By working together, X and Y have expanded the pie and created $120 million in value. Let the celebrations begin!

But wait a minute. Where did that "created" value come from? Unfortunately, it came from the ailing consumers who must now continue paying $4.05 per pill rather than $2.55 or $3.05, the approximate amounts they would pay if Y brought its product to market. In other words, the $120 million was not really *created*; it was just transferred from consumers to producers. Because such agreements restrain competition, the U.S. Federal Trade Commission (FTC)—along with similar entities in other countries—considers them illegal. If such agreements were allowed, X and Y could collude to create value at the expense of consumers. James Gillespie and Max Bazerman use the term *parasitic value creation* to describe what occurs when negotiators create value by taking value away from parties who are not at the bargaining table.[6] We think that the word "parasitic" is appropriate because the benefits that the negotiators achieve come at the expense of others.

Since this type of agreement is clearly illegal, and Firm X could not have approached Firm Y with the kind of offer we described, let's consider how parasitic value creation might actually play out in the real world. What might it look like? In a variation of the scenario described above, the FTC sued pharmaceutical companies Schering-Plough and Upsher-Smith, accusing them of reaching an agreement that restricted trade. Before the FTC lawsuit was filed, Upsher-Smith was planning to introduce a generic pharmaceutical product that would threaten Schering-Plough's dominant product (K-Dur 20, a potassium supplement). Schering-Plough tried to stop Upsher-Smith's entrance into the marketplace by filing a lawsuit that accused Upsher-Smith of violating Schering-Plough's patent. The two pharmaceutical firms reached an out-of-court settlement that specified that Upsher-Smith would delay its entry into the market and that Schering-Plough would pay Upsher-Smith $60 million for five unrelated products.

The FTC lawsuit against the pharmaceutical firms argued that the $60 million was a sham payment for the market delay, intended not as fair compensation for the five products but rather to keep Upsher-Smith's generic product off the market. The pharmaceutical firms' lawyers argued that negotiating multiple issues simultaneously (combining the settlement of the pending litigation with the transaction involving five other products) helped create value and was beneficial to society. They even hired a well-known negotiation expert to testify that value creation was good for society.

We know this case well because Max was on the other side, serving as an expert witness for the FTC. Max's view, then and now, was that parasitic value creation had occurred: the companies created value for themselves, with no apparent concern for the harmful effects of their actions on consumers and, more broadly, on society. In Max's opinion, the five patents simply provided a cover story.[7]

Sadly, many of the negotiation exercises conducted in training seminars implicitly encourage students to engage in parasitic value creation. In one common simulation, students represent firms in an industry that has few players. Across a number of rounds, each firm must decide whether to charge a high or low price. When one firm charges a high price and the other firm charges a low price, the low-price firm picks up market share and wins at the expense of the high-price firm. Yet the game is set up so that both parties would be better off if they both charged high prices. Such exercises are based on the well-known *prisoners' dilemma* problem, in which players are individually better off playing a noncooperative strategy (setting a low price), but collectively better off playing a cooperative strategy (setting a high price).[8] In such simulations, instructors praise the students who figure out how to develop a pattern of mutually high prices that lead to successful value creation for both firms. Given what we know about parasitic value creation, it is troubling that much of this training occurs without any consideration of where the extra profit comes from—the consumer!

When we use the term "parasitic value creation," we do not mean to insult most value-creating agreements, nor are we objecting to companies charging whatever prices the market will bear. Most of the time, value creation should be allowed even when it will impose costs on parties who are away from the table. For example, we view the U.S. pharmaceutical industry as one of the great success stories of the past century. If these firms hadn't achieved healthy profits, many drugs that save lives, reduce the need for surgery, and relieve pain would not exist.

On the other hand, any analysis that focuses only on the profits of coordinating pharmaceutical firms and ignores the harm done to consumers would be incomplete—and possibly unethical. We believe that these companies (and their negotiators) should consider, in much the same way antitrust laws ask firms to consider, whether they are creating societal value or simply helping each other extract as much money as possible at the expense of the consumer or other stakeholders. When your negotiations will affect people who are not seated at the table, such as consumers or future generations, make sure that your ethicality is not bounded by the unintentional exclusion of these parties' concerns.

How can you judge whether the value you create in your negotiation benefits society? One criterion would be to call value creation socially beneficial when the value created for the parties at the table exceeds the costs imposed on outsiders; in such cases, while some of the value created may result from parasitic value creation, the overall result is still a net benefit to society. More generally, to remain alert to the potentially parasitic aspects of your value creation, we recommend that you ask the following questions:

- Who are all of the parties affected by this agreement?
- How is each party affected?
- Should I be concerned about any of these parties?
- How do the effects of the agreement on parties not at the table compare with the effects on the parties involved in the agreement?

We close this section with a political note. One legal, yet disturbing, example of parasitic value creation concerns the role of special-interest groups in elections. In the United States, special-interest groups, including corporations and nonprofit organizations, contribute large sums of money to political campaigns. Politicians, in turn, provide special-interest groups with access to the federal government and influence over policy. Politicians benefit, as the funds keep their campaign coffers full. And the vast sums that special-interest groups spend year after year on lobbying suggest that they are receiving a fine return on their investment. From a simple value-creation perspective, this negotiation achieves gain for all parties—unless you happen to be an average citizen without a powerful lobby! Ideally, elected officials would implement wise policy for everyone, rather than enacting distorted policies that benefit special-interest groups at the expense of the broader public. Then again, for the many reasons we have already covered in this chapter on bounded ethicality, we fear that few, if any, politicians or lobbyists are having a hard time sleeping at night. They have lots of ways to justify their behaviors and little incentive to question their profitable strategies.

OVERCLAIMING CREDIT

After twelve years of marriage, Jim and Karen have decided to divorce. Fortunately, they are both nice people, and have agreed to divide their assets fairly and to avoid conflict that could negatively affect their two children. They hire a divorce mediator, who asks both Jim and Karen to tell her privately how the financial assets should be divided.

"I think I deserve 60 percent of the assets," Jim tells the mediator. "In the first year of our marriage, I received a very large inheritance from an uncle that helped us out a lot. We wouldn't have been able to afford the down payment on our house if it wasn't for that money. So, I think I deserve a bit more than Karen."

Next, the mediator meets privately with Karen, who also believes that 60–40 is the correct division of assets, but not in favor of Jim. "I think I should get 60 percent and Jim should get 40 percent. After all, I've earned almost twice as much as Jim over the past twelve years."

Is Jim being greedy? Is Karen? Are they both arguing for more than they honestly believe that they deserve? Has the divorce affected their ethics for the worse? More likely, as a result of egocentrism (described in Chapter 5), they genuinely believe that they have contributed more to the marriage than is actually the case.

Overclaiming credit can hinder the implementation and progress of a variety of joint ventures, from start-up companies to marriages. Because we tend to make self-serving attributions regarding our behaviors, even honest, well-meaning people are likely to believe that they contributed more to an enterprise than they actually did and then to make moral judgments about those who disagree with them. This serves to fuel the conflict. So, when your colleague argues, "My sales team deserves 70 percent of the credit for the corporation's success over the last two years," accept the fact that she probably believes this statement is true even if you are sure it is not. If pushed, she can probably find some data or logic (however frivolous it may seem to you) that supports her claim.

Even at a societal level, overclaiming can inflict great harm. Across the globe, overharvesting has devastated once-thriving fisheries. Many fisheries have collapsed, and considerable uncertainty surrounds the question of when and how they will be brought back to a sustainable level. A significant part of the problem can be traced to the fact that different fishing groups all believe they are only taking their "fair share" of the resource.[9]

How can you control your own natural psychological tendency to overclaim? Max and his colleagues Nick Epley and Eugene Caruso recently asked one group of MBA students from a prestigious program to estimate the percentage of work they personally completed in their study groups.[10] On average, the claims made by members of each group, when added together, totaled 139 percent. Of course, there is only 100 percent to go around. However, the researchers found that the tendency to overclaim diminished when they asked group members to "unpack" the contributions of others—that is, when they asked group members to think about the contribution of each other member, not just their own contribution. Overclaiming did not disappear entirely, but it did drop by about half; consciously and explicitly thinking about the contributions that each person had made reduced the magnitude of the bias. If you want to diminish the tendency of your group or team members to overclaim credit or contribution, one way to do so is to get them to focus not only on what they have done, but on what each individual, considered one at a time, has done as well.

PUTTING IT TO PRACTICE

Most discussions of ethics in negotiation focus on your intentional choices—whether or not it is okay to lie, to hide information, and so on. In this chapter, we have stressed that negotiators are often not even aware that they are engaging in ethically questionable behavior.

Furthermore, the busier people are, the more they will rely on automatic thought processes, and the more likely it is that they will engage in ordinary unethical behaviors.[11] Unfortunately, most negotiators are busy people for whom negotiating is just one of the many tasks that they must accomplish each day. To make matters worse, there is already a lot to think about when negotiating: how to create and claim value, how to be a good investigative negotiator, how to defend against strategies of influence, et cetera. How can a negotiator do all of this and still avoid falling back on the kinds of automatic processes that lead to ordinary unethical behaviors?

Our perspective on bounded ethicality yields specific advice for managing your own ethical behavior and for understanding and managing the behavior of others. In terms of your own behavior, some important steps include:

1. If you are in a situation where you have a conflict of interest, become extra vigilant. To the extent possible, try to eliminate the source of the conflict (e.g., by recusing yourself from decisions in which you have a conflict of interest).
2. Be aware of the possibility that you may be discriminating against others unconsciously. Taking the IAT tests (mentioned earlier) may help you appreciate this natural tendency. Then, be proactive and take steps to offset your proclivity for selectively rewarding those whom you implicitly favor.
3. Whenever you feel that you have created value, try to analyze where exactly that value is coming from. Is anyone being made worse off? Is this trade-off acceptable to you?
4. When allocating credit, be careful not to give yourself too much credit—or to give too much credit to those whom you like. Specifically, be wary of the tendency to overweight those factors and inputs on which you perform strongly and that make you look good.

You can also use your understanding of bounded ethicality to better understand your negotiation counterparts and to develop better relationships with them. Here, we offer three guidelines for leveraging your knowledge to this end:

1. Audit the claims of your counterparts and look for unintentional biases.
2. Accept the fact that they may be unaware of their bounded ethicality. They may not notice that they are biased or that they are being parasitic in their efforts to create value. Avoid sinister attributions. When someone makes a statement that you do not believe, or "creates" value at the expense of others, avoid labeling him a liar or a thief. Instead, help him see the causes and consequences of his judgments and behaviors.
3. Finally, if you are unable to help your counterpart revise his biased perspective, follow the advice in Chapters 6 and 9 to craft a response that takes his misperceptions into account. For example, when you believe a salesperson is overstating the quality of his product, rather than withdrawing from the discussion or accusing him of exaggeration, deal with this ordinary unethical behavior through the use of a contingency contract. Ask how the superior quality of his product can be measured, and attach payment to performance. If the salesperson was being intentionally deceptive, he will back off the claim. But if he is engaging in ordinary unethical behavior—and believes his exaggerated claim—he will accept the contingency clause (to your benefit).

THE ETHICAL NEGOTIATION GENIUS

We recognize that there is no guarantee that you will easily implement these recommendations. Hopefully, however, we have convinced you that an *ethical* negotiation genius is one who wants to try to eliminate *unintended* unethical behaviors along with more obvious intentional ones. Just because many of these unintended unethical behaviors are common does not mean they are "okay." In our view, ethics in negotiation is about actively striving to be a better person, not about reaching—and settling for—an "acceptable" status quo.

CHAPTER 11

Negotiating from a Position of Weakness

One of the questions that we hear most often from our students and clients—many of whom are seasoned dealmakers—sounds something like this: "The framework and strategies you have presented are great. They have helped us a lot. But what can you do when you have no power in the negotiation? Can you get a great deal when the other side is holding all the cards?" When we ask our students and clients to explain their situation, we hear many versions of the same basic stories. Here are the most common:

STORY 1:

"In our business, potential customers constantly tell us that we have to lower our price, and that if we don't lower it, they will go to our competitors. They do not seem to want to talk about anything other than price. And the fact of the matter is, they *can* go to our competitors and get what they want. How can we possibly negotiate a good deal in such situations?"

STORY 2:

"I recently received a job offer from a company that I would like to work for. The one big problem is that the compensation is not as good as I would like it to be. The other big problem is that my BATNA stinks. I have no other job offers, and I'm pretty desperate. How can I negotiate a better deal for myself?"

STORY 3:

"I am involved in a dispute and the other side is threatening to sue. Their lawsuit is entirely frivolous, but if we go to court, they can continue to litigate until I go bankrupt. They have a lot of money and can easily afford a long court battle. What can I do?"

STORY 4:

"My country is a small player on the world stage. When it comes to negotiating economic or political international agreements, we are constantly being pushed around. More powerful countries overlook our interests, and we practically have to plead for what we most desperately need. Is there some way to improve our position?"

As these stories demonstrate, weakness in negotiation results when the other side's BATNA is relatively strong and your BATNA is relatively weak. Have you ever felt trapped in such predicaments? How did you respond? In our experience, most people in such situations either panic or quickly accept the futility of trying to negotiate away their misfortune. Few actually do what it takes to negotiate effectively and to improve their outcomes. We have also noticed that those who *do* think carefully and systematically about such situations, and who do not abandon the negotiation framework developed in this book, are often able to achieve outstanding results in the face of seemingly impossible odds.

In this chapter, we will help you to understand the secrets of these negotiation geniuses. We will first present strategies that you can leverage even when you have little power. We will then share with you strategies for upsetting the balance of power—that is, how you can move from being weak to being strong in the negotiation.

NEGOTIATING WITHOUT POWER

There is perhaps nothing that creates more anxiety for negotiators than the feeling of desperation that comes from having no good alternatives. The situation only worsens when you realize that the other side is not as anxious as you are to do the deal. Whether you are negotiating the specifics of your only job offer or a contract with the only vendor who can provide what you desperately need, knowing that "no deal" would be disastrous can place a lot of pressure on you. Unfortunately, this anxiety can cause you to give up the hope of creating or claiming value and to lose sight of the need to prepare and execute negotiations carefully and systematically. Instead, you begin to focus on getting a deal done at any cost. While it would be unfair for us to suggest that there is no reason to be concerned in such situations, it would also be unfair—and wildly inaccurate—to suggest that there is little you can do to improve your prospects. Consider the following strategies:

STRATEGY 1: DON'T REVEAL THAT YOU ARE WEAK

Think back to the story we presented in Chapter 1, in which President Roosevelt's campaign manager was negotiating with a photographer over how much to pay for the use of three million copies of a photograph. The problem was that the campaign had already printed the three million copies, and the photographer (who owned the copyright to the photograph) had the legal right to charge $1 per copy. The campaign manager's BATNA was very weak: if an agreeable price could not be negotiated, they would have to throw away the pamphlets or face litigation. Neither of these eventualities came to fruition. Not only did the campaign manager secure the right to use the photograph, but the photographer even offered to *pay* $250 to consummate the deal.

The key to the campaign manager's success: the campaign manager's position was weak, but the photographer did not know that it was weak. Had the photographer known that three million copies of the photograph had already been printed, he would have known that he was in the position of power and could negotiate a more profitable deal.

The obvious lesson: having a weak BATNA is not terribly problematic if the other side does not know that your BATNA is weak. If you have a weak BATNA, don't advertise it!

Surprisingly enough, many people do not heed this advice; in fact, they often make their bad situation worse by unwittingly revealing the weakness of their BATNA. You do this whenever you tell your customer that "time is of the essence" or that "we can meet with you whenever you have the time." Often, it is important to convey that you are facing time constraints or that you have a flexible schedule. But you can send the same messages without making your desperation transparent. For example, you might say that "one of our preferences is to move ahead quickly" or that "we have some flexibility with regards to meeting with you." When you are under pressure and focused on the weakness of your BATNA you may need to remind yourself to use this less revealing language.

STRATEGY 2: OVERCOME YOUR WEAKNESS BY LEVERAGING THEIR WEAKNESS

Recently, an executive student came to Deepak for help with a negotiation. He was attempting to sell his 50 percent stake in a company to his business partner, who controlled the other 50 percent. The seller (Deepak's student) was focused on the desperation of his situation: he needed liquidity very soon, and his partner was the only viable buyer of his shares. The first thing the seller wanted to discuss was the degree to which he should be willing to devalue his shares in order to make the deal happen. "How low should I be willing to go?" he asked.

Nowhere in his analysis was there a consideration of how much the shares might be worth to the business partner—that is, how high a price the buyer might be willing to pay. When Deepak began to probe in this direction, it became clear that the business partner had much to gain by buying out the seller: the buyer had a lot of money, he had long desired to take the company in new directions that the seller had resisted, and purchasing the shares would give the buyer full control over the company's future. As the discussion continued, the student began to realize that he was not the only one who was "weak"; the buyer was also weak, albeit for very different reasons. Focusing on these factors helped the seller to increase his target and change the trajectory of the negotiation. In his discussions with the buyer, he outlined the many benefits to the buyer of making this purchase, downplayed his own desperation, and anchored aggressively in his opening offer. What was the eventual outcome? The two sides agreed to a deal in which the student sold only 40 percent of the company back to his partner—at a total price that was higher than he had originally hoped to receive for his entire 50 percent.

This story highlights the distinction between negotiators who focus only on their own BATNA and those who evaluate the other side's BATNA. If their BATNA is weak, that means that you bring a lot of value to the deal—and you should be able to claim some (or much) of that value. In other words, having a weak BATNA is not particularly problematic if the other side's BATNA is weak as well.

Consider again the success of Roosevelt's campaign manager. Imagine that the photographer had discovered that the campaign manager's BATNA was very weak. Would that guarantee a good outcome for the photographer and a poor outcome for the campaign manager? Not necessarily—because the photographer's BATNA was also weak! If there were "no deal," the campaign would suffer the costs of reprinting three million pamphlets, but the photographer would also lose a huge ("once in a lifetime") opportunity to get tremendous public exposure for his artistic work.

What typically happens when both sides are in a position of weakness? If you think back to the fundamental framework developed in Chapter 1, you will recognize that when both parties have a weak BATNA, it means that the ZOPA is large. In other words, a lot of value is created when the two sides reach an agreement. Who claims more of this value? Usually it is the one who understands the fundamentals and leverages the strategies we discussed in Chapter 1. In this case, the one who fares better is the one who makes the other side's weakness more salient throughout the negotiation. By focusing on the photographer's opportunity for publicity, the campaign manager was able to secure a great outcome for his side. Meanwhile, the photographer was so focused on the prospect of losing a great opportunity that he failed to consider the value that he could bring to the Roosevelt campaign.

STRATEGY 3: IDENTIFY AND LEVERAGE YOUR DISTINCT VALUE PROPOSITION

Firms that bid for business (such as consulting firms, offshore services firms, quasi-commodity suppliers, construction and landscaping professionals, et cetera) often find themselves in a position of weakness. Here is a common complaint: "In our industry, our customers hold an auction for every deal. They solicit bids, and then accept the lowest one. There is no opportunity to create value by introducing multiple issues. Our customers tell us that we must lower our price further, otherwise they will go to our competitors."

These negotiators are stuck bargaining over only one issue (usually price) in an arena where their competitors can compete effectively on the issue being discussed. Though these situations represent a very specific example of "weakness," we devote special attention to them here because these are among the most common problems our students and clients face.

How can you create and claim value when your counterpart (typically, your customer) is only interested in discussing price? In many such situations, you can improve your prospects by changing the game you are being forced to play. Consider that, in negotiation, your ability to legitimately *claim* value is a function of your ability to *create* value. If you bring nothing to the other side that they cannot get elsewhere, then your offer is no better for them than their BATNA. In other words, the ZOPA is small or nonexistent. Why would they want to make a deal with you?

The good news is that, very often, you *do* bring something to the table that distinguishes you from your competitors. This is your *distinct value proposition* (DVP), and it need not be a lower price. You may have a better product, a higher-quality service, a good reputation, a strong brand, or a host of other assets that your customer values and that you can provide more effectively or cheaply than your competitors. Keep in mind that your DVP is not just something you *think* your customer should value, but something they *actually* value. If you bring such value-adding elements to the deal, you have the possibility of using them to get what you want (for example, a higher margin, repeat business, et cetera). The key is to figure out how to make your DVP a factor in the negotiation. This can be difficult when you are stuck in a price-only auction, when the other side seems uninterested in discussing any issue other than price, or when the other side is not familiar with the principle of creating value by negotiating multiple issues. Fortunately, all of these obstacles are surmountable. The following four strategies can help you make your DVP a factor the next time you take part in a negotiation or auction:

Submit multiple proposals. It is not always possible to adequately gauge, prior to making an offer, whether the customer has any interests other than a low price. For this reason, bidders often wonder whether they should bid the lowest possible price or a slightly higher price that includes additional features (such as a higher-quality product or additional services). Next time, try doing both! Instead of submitting one bid, consider making two or more bids simultaneously, a strategy that we initially described in Chapter 3. For example, one bid might be low on price and on service, while the other is somewhat higher on both. If the customer values service, they will appreciate knowing that they can get extra attention from your firm at an additional cost. This strategy will also increase your chances of submitting the winning bid: if they only value price, your low bid will be competitive; if they value other features, your higher bid will be competitive.

Lower your bid just enough to get into the second round. One reason why many companies use price-only auctions is that there are too many potential vendors from which to choose. But not all auctions end with a signed contract. Often, the auction is designed simply to "narrow the field." For example, a customer might invite ten or more firms to bid for a project, and then winnow the list down to the two or three firms with the lowest price bids. These candidates are then invited to engage in one-on-one negotiations. Our

Harvard colleagues Guhan Subramanian and Richard Zeckhauser have coined the term *negotiauction* to describe this two-stage process.[1] In such situations, you need not submit the lowest bid; rather, you should submit a bid that is low enough to pass the initial hurdle, and then try to create value when negotiating multiple issues with the customer.

Keep in mind that your customers may not necessarily "announce" a formal negotiauction (most will not have heard the term) or explain the rules ahead of time. But they may still proceed as though that is the process they are following. Moreover, many customers will be willing to discuss your multi-issue proposal even after the auction is over if you were a "low enough" bidder. As such, it is often a good idea to reach out to your customers after you have "lost" the auction to see if you are in a position to offer a package deal that they value.

One of our students recently described to us how his firm ended up on the losing end of this strategy. His firm was competing against five other firms who were all vying for the same prized customer. The customer held an auction and announced that two of the five firms would advance to the final round of negotiations. The student's firm was one of the two to advance. "We were pretty excited," recalled the student. "We knew how to position our firm in relation to this [one remaining] competitor, and we were confident that the deal was ours. But we lost the deal—to a competitor who had not even made it past the initial auction!" While our student and his colleagues were celebrating, the sales team of the third firm had gone back to the customer and made the case that they could provide the best package deal, despite how the auction had turned out.

Take the agent out of the game. A common complaint among negotiators who are forced to compete solely on price sounds something like this: "We are a high-value partner for our customer. Unfortunately, the customer uses a purchasing agent to negotiate its deals, and this agent is compensated entirely based on how low a price she negotiates. The next thing we know, we're stuck in an auction where the only thing that matters is who can provide the cheapest product. We lose—and the customer loses, too. The only winner is the purchasing agent!"

Intermediaries such as purchasing agents—whose incentives are not always aligned with those who have hired them to negotiate on their behalf—constitute one of the biggest barriers to efficient deal-making. But there are ways to keep such intermediaries from derailing your negotiation. Here are two strategies for doing so, based on the successful experience of our executive students and clients:

- *Send a copy of your proposals to the customer.* Some months ago, one of our students decided to try the strategy of submitting multiple proposals to the purchasing agent, and so he submitted a high-price/high-value offer and a low-price/low-value offer. His low-price offer was accepted. Some weeks later he discovered (in a conversation with the customer) that the customer had never even seen the high-price proposal! In other words, the agent had conveniently eliminated it from the "short list" that was submitted to the customer. Having learned from that experience, our student now makes a habit of sending to his customers ("as a courtesy") a copy of any proposal he submits to the purchasing agent. "Even if the customer chooses not to look at the information I send," explains our student, "the very fact that it's sitting on the boss's desk makes the purchasing agent think twice before he tries to disregard my high-value proposal."

- *Negotiate a post-settlement settlement with the customer.* When our clients and executive students tell us that pressure from the agent is forcing them to sideline their distinct value proposition in an effort to lower the price, we often tell them not to worry. Typically, purchasing agents exit the scene once they have served their purpose (albeit self-servingly) of choosing a vendor. If you really have the ability to create additional value for the customer (beyond cutting price), you will be in a strong position to pitch your proposition once you are dealing with the party that stands to benefit from "hearing you out." In other words, don't assume you are stuck with an inefficient agreement; if both sides can be made better off, you can always revise the agreement after you have won the deal.

Educate your customers between deals. How often do you communicate with your customers (or potential customers) when there is no potential deal on the table? You might send your customers a holiday card once a year, but how often do you reach out to educate them about your ability to provide them with new sources of value? If you are like the vast majority of negotiators, you spend little (if any) time doing so. But if your customers do not understand your distinct value proposition, then that is exactly what you should be doing. It should come as no surprise that customers will value your input and insights most when they have the time to listen to you, when they are least concerned about cutting costs, and when they are under no pressure to commit to anything. These conditions are most often in place when there is no deal on the table—that is, when they are not likely to disregard your comments as an attempt to manipulate them. In the middle of an auction, time pressure, cost concerns, and pressure to make a final decision all work against you. But those who reach out to their customers (and potential customers) *in between* auctions have the possibility of building relationships, learning about their customers' interests and, most important, making their DVP a factor in the *next* negotiation or auction. Most customers are willing to discuss these matters openly and will appreciate your desire to understand their needs. In at least a few cases that we know of, vendors were able to preempt their customers' next auctions entirely; by signaling an interest in understanding and meeting the customers' needs and negotiating multiple issues simultaneously, they were able to sign deals before they ever went to auction! This should not be too surprising: both sides stand to benefit by engaging in negotiations that extend beyond discussions of price. Sometimes all the customer needs is a little bit of encouragement—or education—to push him in the direction of his own self-interest.

STRATEGY 4: IF YOUR POSITION IS VERY WEAK, CONSIDER RELINQUISHING WHAT LITTLE POWER YOU DO HAVE

Many years ago, when Deepak was a senior in college, he received a job offer from a consulting firm. Deepak loved the offer, with one exception: the salary was lower than he had hoped it would be. Deepak called the HR manager and asked whether salaries were negotiable. The HR manager told him that salaries were not negotiable, but offered to set up a lunch with the managing partner so that Deepak could discuss any issues that concerned him. At lunch, after an hour of pleasant conversation, the managing partner explained that the firm calculated starting salaries using a very simple formula in which only three factors mattered: the college the new hire had attended, his or her academic major, and prior work experience. Since they had already considered these factors, they could not increase Deepak's salary.

Deepak knew that he had very little power in the negotiation: he had no better offer to use as leverage, and he estimated that "holding out for more" would result in little, if any, increase in salary. He decided to try a different kind of strategy altogether.

Deepak responded by saying that he understood the partner's perspective, that he really loved the firm, and that he would definitely accept the offer. Having said that, Deepak continued, would the partner be willing to continue the discussion regarding his salary? With the partner's consent, Deepak made an extensive argument that boiled down to the following: he would bring more value to the firm than the simple formula suggested. He concluded by emphasizing that salary was not the most important issue to him—he had already accepted the offer because he was very excited about the opportunity to work at this firm—but that salary was nonetheless *an* issue, as it would be for any young person starting out in life. If there were any help that the firm could give him, it would be greatly appreciated.

The partner liked what he heard, and promised Deepak that he would at least give this perspective some thought. The following day, the partner called Deepak to tell him that the firm would give him a 10 percent increase in salary because they had "taken another look at his [summer] work experience and decided that it probably should have been given more weight in the first place."

Was that really the reason for the raise? Deepak thinks that is unlikely. The more likely reason is a simple but significant insight regarding power: if you have very little power, you may be better off giving it up entirely. Put another way, if you can't outmuscle the other side in a negotiation, you may want to stop flexing your muscles and, instead, simply ask them to help you. When negotiators try to leverage their power, others reciprocate. This pattern can be disastrous when you are the weaker party. But when you make it clear that you have no intention of fighting or negotiating aggressively, others may also soften their stance. Once the managing partner decided that he wanted to help Deepak, he simply needed to find a way to justify this decision. Once he found a way, Deepak got what he wanted.

STRATEGY 5: STRATEGIZE ON THE BASIS OF YOUR ENTIRE NEGOTIATION PORTFOLIO

Max recently consulted with a firm in an industry where profit margins have fallen from about 20 percent to less than 5 percent over the last decade. This decline in margins has been due to an increase in new market entrants and to a growing perception among customers that the competitors in the industry are interchangeable. In an attempt to learn about the firm and industry, Max asked the firm's executives how often they simply refused to reduce their margins below 10 percent. In other words, how often did they risk losing the deal in hopes of earning a higher profit margin? The executives responded that the days were long gone when they could try to be so tough—they needed every dollar of revenue that they could get. Max then asked them to estimate what percentage of their business they would lose if they held out for 10 percent margins. Their estimate: at least 25 percent. At that point, Max simply recommended doing some arithmetic: "If you double your margins [from 5 percent to 10 percent]," Max noted, "and you lose even 49 percent of your business, you are still better off in terms of overall profit."

The results of this simple analysis came as a surprise to the executives. But their surprise is not, in fact, surprising. Too often, when negotiators are myopically focused on the current negotiation, the strategy they adopt is not an effective one for their portfolio of negotiations. If you had only one deal to negotiate, it would make sense for you to reduce your margins as much as necessary to win the deal; after all, any amount of money is preferable to no money at all (assuming that no money is what you will get by pursuing your BATNA). But because there are almost always multiple negotiations to consider, you need a strategy that makes sense for your entire portfolio of negotiations. If you are going to negotiate many deals with many different customers, you may be willing to lose some money in one negotiation (because you held out for a higher margin and lost the deal) in order to win even more money in another negotiation (because you held out for a higher margin and they accepted). Better yet, if you can distinguish between those negotiators who will accept a higher margin and those who will not—and if you can justify charging different prices to different customers—you may be in a position to increase profits even further by charging higher margins only to those who can stomach it.

The key is to audit the implicit assumptions you make when formulating your negotiation strategy. You may perceive yourself as being "weak" if you measure strength only as the ability to push hard in any given negotiation without losing the deal. But you may discover that you are actually quite "strong" once you begin to think about your ability to withstand losing some deals because you are maximizing the value of your entire negotiation portfolio. When you consider your entire portfolio, it is far easier to imagine taking bigger risks, keeping the clients for whom you can add the most value, and becoming more profitable.

UPSETTING THE BALANCE OF POWER

Weakness is always frustrating, but perhaps never more so than when the other side acknowledges the value you create, but still pushes you around—simply because they are bigger and stronger and can do whatever they want. Maybe your largest customer thinks it has the right to make onerous last-minute demands or to ignore some of its contractual responsibilities. Or perhaps your competitor has decided to sue you for infringing on their patent—a case that has little merit, but that they can litigate to the hilt thanks to their deep pockets. If you want to stay in business, such bullies implicitly say, you will have to play by their rules. In some cases, small business owners are held hostage by their *employees;* their top salesperson might be rude, unprofessional, and overpaid, but if he leaves the firm and joins the competition, they will lose half of their business.

In each of these situations, your prospects seem bleak for two reasons. First, you are in a position of weakness. Second, you are dealing with a person or an organization that is inconsiderate of your needs and entirely cavalier in the pursuit of their own self-interest. How might you negotiate in such instances? Begin by considering the various strategies we have outlined above for negotiating without power. If these are not sufficient, consider exercising a different, potentially powerful option: shifting the balance of power in your favor. As we will demonstrate, some negotiations require us not to improve our ability to play the game as it has been defined, but to change the nature of the game itself. The following strategies will help you turn the tables on would-be bullies and achieve outcomes far superior to those you might otherwise expect.

STRATEGY 1: INCREASE YOUR STRENGTH BY BUILDING COALITIONS WITH OTHER WEAK PARTIES

In their book *Negotiating Rationally,* Max Bazerman and Margaret Neale tell the story of how Lee Iacocca, then CEO of Chrysler, found a way to mitigate his company's weakness by building a coalition with other weak parties: his U.S. competitors.[2] In 1986, the three U.S. auto companies (General Motors, Ford, and Chrysler) were engaged in extremely unhealthy competition, as each tried to gain market share through the use of rebates. Each time one company announced a rebate, the other two rushed to raise their own rebate offer. Before long, the auto companies were losing money, on average, on every car they sold! Iacocca recognized that, because of this escalation problem, the automakers were in a very weak position vis-à-vis the consumer. He decided to put an end to this by announcing to the press that Chrysler would discontinue its rebate program—but that if either of the other two companies continued to offer rebates, Chrysler would match those rebates. This action by Chrysler helped to end the rebate war, stopped profit erosion in the industry, and returned all three U.S. automakers to profitability.

Why was Iacocca's strategy effective? Because it shifted power away from buyers and toward sellers. When a company offers to match its competitors' offers, this can turn out to be a very *bad* deal for consumers; such initiatives eliminate the incentive that competitors have to lower their prices (or offer rebates) to attract customers. As a result, the three U.S. automakers, which could no longer be pitted one against another on price alone, gained bargaining power.

You can use the same strategy—building coalitions with other weak parties—in your own negotiations. Consider that, when your customer has many other companies from whom he can purchase, you are in a weak position, but so is each of your competitors. When your boss has the option of hiring or firing you, you are in a weak position, but so is each of your coworkers. And when your country is small and has little voice in international negotiations, your country is in a weak position, but so are many other small countries. Fortunately for those who have little power in their negotiations, it is sometimes possible to shift the balance of power by aligning with these other weak entities.

For example, when bargaining with management, individual employees have often banded together to form unions. If a company were to negotiate with employees one at a time, it could credibly threaten to hire someone else if the employee's demands were perceived as excessive. When employees bargain collectively, however, they avoid competing against one another. The result is typically an above-market wage for all employees. This process effectively shifts power and money from shareholders to employees. A similar rationale has led many small businesses in the United States to negotiate collectively with insurance companies in order to lower the cost of health insurance, and has led many small farmers in developing countries to form "cooperatives" that allow them to negotiate higher prices for the produce they take to market.

In the realm of international relations, a vivid example of the power of coalitions surfaced during the 2003 World Trade Organization negotiations in Cancún, Mexico. Disgruntled by the continued lack of attention paid to the issues of concern to developing nations (such as reducing agricultural tariffs and farm subsidies), twenty-one "weak" countries banded together to create the Group of 21. This group is now in a much stronger position to negotiate for the interests of its members than any member nation would have been on its own.

In each of these examples, coalition building among weaker parties led to a weakening of the previously more powerful side's BATNA. When you build—and are able to sustain—a coalition with other weak parties, you make it difficult for the other side to pit one weak party against another, or to credibly threaten to walk away from the deal.

STRATEGY 2: LEVERAGE THE POWER OF YOUR EXTREME WEAKNESS—THEY MAY *NEED* YOU TO SURVIVE

In 1919, after the end of World War I, the leaders of the victorious Allied forces (most notably, the United States, Great Britain, and France) met in Paris to conduct many months of negotiations that would determine the fate of Europe and much of the rest of the world. Many of the countries affected by the war were invited to make appeals and arguments to the Allies regarding their fate. Most of these arguments pertained to the reshaping of geographic boundaries. The negotiations led to the birth of some new nations, as well as to the reshaping of existing boundaries that helped some countries while hurting others. Most nations that gained territory had been strong allies of the victors and could thus justify a claim to the "spoils" of war. But among those that profited from these talks was a weak country that had contributed relatively little to the Allied war effort: Romania. When the negotiations ended, Romania had roughly doubled in size. How was this possible? Why was Romania able to claim so much value when it had done little, if anything, to create value?

Romania's power lay not in its strength but in its weakness. Here's why: When the war ended, the greatest perceived threat to the Allied nations (in particular, to Great Britain and the United States) was not a resurgence of the defeated enemy. Rather, it was communism, the recently empowered political philosophy that had made its debut with Russia's 1917 October Revolution. Because of the great fear of communism's potential to spread westward, Romania, which lay immediately to the west of Russia, suddenly became an important consideration. If Romania fell, communism would gain another large foothold in Europe. The leaders of Romania did not want this to happen; more important, they knew that the Allied forces did not want this to happen—and that is how they were able to extract more value from the postwar negotiations than they might have otherwise "deserved." Romania's argument can be simplified thus: give us what we ask for, or else we will remain weak; then we will be destroyed, and you will suffer as a consequence.

Similar dynamics play out in business contexts as well. In one case, two companies that had signed a joint-venture (JV) agreement found themselves enmeshed in a bitter dispute when one of the companies, anxious about the other's growing presence in a market in which they competed, threatened to sue for patent infringement. The defendant knew that the case was frivolous, but also knew that the plaintiff, a much larger company, could afford to litigate until the defendant went into bankruptcy. Despite its seemingly precarious situation, the defendant managed to convince its JV partner to drop the lawsuit and to reach a mutually agreeable settlement. The defendant's argument was essentially the following: "If you take us to court, you have the power to push us into bankruptcy. Clearly, we do not want this. But let's also think about what this would mean for you: you would lose a valuable partner. It would be best for both of us if we could set aside the threat of patent litigation and see whether we can work out an agreement that allows us to continue using the disputed technology, for you to feel more secure about your market position, and for us to continue a value-creating relationship that capitalizes on our synergies."

What is the underlying principle of this strategy? If you create value for others, you gain at least some power to claim value for yourself—regardless of whether the other side wishes to reward you for what you bring to the table. In extreme cases, when they push too hard, they potentially hurt themselves. They may not recognize this, however, which is why it is worth reminding them that strength is not simply measured by "what you can force others to do" or "how easily you can make someone's life miserable"; rather, it may be better measured by "what value you can create for others." As a result, it is often useful to tell the negotiation "bully" that an overly strong show of force can be counterproductive: "If you push me too hard, you'll destroy me—and lose a value-creating partner."

STRATEGY 3: UNDERSTAND—AND ATTACK—THE SOURCE OF THEIR POWER

For many years now, Planned Parenthood medical clinics across the United States have faced a recurring problem. Every so often, anti-abortion protestors picket outside the clinics in the hope of discouraging women from entering them. The strategy seems to work quite well; many women who might otherwise visit the clinics are daunted by the prospect of passing through a large crowd that is waving signs and hurling verbal abuse. Setting aside the moral and political elements of this conflict, how might the clinics deal with the strategic problem of reducing the number of intimidating protestors?

A number of Planned Parenthood clinics around the country have adopted a particularly creative strategy for fighting back, usually referred to as the "Pledge-a-Picket" program. Here's how it works: The clinic asks its supporters to pledge donations to the clinic on a *per protestor* basis. The more protestors that show up to picket the clinic, the more money the clinic raises in donations! For example, if someone pledges 50 cents per protestor, and one hundred protestors show up at the clinic, that supporter will donate $50 to the clinic. Many clinics have used this strategy to effectively reduce the incentive of protestors to show up to picket, and some have raised tens of thousands of dollars in pledges. The Planned Parenthood of Central Texas (PPCT) in Waco has even posted a sign outside its clinic that reads: "Even Our Protesters Support Planned Parenthood."

As the Pledge-a-Picket story reveals, it is not enough that you recognize the strengths and weaknesses of each side. It is also critical that you understand the *source* of each side's strengths and weaknesses. Once the Planned Parenthood clinics understood that the source of their opponents' power was the ability to draw large numbers of protestors outside the clinic, they were able to think of a novel way of diminishing the benefits of doing so.

A student of Deepak's who owns a highly successful real-estate development company recently used this strategy to deal with a problem that will seem strange to many Americans. His company is located in a country where blatant political corruption is much more common than in the United States. In this particular case, the developer was awaiting governmental approval for a very lucrative construction project that he had signed. Everything was ready to go when, suddenly, the approval process was stopped dead in its tracks. The reason became clear days later when the developer received a phone call from the son of the powerful elected official who was in charge of signing off on the approval. The son wanted a stake in the project, and he made it clear that if the partnership were accepted, the approval would be granted quickly. The developer knew that it was possible to circumvent the son (and his father) by going through the court system and by contacting other officials with more seniority, but that process would take a long time. Unfortunately, time was of the essence; his company was about to go public, with an initial public offering (IPO) scheduled in three months. If potential investors were to discover that the project might not be approved, the company would be valued somewhat less. More problematic would be the timing of such a rumor. If the politician's son was rebuffed, he could decide to publicize the approval problems just when the company was about to go public. What to do?

Deepak advised the following strategy, which the developer executed with much success: go public immediately with the information regarding potential delays in approval. In other words, reveal to the media that the project is under way, but that its approval will probably not be finalized until some months after the company goes public. At the same time, the developer should release all of the documents related to the merits of the project, as well as the letters that the politician sent earlier in support of the project's approval. That way, investor confidence will remain high.

This strategy has at least three obvious merits. First, by getting ahead of the story, the developer controls how the news is reported and interpreted. Second, by making this information public two months before the IPO, the news itself is made less salient to investors by the time the company goes public. Third, and perhaps most important, with the news already in the press, the politician's son loses his only source of leverage. Because the son's power lies primarily in his ability to damage the developer when he is most vulnerable (during the IPO), that is the element to be targeted. As with the Pledge-a-Picket strategy, this strategy identifies and destroys the primary source of an opponent's power.

The same principle applies to negotiations of all sorts. If you are afraid to confront your powerful salesperson, or are wary of denying his request for yet another exorbitant raise, consider the source of the salesperson's power. In this case, it may be that the salesperson has stronger relationships with your customers than you do. Knowing this, how might you strategize? In the weeks and months ahead, begin building relationships with each of your key customers. You might even lock them in with attractive multiyear contracts. Then, when you stand up to your salesperson's demands, there is little with which he can threaten you. He may choose to leave the firm and go to a competitor, but his ability to take your customers with him will be significantly weakened.

THE POWER OF GENIUS

All of the strategies and insights discussed in this chapter stem from one crucial insight: while being in a position of weakness is sometimes unavoidable, you will negotiate most effectively when you leverage the fundamentals—systematic preparation and careful strategy formulation. Unfortunately, many negotiators compound the problem of weakness by becoming obsessed by the factors that make them weak. This does not mean that you should ignore your weaknesses. But, as dangerous as it is to ignore your weaknesses, it can be equally devastating to overlook your strengths or to assume you have none.

Those who "think weak" inevitably also "act weak." If you are obsessed by your weaknesses, you will be less likely to set reasonably high aspirations, to feel confident asking for more information, to demand that your concessions be reciprocated, or to push the other side to consider the value proposition you are offering. You will also be more susceptible to influence tactics and threats.

Negotiation geniuses recognize their weaknesses and try to mitigate them. Once they have done so, they know they must also focus on their strengths, prepare systematically, and negotiate with an eye toward improving their negotiating position. Doing so will not guarantee "victory," but it will ensure that you have done as well as possible given the situation. Indeed, the power of negotiation genius may be most valuable to you in precisely those situations where the alternative is to despair—or to rely on gut instinct.

CHAPTER 12

When Negotiations Get Ugly: Dealing with Irrationality, Distrust, Anger, Threats, and Ego

By most expert accounts, the Cuban Missile Crisis brought the world closer to nuclear annihilation than it has ever been—before or since. The crisis entailed an escalation of conflict between the United States and the Soviet Union that took place between October 16, 1962, and October 28, 1962. What drove two civilized nations to the brink of mutual destruction? More important, how did they manage to negotiate their way to a safe, mutually acceptable peace?

In his book *Thirteen Days*, Robert Kennedy described the events leading up to the crisis, arguably the most dangerous two weeks in all of human history.[1] The conflict was instigated when United States spy planes revealed that the Soviet Union had begun placing missiles in Cuba that would be capable of delivering nuclear weapons to the United States. Due to the close proximity of Cuba, the U.S. government became very anxious. Making matters worse, just weeks earlier, Soviet ambassador Anatoly Dobrynin had explicitly promised the Americans that no such missiles would be placed in Cuba.

In the days that followed the Americans' discovery of the missiles, the two enemies exchanged threats and counterthreats. As the conflict escalated, emotions mounted and distrust heightened. Both sides were aware that an attack by either country would lead to retaliation, and so it would be entirely irrational for either side to take any steps that could lead to war. But both sides were also aware that irrationality might prevail. As Soviet chairman Nikita Khrushchev wrote in a letter to President John F. Kennedy during the crisis, "If indeed war should break out, then it would not be in our power to stop it, for such is the logic of war."

Acutely aware that both sides were armed and ready to launch nuclear weapons, President Kennedy reflected on the growing sentiment among many of his advisers that a tough military response against Cuba was the best option. Kennedy instead chose the less aggressive option of instituting a naval blockade of Cuba, explaining to his advisers that "the great danger and risk in all of this is a miscalculation—a mistake in judgment." More belligerent actions, Kennedy argued, would likely drive the conflict to a point of no return: "It isn't the first step that concerns me, but both sides escalating to the fourth and fifth step—and we don't go to the sixth because there is no one around to do so." According to Robert Kennedy, "the President believed from the start that the Soviet Chairman was a rational, intelligent man who, if given sufficient time and shown our determination, would alter his position. But there was always the chance of error, of mistake, miscalculation, or misunderstanding, and President Kennedy was committed to doing everything possible to lessen that chance on our side."

But clear communication and rigorous analysis would not be sufficient to resolve the crisis. There was also the matter of personal egos and national pride. The entire world was watching, and neither Kennedy nor Khrushchev could afford to be seen as weak by his citizens, political opponents, media analysts, or the international community at large. Robert Kennedy recalled a discussion that took place between the president and his advisers one evening: "Neither side wanted war over Cuba, we agreed, but it was possible that either side could take a step that—for reasons of 'security' or 'pride' or 'face'—would require a response by the other side, which, in turn, for the same reasons of security, pride, or face, would bring about a counter-response and eventually an escalation into armed conflict."

There was every reason for the situation to spiral entirely out of control. How, then, were the two sides able to negotiate a peaceful settlement? According to Robert Kennedy, it was the negotiation genius of his brother, President John F. Kennedy, that saved the world from nuclear war: President Kennedy made it his top priority to understand as well as possible the interests, needs, constraints, and perspective of the other side. "The final lesson of the Cuban missile crisis," wrote Robert Kennedy, "is the importance of placing ourselves in the other country's shoes. During the crisis, President Kennedy spent more time trying to determine the effect of a particular course of action on Khrushchev or the Russians than on any other phase of what he was doing. What guided all of his deliberations was an effort not to disgrace Khrushchev, not to humiliate the Soviet Union, not to have them feel they would have to escalate their response because their national security or national interests so committed them."

The final deal, negotiated heavily through back channels in an effort to help the parties save face, was this: the Soviet Union would remove the missiles from Cuba; in return, the United States would pledge not to invade Cuba and to remove American missiles from Turkey (which were seen as a threat by the Soviet Union). Out of a concern for how this latter concession would be judged by the public, Robert Kennedy insisted to Soviet ambassador Dobrynin that the removal of missiles from Turkey could not be seen as a quid-pro-quo concession for the removal of missiles from Cuba. As a result, this element of the deal was not made public for years.

In retrospect, the outcome of this crisis seems unremarkable: both parties removed their offending missiles and the conflict deescalated. But it is worth asking: what would have happened if President Kennedy, instead of focusing so intently on Khrushchev's needs and interests, had instead listened to his military advisers, most of whom strongly supported air strikes against Cuba rather than the less aggressive blockade option? Consider the following. During the Cuban Missile Crisis, U.S. intelligence reports concluded that while Cuba had missiles capable of *carrying* nuclear warheads, it had no actual nuclear warheads. It was only years later that the truth—previously known only to the Cubans and the Soviet Union—was made public: at the time of the crisis, Cuba had enough nuclear warheads to obliterate the eastern seaboard of the United States—and they had the authority and intent to use these warheads if they were attacked. In other words, the unremarkable outcome of the Cuban Missile Crisis was by no means assured. If, instead of negotiating with his enemy, President Kennedy had chosen to act tough, flex U.S. military muscle, and follow the advice of his top brass, his decisions would have resulted in the deaths of tens of millions of Americans.

Throughout this book, we have encouraged you to try to understand the interests, needs, constraints, and concerns of the other side and to work with your counterparts to create value. But what happens when this seems virtually impossible? What happens when your counterpart is your "enemy," unwilling or unable to work with you to reach a mutually agreeable outcome? It is worth remembering at such moments that President Kennedy confronted, simultaneously, the very worst of what is possible when negotiations turn ugly—irrationality, distrust, anger, threats, and ego—and succeeded nonetheless. Here we will consider each of these five factors and, in doing so, provide you with a set of principles and strategies that you can leverage when your own negotiations turn ugly.

DEALING WITH IRRATIONALITY

"All of the strategies you have described work when you're dealing with people who will listen to reason," an exasperated executive student remarked recently. "But the people I deal with are completely irrational. How can you possibly negotiate with someone who is irrational?" As the executive's question reveals, negotiators often struggle with the task of trying to negotiate with those who behave recklessly, strategize poorly, and act in ways that seem to contradict their own self-interest; any would-be negotiation genius needs to understand how to deal with these obstacles.

Our advice is this: be *very* careful before labeling someone "irrational." Whenever our students or clients tell us about their "irrational" or "crazy" counterparts, we work with them to carefully consider whether the other side is truly irrational. Almost always, the answer is *no*. In most cases, behavior that appears to be irrational has a rational—albeit hidden—cause. Here, we will share the three most common reasons that negotiators erroneously judge others as irrational.[2] We will also describe the dangers of doing so and explain how to avoid making such mistakes.

MISTAKE 1: THEY ARE NOT IRRATIONAL; THEY ARE UNINFORMED

An executive (who is one of Deepak's students) was recently involved in a dispute with an ex-employee. The employee claimed that he was owed $130,000 in sales commissions for the work he had done prior to being fired from the firm a few months earlier. The executive, on the other hand, claimed the employee was owed nothing—in fact, he insisted the employee had been overpaid by $25,000.

What was the reason for this discrepancy? At the time the employee was fired, the company's accounts were a mess; records had been kept poorly. Since then, the firm had hired a new accountant and updated all of the records. These records now clearly revealed that the employee's claim was entirely illegitimate; if anyone had a claim to make, it was the firm. The executive was uninterested in going to court to recoup the $25,000 that the firm was owed and wanted to drop the matter entirely.

The executive called the employee and told him what the accounting records revealed; he also offered to send a copy of the records. He then made it clear that his case was airtight, but offered to forgive the $25,000 overpayment if the employee agreed to forgo his groundless suit as well. The employee's response: "No way. I don't need to see the records. I'll see you in court!"

The CEO was very confused. There was no way for the employee to win in court. Why was he behaving so irrationally?

Deepak suggested to the executive that the problem was probably not that the employee was irrational, but that he lacked credible information. The executive was convinced that the employee would lose the court battle, but it was possible that the employee was still confident that he would win the case because he did not trust the executive or the firm's record keeping. How could the executive educate the employee regarding his prospects for winning in court? Deepak advised him to have an objective third party, specifically a professional accounting firm, conduct an audit of the records pertinent to this dispute and to mail the results to the employee. (This would be far less expensive than going to court.) Having this information would diminish the employee's perceived likelihood of winning in court and make litigation a less attractive option. What was the result? The employee dropped the suit.

When Deepak was in graduate school, an economics professor began the first day of class with the following statement: "I want you all to remember something—you are not stupid, you are just ignorant. If you were stupid, we could not do much about it. But ignorance we can fix." This insight is as relevant to negotiators as it is to graduate students. Often, when the other side appears irrational, they are in fact uninformed. If you can help educate or inform them—about their true interests, the consequences of their actions, the strength of your BATNA, and so on—there is a strong likelihood they will make better decisions. For example, if someone says no to an offer that you know is in her best interest, do not assume she is irrational. Instead, work to ensure that she understands *why* the offer is in her best interest. She may simply have misunderstood or ignored a crucial piece of information.

MISTAKE 2: THEY ARE NOT IRRATIONAL; THEY HAVE HIDDEN CONSTRAINTS

In 2005, the U.S. government passed legislation to increase food aid to countries that were in dire need of such assistance. There was much support among politicians and activists for this initiative. Not surprisingly, however, there were also certain special-interest groups that opposed this legislation. Here's what *was* surprising: one of the groups that voiced opposition was a consortium of nonprofit organizations whose mission it was to lobby for an increase in food aid to disadvantaged countries! What explains such seemingly irrational and self-defeating behavior? Why would this group oppose legislation that achieves precisely what it purports to want?

The answer lies not in understanding the group's interests, but in understanding its constraints. In order to increase the amount of food sent to disadvantaged countries, the consortium had in the past partnered with American farmers to lobby the U.S. government jointly for greater aid. Why did the farmers join in this campaign? Because when the U.S. government increased food aid, it bought more food from American farmers. As a result, both the farmers and the nonprofits got what they wanted.

This case, however, was different. Mindful of escalating budget deficits, Congress had decided that the only way to increase foreign food aid was to purchase the food more cheaply—not from American farmers, but from developing countries. What would appear to be a double win for the nonprofits (increased food aid *and* increased support for poor farmers in developing countries) instead created a predicament. If the nonprofits supported the legislation, they would be severing ties with their longstanding coalition partner, the American farmer. Instead, the nonprofits decided that their long-term interests were best served by opposing the legislation. This may still seem like a questionable decision on moral, ethical, or other grounds, but it seems irrational only when we overlook the hidden constraints facing the nonprofits.

The problem of hidden constraints is present in many negotiations. When a firm loses a star employee because it refuses to raise her salary to match a competitor's higher offer, the firm is not necessarily behaving irrationally; it may instead be constrained by an HR policy that restricts it from creating huge pay differentials in the firm.

Similarly, when your counterpart seems unwilling to make even small, reasonable concessions that could seal the deal, you might tell yourself he's a fool, or you might try to discover how much authority he has to negotiate a comprehensive, value-maximizing deal. If he is heavily constrained, you might try to negotiate with someone who has greater dealmaking authority.

In negotiation, a wide variety of possible constraints exists. The other side may be constrained by advice from her lawyers, by the fear of setting a dangerous precedent, by promises she has made to other parties, by time pressure, and so on. Negotiation geniuses try to discover these constraints—and to help other parties overcome them—rather than dismissing others as irrational.

MISTAKE 3: THEY ARE NOT IRRATIONAL; THEY HAVE HIDDEN INTERESTS

Some years ago, a group of managers decided to promote Leslie, one of the firm's administrative assistants. Leslie had worked for the firm for thirty years and was only two years away from retirement. She had performed well throughout her career and had received salary increases commensurate with her performance. Because she was already at the top of her salary bracket, it was not possible for the managers to pay her more money; nor was she scheduled for a formal performance appraisal. Rather, the managers simply wanted to do something nice for Leslie, so they decided to surprise her with a promotion. Her job responsibilities would not change, but the new title would give her greater status and prestige.

When she heard of the promotion, Leslie was delighted. She understood that her salary or job responsibilities would not increase, but that was fine with her.

Soon after receiving the promotion, however, Leslie learned that she was now among the lowest-paid employees with her job title. She also began to feel uneasy about having a "fake" job promotion—she was doing no more work and receiving no more pay than she used to, and this made her feel self-conscious with her coworkers. She asked for a raise and voiced her willingness to accept more responsibilities, but was quickly denied.

Within a few weeks of her promotion, Leslie decided that she would rather quit her job than be treated this poorly. By doing so, she lost two years of compensation and also took a hit in her retirement benefits. The managers, who had only the best of intentions, were left asking themselves, "Why did she behave so irrationally?"

What the managers failed to appreciate was that money and status were not the only issues of interest to Leslie. She also cared about perceptions of fairness and equity. The managers felt they had given her more than she even deserved. But in failing to see how their decision would play out in the future, they created a situation in which Leslie felt undervalued, phony, and embarrassed.

More generally, people will sometimes reject your offer because they think it is unfair, because they don't like you, or for other reasons that have nothing to do with the obvious merits of your proposal. These people are not irrational; they are simply fulfilling needs and interests that you may not fully appreciate. When others appear irrational, negotiation geniuses do not write them off as crazy. Instead, they investigate: "What might be motivating her to act this way? What are all of her interests?"

BUT WHAT IF THEY REALLY *ARE* IRRATIONAL?

If your counterpart truly is irrational—in other words, he is determined to work against what is in his best interest—then your options will be fewer. You can try to push through an agreement despite his irrationality, you can try to "go around him" by negotiating with someone else with authority who seems more willing to listen to reason (such as his boss or colleague), or you may decide to pursue your BATNA because his irrationality has eliminated all hope of creating value. You might also leverage the various strategies for confronting your counterpart's biases that we have outlined in Chapters 4-6.

But we suggest—again—that you reconsider your assessment. Negotiators who are quick to label the other party "irrational" do so at great potential cost to themselves. When you use the "irrational" label, you limit *your* options, because there is not much you can say to someone who you truly believe is unable to reason, uninterested in fulfilling her own interests, and incapable of negotiating effectively. Your options greatly increase when you recognize that the other party is not irrational, but simply uninformed, constrained, or focused on interests that you did not anticipate. And as you know, the more options you have, the more effectively you will negotiate.

DEALING WITH DISTRUST

Some years ago, a dispute arose between a U.S. manufacturer of electronic equipment and one of its foreign distributors. Each side felt that the other had reneged on its responsibilities, and both were ready to go to court to settle the matter. Not surprisingly, the two sides had very different perspectives regarding what had gone wrong.

The manufacturer claimed that the distributor had failed to meet its minimum purchase-order requirement for a key product and that the distributor did not have enough distribution channels in place to fulfill its contractual responsibilities. The manufacturer simply wanted to be paid for the equipment it had already delivered and to terminate its agreement with the distributor. The manufacturer claimed that it could no longer trust the distributor and wanted nothing more than to end their relationship.

Meanwhile, the distributor claimed that, within months of signing their agreement, the manufacturer had introduced a new and improved model of the same product and had refused to offer the distributor rights to sell it. By all indications, the distributor claimed, the entire agreement had been a scheme to dump old, obsolete models in the distributor's region. In doing so, the manufacturer had defrauded the distributor. The distributor was demanding millions of dollars in reparation. It, too, felt that the breach of trust was so severe that there was no way to revive the relationship.

As it turns out, the story has a happy ending. The two sides opted for mediation rather than litigation. With the mediator's assistance, they were able to reach an agreement that pleased both sides and that avoided a lengthy court battle.

What was the agreement? Instead of ending their relationship and deciding which party would pay the other for a breach of contract, the two sides agreed to continue their relationship with a restructuring of their existing agreement. The manufacturer agreed to give the distributor the right to distribute the new equipment (including the *exclusive* right to distribute in some parts of the region), and both sides dropped their financial claims.

When we present this case to our executive students, many of them are surprised that either of the two parties would be willing to agree to such a deal. The most important element of any relationship is trust, these executives argue; because the two sides had lost trust in each other, it was unwise to negotiate a continuance of the relationship. When we ask the executives to elaborate on this perspective, they often make one or more of the following statements:

- "If there is no trust, you will get nothing done."
- "Why do a deal with someone you don't trust? It's not worth the risk."
- "If they've exploited your trust before, they will do it again."

We agree with the sentiment captured in each of these statements: indeed, trust is essential in relationships; hence, it is a critical ingredient in negotiation. But we disagree with the belief that trust cannot be regained. More fundamentally, we disagree with the belief that you should end a negotiation (or terminate a relationship) the moment you think that the other side is untrustworthy. Negotiation geniuses consider distrust to be a major obstacle to negotiation. But before they abandon hope of regaining the trust that has been lost, they work to rebuild it.

The first step in rebuilding trust is to diagnose the distrust that exists. Negotiators often think of trust as one-dimensional: either your counterpart is "trustworthy" or she is not. But consider that there are many different kinds of trust.[3] For example, you will trust your surgeon primarily on the basis of whether he or she has the competence to perform a surgery on you, but you will trust your spouse more on the basis of whether he or she is honest with you. Similarly, there are many dimensions along which we might trust our business partners, lawyers, employees, children, friends, and so on. It is also the case that we can trust someone on one dimension ("my lawyer is very competent") but not on another ("my lawyer is sometimes dishonest"). When this happens, you must decide which dimension of trust is most critical to the relationship. If someone cannot be trusted on the critical dimension, you must either fix the trust problem or consider your alternatives to dealing with her.

Two broad categories of distrust are relevant to many negotiations: distrust of another's *character* and distrust of another's *competence*.[4] Consider that, in the manufacturer-distributor dispute, both sides distrusted each other—but for different reasons. The manufacturer believed that the distributor was incompetent: it did not have the infrastructure or know-how to sell the equipment it was licensed to distribute. Meanwhile, the distributor's distrust was more an issue of character: only a dishonest and unethical company would dump outdated equipment in his region and hide information regarding newer models during the initial negotiation.

Once you have diagnosed the source of distrust, you can identify the steps needed to regain it. How might the distributor and the manufacturer regain trust in each other? Because each side is dealing with a different type of distrust, the process will be different for each of them. In the case of the distributor, its management must demonstrate to the manufacturer that their company is in fact competent. How might they do this? They might invite the manufacturer to visit their region to see the distribution channels firsthand, they might show purchase-order data that confirm their ability to achieve high sales, or they might provide reasonable justifications as to why their initial order did not meet the minimum purchasing agreement.

Meanwhile, to gain the trust of the distributor, the manufacturer's management must demonstrate that they are honest and ethical. They might do this by explaining to the distributor that it is common practice in the United States not to reveal information regarding products in development—though they now understand that this practice may be viewed negatively in some other countries. The manufacturer might also offer to extend a peace offering (in the form of financial or other considerations) as an apology for unintended wrongdoing. Finally, the manufacturer's decision to allow the distributor to sell the new product may in itself help overcome the perception that the manufacturer intended to exploit the distributor all along.

If the two sides in this negotiation—or in any negotiation—are able to identify and eliminate the source of distrust, trust can clearly be rebuilt. Unfortunately, negotiators are often dismissive of this possibility. Instead, once they have labeled the other party "untrustworthy," they look only for information that confirms this belief. Moreover, when they are themselves distrusted, they often become defensive or angry rather than focused on trying to systematically eliminate this perception. Negotiation geniuses understand that when the other side says (or implies) that you are untrustworthy, it is time to investigate: "Why does he think so? What would it take to overcome this perception?"

DEALING WITH ANGER

A few years ago, Deepak was shooting pool at a bar with a friend and two strangers. Suddenly, a group of about eight college students stormed into the room. They threw a pool stick onto the table, disrupting the game, and started to scream and curse. Needless to say, Deepak and his friend were taken aback. The two strangers who were playing with them immediately charged at the leader of the gang of students. In a matter of seconds, the friendly game of eight ball had become a shoving match. A fight was about to break out—and it was not at all clear why.

Trying to stop the fight, Deepak and his friend wedged themselves between the two main combatants. It soon became obvious that the college students were upset because they believed that, moments earlier, someone at Deepak's table had disrupted *their* game in the adjacent room. Deepak knew this was not true, but the accusation only fueled the rage on both sides. Deepak and his friend wanted to clear up the misunderstanding, but the situation was getting more physical by the moment. It would have been quite easy for Deepak and his friend to simply walk away—by now, the fight was entirely between the college students and the two strangers—but that did not seem like the right thing to do.

Once it became clear that the provocateurs were unwilling to consider the situation a misunderstanding, Deepak tried a different approach. "Okay," he said to the leader of the college students. "We understand that you think someone 'messed with you.' But what do you think needs to happen now to avoid a fight?"

The leader looked at Deepak just long enough to answer. "I don't know, but you guys messed up our game, so it's a bit late to apologize," he said before rejoining the fray.

Deepak decided to try again: "Okay, but now you've messed up our game as well—so aren't we even?"

"No, we're not *even*," the student shouted. "You started it!"

"I see. Well, let's say someone in this room did start something," Deepak said. "Can you imagine something that could happen now that would make you prefer not to fight? What would that look like? What would you rather be doing?"

The leader was in disbelief, but took a moment to consider the question. "Well, I'd rather be playing pool," he answered, "but we're going to have to start a whole new game."

"And how much will that cost?" asked Deepak.

"One dollar," the student responded.

Deepak took a dollar bill out of his wallet and handed it to the leader. "How about it? Your next game is on me."

The leader smiled as he slowly reached for the dollar. "You know, that's very cool," he said. "That's really very nice of you." He spent the next few minutes calming down his friends, and then escorted them out of the room. The fight was avoided, no blood was spilled, and no bones were broken. All it took was one dollar.

As this story shows, negotiators often confront counterparts who are angry or upset. And while we may think that these emotions are entirely unjustified, this does not change the fact that the angry party thinks that his or her anger is warranted.

How do you typically handle such situations? While another person's anger may evoke your own, many of us recognize that this is not the most effective response to someone's emotional outburst. Instead, there is obvious merit in trying to defuse the other side's anger and refocus attention on the substantive issues at hand. But defusing someone's anger is often easier said than done. Most negotiators do not have a systematic way to deal with the anger of those with whom they are negotiating. Furthermore, seemingly unjustified anger often erupts when you least expect it. What should you do when this happens? The following strategies will enhance your ability to handle angry negotiators in ways that salvage the deal and the relationship.

STRATEGY 1: SEEK TO UNDERSTAND WHY THEY ARE ANGRY

When your negotiation counterpart is angry, you must first find out why. The answer will point you toward an appropriate strategy for handling the situation. For example, if the other party is angry because she is misinformed, the solution is to inform her; if she is angry because she feels disrespected, the solution is to respect her; if she is angry because she misheard what you said, the solution is to clarify your intentions, and so on. Just because *you* know that your counterpart has no reason to be upset does not mean that *she* knows this. In the pool hall dispute, for example, the students' anger was explicable (although it was still an overreaction) once they made clear that they *thought* they had been attacked first. Consistent with the approach we have underscored throughout this book, the best way to deal with emotions you do not fully understand is to investigate their source.

STRATEGY 2: GIVE VOICE TO THEIR ANGER

Most negotiators recognize that anger is usually counterproductive. As a result, when dealing with someone who has lost his temper, most negotiators are likely to do whatever they can to suppress his expression of anger. "Getting angry will get us nowhere," you might be tempted to say, or, "We're not going to sit here and listen to you shout," or, "It's in everyone's best interest if you calm down."

These are all reasonable statements, but they overlook an important fact. If you do not give an angry negotiator the opportunity to voice his frustration, he will likely become even more angry—or, at the very least, resentful. A much better approach is to encourage people to voice their anger and to help you understand its source. You might say, for example, "I can see that you're angry, and I want to understand why that is. Tell me what's on your mind." The key is to give legitimacy to the other person's feelings. You can (and should) question the legitimacy of what he believes, but you should not waste time questioning the legitimacy of a person's anger *given* what he believes to be true.

STRATEGY 3: SIDESTEP THE EMOTION

Some years ago, Deepak's martial arts instructor gave him some important advice regarding how to block a kick or a punch: "The best block is *don't be there.*" In other words, when you try to stop someone's physical attack with your own physical maneuver (a block), you are pitting power against power—and the stronger party will have an advantage. But if you can sidestep the attack, you will avoid the hit, retain your balance, and remain in control of the situation.

The same is true when it comes to emotion in negotiation. When the other side is angry, do not allow yourself to be the target by taking it personally. Instead, understand that her anger is a natural consequence of her beliefs. If she believed differently, she would not be angry. The best thing for you to do, then, is to keep your composure and help her change her beliefs. Sidestepping emotions is certainly not easy—especially when the other side is launching personal attacks and seems intent on provoking a response. To aid in sidestepping the emotion, ask yourself the following questions:

- If I were in her position, would I be acting the same way?
- Is this genuine emotion, or is it a tactic aimed at intimidating me?
- Is this how she behaves with everybody?

If you can conclude that their anger is natural given where they stand, or that they are simply acting tough to manipulate you, or that this is how they treat everyone, you will find it easier to sidestep the attack and maintain control of your own emotions.

STRATEGY 4: HELP THEM FOCUS ON THEIR TRUE UNDERLYING INTERESTS

The most difficult part of Deepak's pool hall negotiation was not figuring out the other party's underlying interests (which were to play pool and not lose face). Rather, it was making the other party's underlying interests salient to *them*. Anger prevents people from staying focused on the substantive issues about which they care deeply. Your task is to help the angry negotiator shift attention away from those elements that fueled his anger and toward those elements that would fulfill his interests. Try asking questions such as these:

- "What would you like to see happen now?"
- "What would you rather be doing?"
- "What would help us put this behind us?"
- "Is there anything else you would like to discuss or clarify before we return to the substantive issues you highlighted earlier?"

All of these questions facilitate a transition away from anger and toward interests.

DEALING WITH THREATS
AND ULTIMATUMS

Deepak has a client, the CEO of a large agricultural firm, who was recently negotiating with a large commercial bank for a multimillion-dollar line of credit. Because the CEO had personal connections with a director at the bank, he did not bother to procure competing bids from other banks. After months of negotiations, the deal was structured and both sides were ready to sign the agreement. Before this could happen, however, the CEO discovered during a conversation with an industry expert that the bank was charging his company a risk-adjusted rate that was significantly higher than what other banks would have charged. The CEO was both surprised and upset. Had his "friend" at the bank taken advantage of him? Even if this was the case, it was not clear whether the CEO could threaten to go to the bank's competitors; this option had been viable some months ago, but now the company needed the line of credit very soon. Restarting the entire negotiation process with another bank could be extremely costly.

The CEO called the bank director, shared what he had learned, and proposed a revision of the terms of the agreement. Upon hearing the CEO's proposed revision, the director became very angry. In particular, he was "very turned off" by the suggestion that the CEO wanted to "renege" on their verbal agreement. In a long e-mail that followed the conversation, the director began by writing: "My flexibility on pricing is none." If this was unacceptable to the CEO, he continued, then they "should have serious discussions" regarding the types of proprietary information the CEO was barred from sharing with the bank's competitors. The threat was implicit, but clear: "We cannot move on this issue. You are welcome to go to our competitors."

The CEO approached Deepak for advice on how to respond to the director's e-mail. He had a variety of questions: Was this a "true ultimatum" or simply a negotiation "tactic"? Should he continue to push for a better pricing structure, or should he instead ask for smaller concessions on other, less thorny issues? Should he be forceful or pleasant? Should he continue to appear upset, or should he appear calm and in control? Deepak's advice, described below, leveraged three strategies for dealing with threats and ultimatums in negotiation.

STRATEGY 1: IGNORE THE THREAT

Deepak began by advising the CEO to completely ignore the ultimatum ("My flexibility on pricing is none")—to pretend that this statement had never been made. Instead, the CEO should respond to the less harshly written, more substantive elements of the e-mail, which referred to "reliance on market rates," "competitive pricing," and "structuring fees that reflect the market standard." Specifically, he told the CEO to *thank* the director for agreeing to think about the deal from the perspective of what is consistent with prevailing market rates—and to make no mention of the director's alleged inflexibility on pricing. Why? If the director issued the ultimatum out of frustration, ignorance, or the desire to save face, the worst thing for the CEO to do would be to draw attention to the ultimatum and make it more difficult for the director to back away from his statement in the future. It would be much better to ignore the ultimatum and give the director space to retreat from it in the ensuing days and weeks. It is worth pointing out that this advice is sound even if the ultimatum *is* real—that is, even if the other side is truly unwilling or unable to offer you any more concessions. If this is the case, and you have ignored their ultimatum, rest assured that they will mention it to you again.

President Kennedy used a similar strategy during the Cuban Missile Crisis. During the height of the crisis, he received two different (and somewhat contradictory) messages from Khrushchev within the span of twenty-four hours. One of them (the "hard" message) was very aggressive; in it, Khrushchev demanded the removal of U.S. missiles from Turkey in exchange for the removal of Soviet missiles from Cuba. In the "soft" message, which was much less antagonistic, Khrushchev offered to remove the missiles from Cuba in exchange for the United States ending the blockade and promising that there would be no attack on Cuba. As Kennedy's advisers discussed how to craft a response that would address all of the issues contained in both messages, Robert Kennedy suggested a different approach: ignore the hard message. Robert Kennedy was among those who believed that the hard message (which was the only one that was sent publicly) was designed more to help Khrushchev save face in the world community than it was to promote substantive discussions. Ignoring the hard message—whose terms the U.S. government could not immediately accept—and instead agreeing to the terms of the soft message, Robert Kennedy argued, would be a much more productive strategy.

More generally, it is possible to ignore the other side's ultimatum even when it includes no soft message. Consider the following ultimatum: "This is our final offer: take it or leave it." How might you respond to this statement while still ignoring the ultimatum? Consider the following viable responses:

- "It seems pretty clear that you find it difficult to make further concessions on the issues we've been discussing. I suggest we focus on other aspects of the deal and come back to this point once all other elements are on the table."
- "I can see that you fully believe that you have already conceded as much as should be necessary to close the deal. As it turns out, we feel the exact same way regarding our concessions. Hopefully, this means that we *are* close to reaching an agreement. So let's keep working."
- "I can understand your frustration. We both know there is a deal to be made, and yet we can't seem to find it. Can you help me better understand your perspective? Why do you think we're not there yet?"

Notice that each of these responses ignores the "take it or leave it" demand. Instead, the responses are aimed at softening the other side's statement so that it will not be a barrier in the future if, in fact, it is possible for them to make further concessions.

STRATEGY 2: NEUTRALIZE ANY ADDITIONAL THREATS THEY MIGHT BE TEMPTED TO MAKE

Returning to the bank negotiation story, Deepak next advised the CEO to pre-empt (to the extent possible) any additional threats the director might be tempted to make. He did so by helping the CEO anticipate the threats and counterarguments that his draft e-mail reply would generate, and then encouraged him to respond comprehensively to these potential reactions. For example, one potential response by the director would be to threaten (implicitly) to drag out the negotiations, knowing that the prospect of lengthy discussions would likely force the CEO to capitulate. Anticipating this, Deepak advised the CEO to include the following text in the e-mail: "We understand that these new issues may cause delays in structuring and implementing a final agreement. If you also anticipate such delays, we suggest involving other senior bank officials in this process from the very start." Why might this statement neutralize the director's potential threat? Because the CEO knew that the involvement of senior bank officials would make the director lose credibility at his bank, a consequence he would be highly motivated to avoid.

Pre-empting the other side's aggression is also a useful tactic when you are dealing not with threats, but with their legitimate complaints or concerns. For example, the director may have been genuinely concerned that having to restructure the deal at this late stage in the negotiation would cause him embarrassment, as he would be forced to tell his boss that the deal would bring in less money than he had earlier announced. In such instances, you can make your own position stronger if you are able to voice the other side's legitimate complaints or concerns for them, rather than waiting for them to raise these issues. For example, you might say: "We understand that corporate politics and other institutional hurdles sometimes make it difficult to make even reasonable changes to a deal this late in the game. But we would like to work with you to figure out ways to make this happen. We also feel—and hope that you agree—that the most important issue continues to be reaching an agreement that is consistent with prevailing market rates." When you are the first to voice *their* concerns, you lessen the degree of antagonism with which they can argue against you. They may still fight back, but they will be in no position to suggest that you are concerned only about yourself, or that you don't understand their perspective.

STRATEGY 3: IF YOU DON'T FIND THE THREAT TO BE CREDIBLE, LET THEM KNOW

If the director's threat had been credible—if he would have truly preferred "no deal" to a change in pricing—then the CEO would have had little room to maneuver. Often, however, a threat is not credible—you know they will not follow through on it—but it is still impossible to entirely ignore or pre-empt it. How should you respond? In as positive a tone as possible, signal to the other side that, because you understand *their* constraints and *their* interests, you don't find the threat to be credible. Consider, for example, how the CEO could have responded to the bank director's threat to walk away from the deal:

Signal 1: Your constraints will not allow you to follow through on this threat: "Finally, with regard to the interest rate: we feel comfortable in knowing that you will, as always, follow your bank's policy of pricing risk according to market standards. This gives us confidence that, as you run the numbers and look at the data, you will find ways to lower the rate you have quoted. As you've mentioned in the past, this is one of the benefits of working with a large bank like yours: at the end of the day, we don't have to argue about what is fair—we can all take a look at the market."

Signal 2: Your interests will not allow you to follow through on this threat: "It is obvious that there are some discrepancies on how we are calculating risk in this case. But we know that, like us, you have been working on this deal for many months now and will not want to see it unravel over one issue. So let's work on resolving this in a way that is agreeable to all parties involved."

Both of these responses are friendly and gracious, but both make it clear to the director that you do not perceive his threat (whether veiled or explicit) to be credible.

DEALING WITH THE NEED TO SAVE FACE

When you have exposed the fact that the other side's threat is not credible, that their anger is baseless, or that their lack of trust in you is unfounded, you have every reason to celebrate: you were right and they were wrong. But you are not in the clear yet. Unless the other side is able to save face—that is, to avoid embarrassment or humiliation—they may be very reluctant to change their perspective or their behavior. Instead, they may act in ways that help them preserve their dignity or salvage their ego, but that destroy value.

Negotiation geniuses will not only give their counterparts the opportunity to save face, they will *help* them to save face. "Above all, while defending our own vital interests," President Kennedy said in a speech at American University soon after the Cuban Missile Crisis, "nuclear powers must avert those confrontations which bring an adversary to the choice of either a humiliating defeat or a nuclear war."[5] In your negotiations, the stakes will not be nearly as high. But if President Kennedy was worried that someone would enter a nuclear war to avoid humiliation, consider how much more likely it is that someone will walk away from thousands or millions of dollars in order to save face.

Suppose you are negotiating the purchase of a product or service, and the seller tells you: "There's no way for us to lower our price—this is our final offer." Later, it becomes clear to both of you that she will have to lower her price in order for you to make the purchase. Here are some ways to help this counterpart save face:

- "I'm glad I was able to find ways to compensate you for a lower price, because I know you could not have lowered it otherwise."
- "I realize that you are doing me a favor by reducing the price beyond what is normally possible, and I greatly appreciate it."
- "We're fortunate that we were able to get past the discussion of price, in which you had already conceded all you could. Instead, we were able to focus on creating a package deal that pleased us both."

Each of these responses reduces the likelihood that the other side will stick to her ultimatum, because each gives her a legitimate, face-saving way to frame her decision to change course. Often, your counterparts will find their own way to justify backing away from their original claims; if they can't, it helps if you can give them a story to tell themselves—and to others who might question their decision to back down. It is worth pointing out, however, that each of these responses would be less necessary if, from the start, you had followed the strategy of ignoring their ultimatum altogether.

It is also worth keeping in mind that it's not only your counterpart who has a strong need to save face. You are just as likely to sabotage your self-interest when pursuing it would make you lose face. So when you're involved in a disagreement or dispute, don't place your ego on the line. This means refraining from making empty threats or ultimatums. It also means carefully thinking through the implications of calling someone a liar, lashing out in anger, or staking a firm claim on a position that you may one day have to abandon. Negotiation geniuses avoid these behaviors and instead focus on alternatives that serve the same purpose, but that entail less risk. Instead of calling someone a liar, ask him to substantiate his claims. Instead of lashing out in anger, tell your counterpart why you are upset. And instead of swearing that you will never back off from a particular position, anchor aggressively and provide a justification for the anchor.

WHAT LOOKS GOOD VERSUS WHAT WORKS WELL

Many of the strategies and tactics we have presented for dealing with tough negotiation situations are not the kind you would see in a Hollywood movie. In a movie (and, regrettably, in some negotiation texts), the protagonist fights fire with fire, slams his fist on the table, and doesn't back down from a fight. These tactics look good on the big screen, but most of them do not work well in practice. Negotiation geniuses approach "ugly" negotiations the same way that they approach "beautiful" ones—with an investigative approach that focuses on each side's underlying interests. We will end with another sage quote from Deepak's martial arts instructor: "If you're in danger, don't throw a spinning back-kick to their face. Instead, attack their kneecap. The kick to the face looks good, but the kick to the knee will save your life." The same principle applies here: save the histrionics for the stage, and bring your negotiation genius to the bargaining table.

CHAPTER 13

When *Not* to Negotiate

This story takes place on April 1, 2005—yes, on April Fool's Day—but as strange as it may seem, this tale is entirely factual. It started with a Harvard economics professor who wanted to procure some manure (yes, you read that correctly). For years, this professor (who is *not* one of the authors) had been driving to a piece of farmland located about ten miles from his million-dollar home, shoveling manure into his truck, and carting it back to use in his garden. Of course, taking something from someone else's property without their knowledge and without payment is illegal—even when the thing you're taking is manure. There is some evidence to suggest that the professor was unaware that he had been breaking the law for all these years. Nonetheless, it was very clear to him on that night, April 1, 2005, that he was in big trouble. One of the farmhands spotted the professor as he tried to exit the property with the manure in his truck and promptly blocked the professor's path with his own truck. The farmhand, who was also the nephew of the property owner, was clearly upset. The farmhand threatened to call the police, and the professor had to think fast. He had two clear options: he could rely on his people skills (apologize, plead ignorance, promise to make amends, et cetera), or he could rely on his training as an economist. He chose to do the latter.

Valuing the manure in his truck at no more than $20, the professor offered the farmhand $20. The farmhand became more upset. Believing he had just offered the farmhand more than his reservation value, the professor was probably surprised; nonetheless he upped his offer to $40. In response, the farmhand called the police. The professor was charged with trespassing, larceny, and malicious destruction of property (yes, we are still talking about manure). But these charges would soon become the least of the professor's concerns. Once news of the event became public, it spread quickly through local, national, and international media channels. Even Jay Leno joked about the Harvard professor's misadventure in his *Tonight Show* monologue.

Where did the professor go wrong? Obviously, he erred in not recognizing that he was stealing the manure. Even worse, he overlooked all of the signs that he was not in a position to negotiate his way out of trouble. Had the professor considered how weak his BATNA was ("If there is no deal, I will face legal hassles and public ridicule") and how strong the farmhand's BATNA was ("If there is no deal, he will call the police"), he might have decided not to try to haggle. Furthermore, seeing how upset the farmhand was, the professor might have realized that his "negotiation" might appear to be a bribe and only fuel the fire. Finally, even after deciding that a monetary offering would help settle the matter, why would the professor offer so little? Given the stakes, the strength of the farmhand's BATNA, and his heightened emotions, a much better approach would have been to apologize, plead ignorance, and *ask the farmhand* what it might take to make amends for the unfortunate situation. Instead, the professor decided to negotiate—and that's when the manure really hit the fan.

This book is designed to help you improve your negotiation skills and give you the tools you need to achieve better outcomes for yourself and for the people you care about. Though titled "When *Not* to Negotiate," even this chapter is aimed at expanding your negotiation ability, because one critical aspect of expertise in any domain is recognizing your limits. Upon reading this book, you may be tempted to start trying out your newfound negotiation skills everywhere—all the time and on everyone—to see if you can get others to do what you want.

Our advice: slow down. Recognize that the "softer" aspects of what you have learned (listening, understanding, empathizing, and so on) are some of the most widely applicable tools you can leverage, especially in sensitive situations where adrenaline-driven tactics might only make matters worse. Becoming a negotiation genius is a matter of not only knowing *how* to negotiate, but also knowing *when* to negotiate.

Specifically, negotiation may not be the best option: when the costs of negotiation exceed the amount you stand to gain, when your BATNA stinks (and everyone knows it), when negotiation would send the wrong signal to the other party, when the potential harm to the relationship exceeds the expected value from the negotiation, when negotiating is culturally inappropriate, or when your BATNA beats the other side's best possible offer. This chapter will help you better understand—and better strategize in—each of these situations.

WHEN TIME IS MONEY

Many years ago, Max was teaching a course on negotiation in Bangkok, Thailand. The students, naturally, were curious to know whether Max could negotiate in the real world or whether he simply knew the topic from an academic perspective. So each class began the same way. One of the students would ask Max where he went the previous evening and then ask the key question: "How much did you pay the taxi driver to get back to the faculty dorms?" At the time, in Thailand, one would routinely negotiate the price of the ride with the taxi driver before getting into the car. The students could then judge whether Max paid the rate that locals would pay or whether he paid the price reserved for foreigners—and for those lacking strong negotiation skills. By the end of the first week, Max understood the local taxi market quite well and was able to impress his students regularly with his ability to negotiate a good rate.

Then Marla, Max's wife, arrived in Thailand. On the evening of her arrival, Max and Marla took a long walk across town to a nice restaurant. After dinner, just outside the restaurant, Max hailed a taxi and, in his poor Thai, told the driver the destination. The driver asked for 70 baht ($2.80 at the time), which was a very high price. Max countered with 30 baht ($1.20), the lowest possible price for a local taxi ride and the price Max had paid a few days earlier for a similar ride. The driver quickly dropped his price to 50 baht; Max repeated his offer of 30 baht. The driver came down to 40 baht. Max stuck to 30 baht. The driver decided to pursue his BATNA and drove away.

Max hailed another taxi and shared the destination with the driver. The driver's response was 50 baht—a much more reasonable first offer than the one made by the previous driver. Max countered with an offer of 30 baht. The driver came down to 40 baht, at which point Max repeated his 30 baht offer. Again the driver drove away.

At this point, Marla, exhausted from her trip across the globe, asked Max what was going on. He explained that the drivers were demanding $1.60 for the cab ride and that he knew he could negotiate the price down to $1.20. Marla was not only unimpressed, but also rather annoyed. She offered to "chip in" 40 cents if that would seal the deal and get her home. Max wanted to explain that it was important for him to get a deal that would impress his class the next day, but he decided not to push it. Instead, he learned an important lesson. He had not only been ignoring the value of his own time but, more important, the value of Marla's time.

It is common for negotiators to become so focused on "getting a good deal" or "winning" that they fail to consider the value of the time they are spending (or wasting) in pursuit of fairness or victory. In doing so, they often waste time on trivial negotiations that could be better spent consummating more important deals, completing other tasks, or simply relaxing. Many negotiators claim they are extremely busy people who are constantly short on time—yet these same people do a very poor job of prioritizing their time. If you tend to claim that you have very little free time, consider where your effort would provide the highest payoff. Then focus more on improving your performance in these critical negotiations and less on trivial negotiations, such as those that would give you only a nominal discount on an already acceptable starting price.

Unfortunately, making this change is not as simple as recognizing that time is a limited resource that should not be wasted. You also need to recognize the many ways in which you have been conditioned to make these kinds of mistakes and work hard to change your habits. For example, consider that, across cultures, people are conditioned to look for the best deal, to not waste money, to avoid penalties and fines, and to finish everything on their dinner plate. What's wrong with such advice?

Usually there is nothing wrong with following these rules, but sometimes they motivate us to make irrational decisions that destroy value. Deepak discovered this one evening when his wife, Shikha, asked him to return the DVD they had rented the previous evening. The DVD was due back before midnight; if it was not returned on time, they would have to pay a fine. The problem was that Deepak happened to be sitting very comfortably in the living room. He had no desire to get up, get dressed, and drive two miles to return the movie. Deepak explained that he would prefer to return the movie the following day when he drove by the video store on the way to work, and that he could live with the $3 fine. Shikha saw things differently. She was unimpressed by Deepak's position on the matter, which she characterized as "being lazy."

Deepak suggested that they look at the situation in a different light. "Suppose there was no DVD or penalty involved," he said. "Instead, imagine there's someone standing outside the video store, handing out $3 to anyone who comes by. Would you want me to get up, get dressed, and drive two miles to pick up that $3? No way! So if it isn't worth going out there for $3 in that situation, there really isn't any reason for me to go now."

Shikha agreed with Deepak's argument, but as always, she improved his analysis. "From now on," she said, "perhaps we should plan ahead so that we don't find ourselves in situations where we have to choose between wasting money and wasting time." In fact, she pointed out, Deepak could have returned the DVD on the way to work that morning, avoided the penalty, enjoyed the evening in the living room, and eliminated the need for this entire conversation. But, according to Deepak, that would not have been nearly as fun—or insightful.

As this story reveals, we are often tempted to underestimate the value of our time because we are misapplying seemingly reasonable advice (e.g., get the best deal, don't accept what is unfair, avoid penalties, and so on). Furthermore, as Shikha's solution to the DVD problem reveals, it is often possible to make rational decisions and at the same time avoid unpleasant trade-offs if one has prepared effectively from the start.

WHEN YOUR BATNA STINKS— AND EVERYONE KNOWS IT

In our jobs as professors at the Harvard Business School, second-year MBA students often visit us seeking advice on negotiating their job offers. Quite often, the students sit down and describe the excellent offer that they have received—great company, great location, great boss, and great initial assignment. We congratulate them on obtaining the offer and ask how we can help. They explain that the offer is just a bit low on one issue—salary. It seems that many of their friends have been offered more money by other firms.

At this point, we ask the question they learned to expect from us during their first-year course on negotiation: "What's your BATNA? What other offers do you have?" They often complain that negotiating would be easy—and they wouldn't need our advice—if they had multiple offers. The problem, they explain, is that they only have one offer and that the prospective employer knows this (or will soon know, because the student will not lie about it).

How should these students negotiate for a higher salary? While the advice we give varies by situation, one piece of advice that we commonly offer—based on Deepak's story in Chapter 11—comes as a bit of a surprise to our students: They should call their future employer, express their enthusiasm regarding the company and the offer, and accept the job. Then, *after* accepting, they should ask their new boss for a favor: "Would you mind looking at some data regarding starting salaries of MBA students who have graduated from HBS? I'd like you to consider whether a somewhat higher starting salary might be both possible and fairer." Finally, they should clarify that they have already accepted the offer regardless of whether the salary changes or not— what happens in the salary negotiation will not affect their decision to join the firm.

Our students commonly protest that they would lose too much

power in the negotiation by accepting first. "What power are you referring to?" we ask. "If you try to negotiate with your new employer, and your BATNA is to remain on the job market without an offer, and the employer knows that they have already given you something higher than your reservation value, then you have little power to begin with." In such a situation, you may not want to play the "negotiation" game. You may be much better off playing a different game—for example, the game called "fairness," or the one called "could you please help me?" More generally, you may want to avoid negotiating when a reasonable analysis suggests that you will lose the negotiation game but may win some other type of game. In particular, when your BATNA stinks, their BATNA is fine, and all of this information is common knowledge, you may want to simply say yes in the negotiation and then change the game.

Does this advice work? Think back to how Deepak negotiated a job offer with his preferred employer. His strategy was to accept the offer before negotiating and then to create an environment where the managing partner liked him, wanted to help him, and could find ways to justify a salary increase. The result: a 10 percent increase in starting salary after both the HR department and the managing partner had said that salaries were nonnegotiable.

WHEN NEGOTIATING SENDS THE WRONG SIGNAL

Steve, a senior manager in a highly profitable accounting firm, was surprised one morning when he received a phone call from the president of his company. "What could he possibly want with me?" wondered Steve, who had never before met or spoken with the president. The president told Steve that he was planning to make a lot of changes in the organization and that one of the primary changes would involve restructuring the executive team: some people would be leaving, and some new blood would be brought in. The president asked Steve to meet with him the following day for a brief conversation. The next day, only minutes into their conversation, the president offered Steve a new job at the executive level, a promotion that would move him up three levels in the organization.

Most employees of most organizations would be absolutely thrilled to receive such an opportunity. But this situation was different. In his current position, Steve was not only earning a high salary, but was also a member of a highly coveted bonus pool that usually tripled his annual salary. The new job, while at the executive level, might end up paying him considerably less. The president had not discussed compensation, and Steve wondered whether the president himself knew what his salary would be in the new position. Steve was excited about the new job, but was extremely worried about the prospect of seeing his compensation cut in half, or worse! What to do? Should he ask what compensation he would receive? Should he anchor the negotiation by revealing how much compensation he was currently receiving and then invite a response? Should he ask for more time to make the decision and then try to obtain additional information from other sources? Should he simply accept or reject the offer as it stood?

There may be no single "right" approach to this situation. But let's consider what Steve did and, more important, why he did it.

Based on how quickly the company president made the offer and based on the fact that the president waited to make the offer until they were face-to-face, Steve gathered that the president wanted a quick decision. Furthermore, the president had *chosen* not to bring up the topic of compensation. Steve interpreted this to mean one of two things: either the president was confident that the compensation would be sufficient, or he was purposefully avoiding the topic because he did not want Steve's decision to be motivated primarily by financial considerations. Given the emphasis the president kept placing on "building a new team with a shared vision," Steve reasoned that the latter was almost certainly true. If so, perhaps the worst thing to do would be to bring up compensation.

Steve came to the conclusion that this was not the time to negotiate. For one thing, even if the compensation was very low, he might be in a better position to negotiate a higher salary after he had proven himself in the new role. He might regret his decision not to negotiate if he was unable to negotiate an adequate salary later, but he could stomach the risk. More important, trying to negotiate under the current circumstances would send the wrong signal—that he was more interested in money than in being a part of the leadership team and helping to reshape the organization.

Steve told the president that, while some aspects of the job were obviously still unclear, he shared his vision and was excited to join the team. He added: "I fully trust you to help make my transition into this new role both successful and mutually rewarding."

Later, some of Steve's colleagues told him that he should have negotiated compensation—that he was in a great position to do so because the president had clearly sought him out.

Steve's response? "Maybe I could have tried to negotiate a stellar compensation package, and maybe I'll regret not having negotiated when I had the chance. But I'm absolutely certain that I sent exactly the right signals—that I am a team player, that I trust the president, and that I am not solely motivated by dollars and cents—to a powerful person with whom I expect to have a close long-term relationship."

What eventually transpired? After he received the promotion, Steve's salary was cut in half—but he was given enough in bonuses, stock options, and scope for future advancement that his annual compensation effectively doubled.

As the reasoning behind Steve's decision reveals, the decision to negotiate always sends *some* signal. Typically, the signal you are sending when you initiate a negotiation is that you require more in value before you can agree to a deal. And, typically, this is a fine signal to send. However, in some situations, the signal you send when you decide to negotiate is that you do not trust the other side or that you are more concerned about what you will get from the deal than you are about the relationship, or about the rationale for the deal itself.

If your decision to negotiate will send the "wrong" signal, you have three options.

1. Negotiate anyway. You might decide that what you stand to gain from negotiation outweighs the costs of sending the wrong signal.

2. Change the signal. You might try to actively manage the way in which the other party will perceive your decision to negotiate. For example,

Steve might have initiated a discussion of compensation as follows: "I am very excited about the offer and hope to play a role in transforming this organization. I also appreciate your trust in me. Before I sign on, I do have some questions. I'm sure that's no surprise. Would it be possible for you to give me some more information regarding my role, responsibilities, and compensation? Regarding compensation—I don't want you to get the wrong idea. I am not fixated on the dollars and cents. But it is something that anyone with three young children needs to at least consider. Is this something that we can discuss?" In saying this, Steve might have made it less likely that launching a compensation negotiation would upset or offend the president.

3. Decide not to negotiate. If you think that the cost of sending a negative signal is too high and that it will be difficult to change the signal, you may want to decide, as Steve did, that this is not the time to negotiate.

WHEN RELATIONSHIPS MIGHT SUFFER

Sharon and Mark purchased a piece of land and proceeded with their plans to build their dream house. The home's construction would stretch their budget, but they carefully planned a way to build at the lowest price possible. Fortunately, Sharon and Mark had attended a seminar advertised in their local newspaper on "getting the price you deserve." Their instructor had told them that the more bids they sought, the lower their price would be. Accordingly, they took their architectural plans to eight different builders and were delighted when one builder came in with a surprisingly low bid—a full 10 percent lower than the second-lowest bid.

The negotiation course seemed to be paying off. If the builder is this desperate for projects, Sharon and Mark speculated, perhaps he will accept further concessions. In face-to-face negotiations, they pushed for a lower price. At first, the builder resisted. But when Sharon and Mark offered to sign the contract that day, set a deposit check on the table (another trick picked up in the negotiation class), and then threatened to go elsewhere, the builder had to reconsider. He thought about his desire to keep his crew employed and agreed to lower the price by another 3 percent, shaking his head and grumbling about whether any profit remained. Sharon and Mark seemed to have negotiated the best price they could have hoped to obtain—the lowest bidder's reservation value! Their happiness kept them from noticing the fact that the builder felt trapped and was unhappy with how the negotiation had unfolded.

After the contract was signed, Sharon and Mark's architect came up with a number of changes, all of which they thought looked great. They took these seemingly small "change orders" to the builder and were shocked by the prices that the builder demanded to accommodate the altered work plan. Sharon and Mark pushed hard for lower prices, but this time the builder refused to make concessions. Their excellent initial price continued to rise, due not only to the change orders, but also to an increase in lumber costs (the contract had a cost-of-lumber adjustment). Many difficult conversations took place between the builder, who remained grumpy about his profit margin, and Sharon and Mark, who were frustrated by the price increases.

When the builder told them that the house would most likely be completed in three months, Sharon and Mark sold their condo and set a closing date that coincided with the expected completion date of the house. However, the house was not completed on time, and Sharon and Mark were forced to move into temporary housing. Again and again, they discussed their need for completion with the builder, who repeatedly blamed the delays on subcontractors. Sharon and Mark checked the contract and found no clause dealing with delays.

After nine weeks in temporary housing, Sharon and Mark finally moved into their supposed "dream house." At first they were pleased with the house. But the longer they lived in it, the more problems they encountered: one of the heating systems failed during the winter, two of the appliances were unreliable, some of the carpentry wasn't finished, and cracks started to emerge in the drywall. Some of these items were under warranty; some were not. The builder did not quickly attend even to those items that were under warranty; after all, he had already been fully paid for his work. "I know that I'm obligated to fix the cracks in the drywall," the builder said during one heated conversation with Sharon, "but I'm not obligated to do it at your convenience."

Ultimately, Sharon and Mark regretted that they had ever decided to build their dream house. Their condo had been fine for their needs, and a lot less of a hassle.

Why was the building project such a disaster? Sharon and Mark got a great price for a house that they eventually did not want. They focused on getting a low price at the expense of other important issues, such as timely completion and quality construction. Most important, they pushed for a price that, while desirable, destroyed their relationship with the other party. When Sharon and Mark received the builder's low bid, they probably should have accepted it and then negotiated "friendlier" issues, such as how to deal with change orders, whether to add a small lateness penalty and a small timeliness bonus to the contract, and so on. Sharon and Mark did a good job negotiating the price of their home construction, but they would have done a much better job negotiating their overall outcome had they avoided negotiating the builder down to his reservation value.

As we think about how Sharon and Mark should have handled their negotiation, it is worth recalling (from Chapter 1) what transpired when Albert Einstein was "negotiating" his job offer with Princeton University. Einstein requested an annual salary of $3,000, and Princeton responded by offering to pay him $15,000 annually. Princeton's decision to offer Einstein an appropriate wage, rather than accepting (or haggling over) his low bid, was the right one to make—and not simply because the other party was Albert Einstein. Organizations often face a choice between paying employees the bare minimum required to attract and retain them and paying a "fairer" or more generous wage. Ethical considerations aside, organizations (and consumers like Sharon and Mark) will generally benefit by taking a long-term perspective that entails building a reputation for fairness and for contributing to the well-being of their negotiation counterparts.

WHEN NEGOTIATING IS
CULTURALLY INAPPROPRIATE

Let's revisit Max's taxi negotiations in Thailand and see how these might work—or not work—once Max returns to Boston. Imagine that Max returns to the United States, walks out of the airport terminal, and waits in line for a taxi. When his taxi arrives, Max asks the driver how much it will cost for a ride to his home in Cambridge. The driver says that he will go by what the meter registers, but estimates that it will be close to $20. As other travelers wait impatiently behind him, Max begins to haggle. He offers $10. The taxi driver swears at Max and calls the attendant responsible for managing the taxi stand. The attendant pulls Max aside and tells him that he is holding up the line and will have to either take the ride now or find a different way to get home.

Should Max be surprised that this negotiation failed? Of course not. Nor should he be surprised if he next went to a grocery store and was unable to engage the clerk in a negotiation over the price of a bottle of water. Some of the behaviors that Max found to be perfectly acceptable in Thailand would be laughable, even offensive, back home in the United States. It is worth mentioning that we have had students tell us occasionally about their success in negotiating seemingly non-negotiable items (such as the price of a cup of coffee at Starbucks). You might also recall how Shikha, Deepak's wife, successfully negotiated with a taxi driver in Boston (as described in Chapter 3). But very often, such negotiations will fail because they are not culturally appropriate.

Within our own culture, we tend to know which behaviors are consistent with social norms and which are not. Our knowledge of our own culture tells us what time we should show up for a party that "starts at 7 P.M.," whether it is acceptable to burp after a meal or to show the soles of our shoes, and countless other rules of conduct. Our understanding of our own culture also tells us when it is appropriate to negotiate—and when it is not. Unfortunately, we often violate such norms in other cultures. If Max, when in Bangkok, had simply accepted the 70 baht offer from the taxi driver, he not only would have overpaid, but he would have also given the driver a funny story (about the ignorant foreigner) that he could share with his friends. As another example, consider that in some cultures and contexts, it may be acceptable to anchor aggressively and then negotiate down to a mutually agreeable price; in others, your willingness to retreat from your original, justified anchor may signal to the other party that you were initially lying or being greedy.

How can you know whether it is okay to negotiate in a particular culture? How should you initiate negotiations in a different culture? The first step in answering these questions is always preparation. Before you travel, elicit advice from others who have done business in that culture or who are from that culture. Learn as much as you can, including what is and is not appropriate to say and discuss, how and when to initiate substantive discussions, how to build rapport and trust, how to manage status and respect issues, and how aggressively people can be expected to anchor. The more you know going in, the better prepared you will be to negotiate effectively.

Even if you are not culturally sophisticated, all is not lost. Imagine that you find yourself having to negotiate in a foreign land where you know very little about the local culture or social norms. What should you do? Ask to be educated. Most people in most parts of the world will not be offended by—and will probably appreciate—a statement such as the following:

As you know, we have not done business in this country before. That's one of the reasons we are thrilled to have this opportunity to meet with you and discuss issues of mutual interest. However, this also means that we may not always know the correct way to articulate or convey certain ideas. We hope you will be forgiving if we say or do something that seems awkward. We assure you that we mean no disrespect and that, while we may stumble occasionally, we are fast learners. Perhaps you are feeling similar anxiety, in which case we can assure you that we understand your good intentions. I think we all stand to benefit if everyone feels comfortable discussing issues openly, asking questions, and being patient. I hope that you agree. We're excited about the opportunity we have not only to do business with you, but also to learn about your culture.

How would you respond if someone with whom you were negotiating made this statement? In all likelihood, you would welcome their sentiments and feel more relaxed and comfortable yourself. Unfortunately, when negotiating cross-culturally, many people instead decide to "fake it," rely on cultural stereotypes, or ignore the cultural element altogether. None of these strategies beats the investigative approach that we first introduced in Chapter 3: when you don't know something, try to learn it.

WHEN YOUR BATNA BEATS THEIR BEST POSSIBLE OFFER

In 1981, Roger Fisher and William Ury published a short book entitled *Getting to YES: Negotiating Agreement Without Giving In*. As you may know, the book became a best seller and transformed the practice of negotiation. Previously, most writing on the topic of negotiation focused on protecting "what's yours" and getting as much of "what's theirs" as possible—an approach that many people would describe as "win-lose" negotiation. By contrast, *Getting to YES* encouraged agreement and exalted the pursuit of "win-win" deals.

Overall, *Getting to YES* has had a very positive impact on society. But among some of its enthusiasts, the book seems to have created too strong of a bias toward *always* "getting to yes." The amazing success of *Getting to YES* has contributed to the perception that an impasse, or "no deal," is equivalent to a failed negotiation. But sometimes in negotiation, you should *not* get to yes! Sometimes your BATNA is better than any offer your current negotiation counterpart can make, and "no deal" is the best outcome that two fully rational negotiators can hope to achieve. In these cases, the best you can do is to get to "no" as efficiently as possible. How will you know when "no deal" is the best outcome? Look for the following signs:

- You have told them about your other offers, and they are unable to match or beat the value that these alternatives offer to you.
- Instead of trying to meet your needs, they are trying hard to convince you that your interests are not what you think they are.

- They seem more interested in stretching out the negotiation than in exchanging information, building a relationship, or structuring an agreement.
- Despite your best efforts, they will not answer any of your questions; nor will they ask about your needs or interests.

In such situations, there is no virtue in negotiating for the sake of negotiating or negotiating well past the time it should take for you to discover that no ZOPA exists. When there is no ZOPA, there should be no deal. In such situations, instead of "getting to yes," exercise your BATNA.

CAN'T A GENIUS NEGOTIATE EVERYTHING?

As we have stressed throughout this book, more often than not, negotiating allows you to create value above and beyond your alternatives to reaching agreement. But it is worth keeping in mind that not every aspect of life is a negotiation. By considering the context of the negotiation, the relationships involved, and your alternatives away from the table, you will become adept at identifying when to negotiate, when to accept a deal without negotiating, and when to simply walk away. Some negotiation "experts" will tell you that "you can negotiate anything." Perhaps you can—but that does not mean you *should*. Often, there are better things to do than negotiate. Negotiation geniuses are able to recognize and leverage these alternatives.

CHAPTER 14

The Path to Genius

Some years ago, one of us sat in on an MBA negotiation class that was taught by a well-known negotiation professor. It was the last day of the semester-long course, and the professor kept referring to his students as "negotiation experts" (for instance, "now that you are negotiation experts," and so on). We found this quite disturbing. These students were not experts—certainly not yet. Some of them might never become negotiation experts. And yet the last day of the course was being celebrated as the last step in the learning process. In contrast, we hold no such illusions. Rather, we believe that reading this book is your *first* step toward becoming a negotiation genius—or expert.

Recall the distinction we made in Chapter 6 between experience and expertise. Experience is what you gain when you engage in a particular behavior (such as negotiation) many times. Expertise is what you gain when you are able to infuse your experience with a "strategic conceptualization" of what you are doing.[1] Unfortunately, many people confuse these two ideas and mistakenly think that their vast experience in negotiation qualifies them as experts.

One of our executive students recently told us that he didn't expect to learn much from a course on negotiation. He had accumulated many years of negotiation experience and had "seen it all." In support of his argument for the supremacy of experience, he even quoted Benjamin Franklin: "Experience is a dear teacher." Unfortunately for the student (and his prospects for learning), he had misunderstood Franklin's point. When he used the word "dear," Franklin meant it as a synonym for "expensive," not "precious." This becomes clear when you consider Franklin's full statement: "Experience is a dear teacher, but fools will learn at no other." Yes, experience is an extremely important part of becoming a negotiation genius, but it is not sufficient.

The students whose professor told them they were experts, the dealmaker who came to us with twenty years of negotiating experience, and you, all have one thing in common: when it comes to negotiation, you do some things well, you do some things poorly, and the best way for you to become a more effective negotiator—indeed, a negotiation genius—is to think more deeply and analytically about the framework we have developed. Only by leveraging experience *and* insight will you truly achieve expertise.

WHICH STORY WILL YOU TELL?

Try to remember a recent negotiation in which you reached an agreement, but got a pretty lousy deal. Now imagine that you complained about the outcome to your boss, colleague, friend, or spouse. How did you account for your result? Here are some common explanations that we have heard from negotiators.

- "The other party said that they had a better offer from the competition. There was nothing more that I could do."
- "The market moved against us."
- "There was not enough time to push for a better deal."

And here are some explanations that we rarely hear:

- "I didn't prepare systematically."
- "Our team was not well-coordinated."
- "I didn't collect the information that I needed prior to the negotiation."
- "I blurted out an offer before I thought it through."

The difference between the two lists is crucial. The first consists of *external* attributions. The failure was due to factors beyond your control. The problem was with the situation, not with what you did or did not do. In contrast, the second list consists of *internal* attributions for the failure—there were things you could have done differently to achieve a better outcome. When we think of our successes, we are very quick to attribute them to factors within our control. But when we think of failures, we usually find ways of externalizing the blame.

The *good* news is that these types of external attributions may salvage your reputation with your boss. They will also make you feel better about the "fact" that the bad deal wasn't your fault and that you did the best you could. The *bad* news is that the poor outcome probably was at least partially your fault; thus, you are not being entirely honest with yourself or with others. Most often, when you get a lousy deal, it is because you were in a difficult situation *and* you did not handle it as well as you could have. Now for the *really bad* news: when you attribute your failures to external factors, you make it very difficult to learn from your experience and improve as a negotiator.

As a negotiator, you face a choice: do you want to feel good about yourself or do you want to learn? Because you have reached the last chapter of this book, we presume the latter. If so, your goal is to find ways to integrate the principles, strategies, and tactics presented in this book into your life. We end by suggesting some ways for doing so.

PERFECT CAN BE THE ENEMY OF GOOD

It has been said that "perfect is the enemy of good," a principle that applies to personal change in many areas. If you try to do too much, too soon, you will be overwhelmed. For example, you may want to try to memorize all of the ideas and strategies you found useful in this book so that you will be prepared for every possible eventuality in your next negotiation. If you try to do this, you will inevitably fall short of your expectations—and of your potential.

In addition to recognizing the virtues of incremental (rather than hurried) progress, you must anticipate the various obstacles to change that you will undoubtedly face. You may find it difficult to try new ideas or strategies because you are risk averse or because you find the status quo to be comforting. Or you may find it difficult to change your ways when everyone around you expects you to believe certain things and behave a certain way. It is also possible that you simply won't have the time necessary to devote to change. Recognize that all of these obstacles—and others that you might think of—are typical. Your need to confront these obstacles does not say anything about you or your prospects for effective change; it simply means that you are human. This understanding may give you some relief, but it does not solve your problem. How can you overcome common obstacles to change and effectively leverage the ideas in this book?

Here are some practical steps that you can follow to transition from *reading* about key negotiation ideas and strategies to changing how you actually negotiate:

1. Review the book (or any notes you may have taken as you read) and make a list of all of the strategies and tactics that you would like to try in your own negotiations. Once you have done this, identify which items on the list require further contemplation and which ones you can use immediately.

2. Among those ideas that you wish to contemplate further, identify one key concept that you will spend time working on in the week ahead. Set aside some time in your schedule to think more deeply about this idea. How might you apply it to your negotiations? What are its strengths? What are its weaknesses? How might you integrate the principle into your way of thinking? Do the same for all of the other ideas you would like to contemplate further: tackle one idea each week. If you have the time to explore more ideas in a particular week, add items to your weekly list.

3. Identify other people, such as friends and colleagues, with whom you would like to discuss particular negotiation strategies. Ask them to play devil's advocate to your proposed use of a strategy and to critique your game plan. Trying out new negotiation strategies on supportive friends or colleagues will not only give you the confidence to transfer your new skills to important negotiations, but will also help you identify mistakes you may have overlooked.

4. For those strategies that you are ready to implement immediately, think about your current (or upcoming) negotiations. Write down which specific strategies and tactics you would like to employ in each negotiation. To avoid "shooting from the hip" when you get to the bargaining table, you should also plan how exactly you will implement these strategies.

5. After your negotiations, think about other strategies that you could have applied but did not. Think about how you might do so in the future.

6. Every so often, revisit the book to see if there are other ideas, strategies, or tactics that seem relevant to your current or upcoming negotiations.

CREATING THE RIGHT ENVIRONMENT FOR GENIUS

An executive student who runs a midsize company came back to visit Deepak a year after taking his course on negotiation. The executive had been so energized by the course material that he wanted all of his employees to learn and master the strategies discussed in class. During the course of the past year, he reported, he had put forth a lot of effort to educate his employees. Unfortunately, he had achieved very mixed results. He described the problem:

"In my company, we have two divisions: the 'Openers' and the 'Closers.' It is the job of Openers to bring in potential clients. Once the potential client is sufficiently interested in what we have to offer, they are passed on to the Closers. It is the Closers' job to close the deal. When I tried to teach my employees about investigative negotiation, creating and claiming value, etc., a strange thing happened. The Openers got the message quickly. They were excited to leverage these new ideas in their negotiations with potential clients. But the Closers—they didn't get it. They looked at me as if I was talking complete nonsense. And they went back to their jobs and didn't change a thing. They continue to claim very little value and to do whatever it takes to sign the deal. They seem to have no sense of the merits of value creation, or of the potential for value claiming!"

The executive wondered aloud whether the problem was that he was recruiting more open-minded people as Openers and more closed-minded people as Closers. Deepak responded by asking whether, in his firm, these two divisions were actually referred to as "Openers" and "Closers." "Yes," the executive said. "Why, then," asked Deepak, "are you so surprised that your Closers are closing deals for you?" The executive was not sure what he meant, so Deepak asked another question: "What do you think Closers are most afraid of doing in their jobs?" The executive thought for a moment, then responded: "Losing the deal." Deepak asked if there were any incentive systems in place to reward Closers. There were: their bonuses were tied to the number of deals they closed.

That was the problem. These employees were being told (literally) that their job was to close the deal. They were also being rewarded financially on the basis of closing the deal. Yet the executive was surprised when the Closers ignored his suggestion that they should try to claim as much value as possible. Why would they do anything that might risk losing the deal?

This problem is common. Often, we—or our employees and coworkers—have both the analytic ability to learn new skills and the desire to change our behavior, yet we are constrained by the culture or incentive systems that exist in our organizations. For the ideas in this book to take shape in the real world, you need to take steps to remove these constraints. If you are in a position of authority, assess the culture and incentive systems that govern your team, division, or organization. If you determine that these systems will stifle the changes you hope will take root in the negotiation behaviors of your employees or colleagues, work to facilitate change. If you are not in a position of authority, but can see how your organization's culture or incentive system is creating a barrier to change, consider taking it upon yourself to educate those who can do something about it.

THE DISAPPEARING CIRCLE

When executives and MBA students first enroll in a course on negotiation, they typically arrive with assumptions about the "things that are negotiable" in life. Usually, in their minds, a small circle of negotiable things exists: buying or selling a house, a car, or a business; haggling with a street vendor; negotiating salary with an employer; and perhaps little else. They look forward to learning how to be more effective in these negotiations. But as the course progresses, and we discuss different strategies and tactics for negotiating in a wide variety of contexts, their circle of negotiable things begins to grow. More and more issues, conflicts, and situations seem negotiable. Students often report that this is an empowering feeling. But where does it end? How large is the circle really?

Those who reflect deeply on the ideas presented in their negotiation course—or the ideas presented in this book—in the months and years that follow their classroom (or reading) experience discover that, eventually, the circle grows infinitely large; that is, it simply *disappears*. There are no longer "things that are negotiable" and "things that are not negotiable." Instead, they discover that they have learned a set of basic principles for human interaction. These principles are not about buying, selling, crafting deals, reaching agreements, overcoming bias, and so on. Those activities are mere applications of more fundamental principles for successfully engaging with other people who, like you, are usually well-intentioned human beings who have different interests and perspectives.

A negotiation genius is someone for whom the circle has disappeared—for her, the ideas and principles are what matter, and these are ingrained in her approach to dealing with all types of human interaction. For a negotiation genius, applying the ideas in this book during a complex business transaction is no different from applying the ideas when having a conversation with a spouse, a friend, or an employee. Investigative negotiation principles are as applicable to a legal dispute as they are to a spat with a coworker; influence tactics can be usefully applied not only to the sale of your business services, but also in your negotiations with your children.

NEGOTIATION GENIUS IS ACHIEVABLE

We end with an observation regarding genius. The mistake is to think that some people are born geniuses (Einstein, Mozart, Michael Jordan, et cetera), and others of us are not. In fact, genius is often a combination of natural ability and a lot of hard work. But, you will argue, no amount of hard work will turn you into Michael Jordan or Mozart or Einstein. You are probably correct—you are unlikely to have the "raw materials" needed for their achievements. The good news is that you *do* have the raw materials needed to become a negotiation genius—almost everyone does. Negotiation genius is about human interaction, and the only raw material you need to achieve it is the ability to change your beliefs, assumptions, and perspective. You have this ability. If you now put forth the effort to implement what you have learned, then you will become a negotiation genius—someone who finds it easy to achieve brilliant results in all types of negotiations. We hope you will put forth this effort. We hope this book motivates you to do so and guides you along the path.

analogical reasoning: The process of learning by comparing and contrasting similar lessons from two different episodes or events.

anchor: A number, such as a first offer, that focuses negotiator attention and expectations and helps resolve uncertainty.

behavioral decision research: An area of research that focuses on the systematic ways that the human mind deviates from rationality; has led to scientific revolutions in fields such as economics, psychology, finance, law, medicine, marketing, and negotiation.

best alternative to a negotiated agreement (BATNA): The course of action a negotiator will pursue if and when the current negotiation is unsuccessful (i.e., ends in impasse).

bounded awareness: The systematic failure to see readily available information that is relevant to a decision but is not the object of focus.

cognitive biases: The systematic mistakes that negotiators make because of the way in which their minds operate.

competitive arousal: An emotional state that results from heightened perceptions of rivalry, and that can create in negotiators the desire to "win at any cost."

contingency contract: A provision in an agreement that leaves specific elements of the deal unresolved until a particular source of uncertainty is resolved in the future. Such provisions allow both sides in the negotiation to "bet" on their differing beliefs regarding the probability of a future event.

contingent concessions: In negotiation, concessions that are explicitly tied to specific actions by the other party. These are phrased in a quid-pro-quo manner to clarify that concessions will only be made if the other party does their part.

contrast effect: The tendency to judge the magnitude of something based not on its absolute or objective size, but instead on how it appears relative to a (perhaps arbitrary) point of reference.

co-opetition: Situations in which a party has the incentive to cooperate with another party on some fronts, while competing with the same party on other fronts.

de-biasing strategies: The steps a negotiator takes to reduce his or her naturally occurring decision biases.

distinct value proposition: The host of assets that your negotiation counterpart values and that you can provide more effectively or cheaply than your competitors.

door-in-the-face strategy (DITF): The technique of increasing others' willingness to comply with your request by first asking them to agree to an even more extreme request that they are almost certain to reject.

egocentrism: The tendency for our perceptions and expectations to be biased in a self-serving manner.

fixed-pie bias: Negotiators often fail to create value because they assume "whatever is good for them is bad for us"; that is, they believe there is a "fixed pie" of value or resources even when it is possible to increase the size of the pie.

foot-in-the-door strategy (FITD): A strategy of influence that is based on the premise that the willingness of others to agree with one request leads to an increased commitment on their part to agree with additional requests that naturally follow from the initial request.

framing effects: The common tendency for negotiators to treat risks involving perceived gains differently from risks involving perceived losses.

haggling: The iterative give-and-take that occurs after each party has made its initial offer.

illusion of superiority: A bias that causes people to view themselves as better than others on a variety of desirable attributes.

inattentional blindness: A phenomenon in which people are focused so intently on a particular task that they fail to see obvious information in their environment.

incentive compatible: Negotiated clauses that offer incentives for the other party to behave in ways that are consistent with the spirit of your agreement.

information asymmetry: The fact that each side in the negotiation is inevitably aware of facts and data that the other side does not know.

insider lens: The perspective negotiators typically adopt when they are personally involved in a decision or negotiation. The insider lens is more susceptible to bias, and more likely to rely on intuition, than the outsider lens.

investigative negotiation: A negotiation mind-set and methodology that focuses on discovering the often hidden or guarded interests, priorities, needs, and constraints of the other party.

irrational optimism: A positive illusion that leads most of us to believe that our futures will be better and brighter than those of other people.

learned optimism: The perspective that a person's tendency to overestimate her chances of success is a learned, functional attribute; theoretically, unrealistically high levels of optimism will motivate persistence in the face of rejection.

logrolling: The act of making trade-offs across issues in a negotiation. In particular, logrolling involves giving the other side something that they value relatively more in return for receiving something that you value relatively more.

loss aversion: The tendency for people to be more motivated to avoid losses than they are to accrue gains.

marginal utility: The happiness associated with an incremental change in circumstances; for example, how much happier a negotiator is when he receives an additional concession above what was already received or expected.

motivational biases: A range of misperceptions resulting from the common human tendency to view the world the way we wish it were rather than how it truly is. In particular, the desire to see ourselves as fairer, kinder, more competent, more generous, more deserving, and more likely to succeed than others.

negotiauction: A two-stage bidding/negotiation process in which an initial auction narrows the field to the most promising candidates, who are then invited to engage in one-on-one negotiations.

nonrational escalation of commitment: The act of continuing to pursue a failing course of action based on the strong psychological need to justify (to oneself or to others) one's prior decisions and behaviors.

non-zero-sum negotiation: A negotiation in which what one party gains is not associated with an equivalent loss for the other party. In such negotiations, the total value of the deal depends on how well the parties employ value-creating strategies.

norm of reciprocity: The widely held expectation and understanding that parties should repay or reward others for their benevolent or helpful behaviors. In negotiation, the norm of reciprocity creates the expectation that both sides will take turns making concessions.

outsider lens: The perspective negotiators typically adopt when they are not personally involved in a decision or negotiation. The outsider lens is less susceptible to bias, and less likely to rely on intuition, than the insider lens. The outsider lens helps negotiators to generalize across situations and to identify relevant patterns and lessons.

overconfidence: A bias that describes the tendency of negotiators to be more confident in their assessments than reality supports.

package reservation value: The "walk-away" value that you calculate using all of the issues in the negotiation. This is the minimum total value you will need to obtain in the negotiation if you are to forgo your BATNA. It is often necessary to use a scoring system to help calculate your package reservation value.

parasitic value creation: Value creation that occurs when negotiators at the table are made better off because they have extracted value from parties who are not at the bargaining table.

Pareto-efficient agreement: An agreement in which there is no way to make one party better off without hurting at least one other party.

Pareto improvements: Changes to a deal that make at least one person better off without making anyone worse off.

positive illusions: Unrealistic positive beliefs regarding our abilities and our future. Such beliefs, arguably, contribute to our psychological and material well-being by protecting our self-esteem and motivating us to persevere when faced with difficult tasks.

post-settlement settlements: Agreements that are negotiated after the initial agreement is signed. Post-settlement settlements are pursued in order to create additional value.

prisoners' dilemma: A competitive situation in which both players are individually better off playing a noncooperative strategy, but collectively better off playing a cooperative strategy.

psychological biases: Systematic departures from rationality that can derail an otherwise sound negotiation strategy.

reactive devaluation: The tendency of negotiators to denigrate the value of a concession or idea simply because it was made by someone who is seen as an adversary.

reference group neglect: The common—and harmful—failure of negotiators to adequately consider the strength of the opposition.

reference point: Any salient source of comparison. Reference points can affect the judgments negotiators make regarding the value of a particular issue or offer.

reservation value: A negotiator's "walk-away" point in a negotiation. If the value being offered by the other side is equal to the negotiator's reservation value, the negotiator is indifferent between accepting the offer and rejecting it in favor of pursuing his/her BATNA.

self-serving attributions: The tendency to make causal judgments in ways that help the negotiator feel good about him- or herself.

social proof: A psychological principle that states when there is uncertainty or ambiguity regarding the appropriate course of action, people look to the behavior of similar others for guidance.

stereotype tax: The cost we bear when we base our decisions about others on stereotypes rather than on more useful information about them as individuals.

stereotyping: Identifying a key feature that is perceived to describe some members of a group, applying this description to all members of the group, and failing to notice the uniqueness of specific group members.

target price: The outcome a negotiator hopes to achieve in the negotiation. This is also referred to as a negotiator's aspiration level.

value creation: The act of increasing the total amount of value that is up for grabs in the negotiation. This is done, for example, when negotiators identify each other's priorities and engage in logrolling.

vividness bias: The tendency of negotiators to focus too much attention on vivid features of offers and to overlook less vivid concerns that may nonetheless have a stronger impact on their satisfaction.

want-self versus should-self: The internal negotiation people often face between doing what they want to do versus doing what they think they should do.

winner's curse: Situations in which a bidder wins the deal by paying more than the commodity is worth, due to a failure to consider the information advantage of the other party.

zero-sum negotiation: A negotiation in which whatever one party gains results in an equivalent loss to the other party. Also referred to as "fixed-sum negotiation" and "distributive negotiation."

zone of possible agreement (ZOPA): The set of all possible outcomes in a negotiation that would be acceptable to all parties. In a one-issue price negotiation, this is the space between the seller's reservation value and the buyer's reservation value.

NOTES

CHAPTER 1: CLAIMING VALUE IN NEGOTIATION

1 This story was recounted by David Lax and James Sebenius in their 1986 book *The Manager as Negotiator: Bargaining for Cooperation and Competitive Gain* (published by Free Press).

2 Adapted from D. Malhotra (2005). Hamilton Real Estate: Confidential Role Information for the Executive VP of Pearl Investments (SELLER). Harvard Business School Exercise 905-053. Available, along with the Role Information for "Buyer" and a Teaching Note, from Harvard Business School Publishing.

3 Fisher, R., and Ury, W. (1981). *Getting to Yes.* Boston: Houghton Mifflin.

4 Northcraft, G. B., and Neale, M. A. (1987). Experts, Amateurs, and Real Estate: An Anchoring-and-Adjustment Perspective on Property Pricing Decisions. *Organizational Behavior & Human Decision Processes,* 39(1), 84–97.

5 *Ibid.*

6 Malhotra, D. (2004). Trust and Reciprocity Decision: The Differing Perspectives of Trustors and Trusted Parties. *Organizational Behavior and Human Decision Processes,* 94: 61–73.

7 Shell, R. G. (1999). *Bargaining for Advantage: Negotiation Strategies for Reasonable People.* New York: Viking.

8 Galinsky, A. D., Mussweiler, T., and Medvec, V. H. (2002). Disconnecting Outcomes and Evaluations: The Role of Negotiator Focus. *Journal of Personality and Social Psychology,* 83(5), 1131–1140.

CHAPTER 2: CREATING VALUE IN NEGOTIATION

1 This statement was made by Richard Holbrooke during a panel discussion at Harvard University in October 2004.

2 Adapted from A. Tenbrunsel & M. Bazerman (2006). Moms.com Simulation and Teaching Note. (Dispute Resolution and Research Center, Northwestern University.)

3 Valley, K. L., Neale, M, A., and Mannix, E. A. (1995). Friends, Lovers,

Colleagues, Strangers: The Effects of Relationships on the Process and Outcome of Dyadic Negotiations. *Research on Negotiation in Organizations*, 65–93, eds. R. J. Bies, R. J. Lewicki, B. H. Sheppard. Greenwich, CT: *JAI*.

4 Raiffa, H. (1985). Post-Settlement Settlements. *Negotiation Journal*, 1, 9–12.

CHAPTER 3: INVESTIGATIVE NEGOTIATION

1 *ABC News* (2004, July 13). Nader Campaign Accepts Republican Donations. From http://abclocal.go.com/kgo/story?section=News&id=1873814.

2 Brandenburger, A. M., and Nalebuff, B. J. (1996). *Co-opetition*. New York: Doubleday.

CHAPTER 4: WHEN RATIONALITY FAILS: BIASES OF THE MIND

1 Malhotra, D., and Hout, M. (2006). Negotiating on Thin Ice: The 2004–2005 NHL Dispute. Harvard Business School Cases: 906-038 and 906-039.

2 LaPointe, J. (2004, December 27). Bettman's Vision for the NHL Did Not Include Labor Strife. *New York Times*, D1; (2005, January 10); Worst Managers: Gary Bettman, National Hockey League, *Business Week*, 76.

3 LaPointe, Bettman's Vision for the NHL Did Not Include Labor Strife, *op. cit.*

4 Cannella, S. (2005, February 17). Shameless and Pointless: Bettman, Goodenow Disgrace the NHL More than Ever, *Sports Illustrated* online.

5 Hahn, A. (2005, July 26). NHL: Players OK Pact. *Newsday*, A86.

6 Farber, M. (2005, February 17). Down with the Ship: With Season Sunk, Bettman, Goodenow Should Resign. *Sports Illustrated* online.

7 Originally cited by Ross, L., and Stillinger, C. (1991). Barriers to Conflict Resolution. *Negotiation Journal*, 7(4), 389–404.

8 Bazerman, M., Baron, J., and Shonk, K. (2001). *"You Can't Enlarge the Pie": Six Barriers to Effective Government*. New York: Basic Books.

9 Thompson, L. (2001). *The Mind and Heart of the Negotiator*. Upper Saddle River, NJ: Prentice Hall.

10 Stillinger, C., Epelbaum, M., Keltner, D., and Ross, L. (1990). The Reactive Devaluation Barrier to Conflict Resolution. Unpublished manuscript, Stanford University.

11 Babcock, L., and Laschever, S. (2003). *Women Don't Ask: Negotiation and the Gender Divide*. Princeton, NJ: Princeton University Press.

12 Ku, G., Malhotra, D., and Murnighan, J. K. (2005) Towards a

Competitive Arousal Model of Decision Making: A Study of Auction Fever in Live and Internet Auctions. *Organizational Behavior and Human Decision Processes,* 96(2), 89–103.

13 Sebenius, J. K., and Wheeler, M. A. (1994, October 30). Sports Strikes: Let the Games Continue. *New York Times,* 3, 9.

14 Tversky, A., & Kahneman, D. (1981). The Framing of Decisions and the Psychology of Choice. *Science,* 211(4481), 453–458.

CHAPTER 5: WHEN RATIONALITY FAILS: BIASES OF THE HEART

1 Homer (R. Lattimore, trans.) (1999). *The Odyssey.* New York: Harper-Collins.

2 Schelling, T. C. (1984). *Choice and Consequence: Perspectives of an Errant Economist.* Cambridge, MA: Harvard University Press, 58.

3 Bazerman, M. H., Gibbons, R., Thompson, L. L., and Valley, K. L. (1998). Can Negotiators Outperform Game Theory? *Debating Rationally: Nonrational Aspects in Organizational Decision Making.* Halpern, J. J., and Stern, R. N., eds. Ithaca, NY: ILR; O'Connor, K. M., De Dreu, C. K. W., Schroth, H., Barry, B., Lituchy, T. R., and Bazerman, M. H. (2002). What We Want to Do Versus What We Think We Should Do: An Empirical Investigation of Intrapersonal Conflict. *Journal of Behavioral Decision Making,* 15(5), 403–418.

4 Loewenstein, G. (1996). Out of Control: Visceral Influences on Behavior. *Organizational Behavior and Human Decision Processes,* 65(3), 272–292.

5 O'Connor, K. M., De Dreu, C. K. W., Schroth, H., Barry, B., Lituchy, T. R., and Bazerman, M. H. (2002). What We Want to Do Versus What We Think We Should Do: An Empirical Investigation of Intrapersonal Conflict. *Journal of Behavioral Decision Making,* 15(5), 403–418.

6 *U.S. News & World Report* (2005, January 30), 52. It is also interesting to note that the loser paying the legal expenses of the winner is the law in some parts of the world; e.g., in England.

7 Bazerman, M. H., and Neale, M. A. (1982). Improving Negotiation Effectiveness Under Final Offer Arbitration: The Role of Selection and Training. *Journal of Applied Psychology,* 67(5), 543–548; Babcock, L., and Loewenstein, G. (1997). Explaining Bargaining Impasse: The Role of Self-Serving Biases. *Journal of Economic Perspectives,* 11(1), 109–126.

8 Diekmann, K. A., Samuels, S. M., Ross, L., & Bazerman, M. H. (1997). Self-Interest and Fairness in Problems of Resource Allocation: Allocators Versus Recipients. *Journal of Personality and Social Psychology,* 72(5), 1061–1074.

9 Harris, S. (1946). *Banting's Miracle: The Story of the Discovery of Insulin.* Toronto: J. M. Dent and Sons.

10 Ross, M., and Sicoly, F. (1979). Egocentric Biases in Availability and Attribution. *Journal of Personality and Social Psychology,* 37(3), 322–336.

11 Rawls, J. (1971). *A Theory of Justice.* Cambridge, MA: Harvard University Press.

12 Taylor, S. E. (1989). *Positive Illusions: Creative Self-Deception and the Healthy Mind.* New York: Basic Books.

13 Kramer, R. M., Newton, E., and Pommerenke, P. L. (1993). Self-Enhancement Biases and Negotiator Judgment: Effects of Self-Esteem and Mood. *Organizational Behavior and Human Decision Processes,* 56(1), 110–133. Kramer, R. M. (1994). *Self-Enhancing Cognitions and Organized Conflict.* Unpublished manuscript.

14 Taylor, S. E., and Brown, J. D. (1988). Illusion and Well-Being: A Social Psychological Perspective on Mental Health. *Psychological Bulletin,* 103(2), 193–210; Bazerman, M. H. (2005). *Judgment in Managerial Decision Making* (6th ed.). New York: John Wiley & Sons.

15 Seligman, M. E. P. (1991). *Learned Optimism.* New York: Pocket Books.

16 Babcock, L., and Loewenstein, G. F. (1997). Explaining Bargaining Impasse: The Role of Self-Serving Biases. *Journal of Economic Perspectives,* 11(1), 109–126; Kramer, *Self-Enhancing Cognitions and Organized Conflict.*

17 Brewer, M. B. (1986). Ethnocentrism and Its Role in Intergroup Conflict. In S. Worchel & W. G. Austin (eds.), *Psychology of Intergroup Relations.* Chicago: Nelson Hall; Kramer, *Self-Enhancing Cognitions and Organized Conflict.*

18 Diekmann, K. A., Samuels, S. M., Ross, L., and Bazerman, M. H. (1997). Self-Interest and Fairness in Problems of Resource Allocation: Allocators Versus Recipients. *Journal of Personality & Social Psychology,* 72(5), 1061–1074; Tenbrunsel, A. E. (1998). Misrepresentation and Expectations of Misrepresentation in an Ethical Dilemma: The Role of Incentives and Temptation. *Academy of Management Journal,* 41(3), 330–339.

19 Sorenson, T. C. (1965). *Kennedy,* New York: Harper and Row, 322.

20 Kramer, R. M. (1994). *Self-Enhancing Cognitions and Organized Conflict.* Unpublished manuscript.

21 Salovey, P., and Rodin, J. (1984). Some Antecedents and Consequences of Social-Comparison Jealousy. *Journal of Personality and Social Psychology,* 47(4), 780–792.

22 Kramer, R. M. (1994). *Self-Enhancing Cognitions and Organized Conflict.* Unpublished manuscript.

23 Malhotra, D., and Murnighan, J. K. (2002). The Effects of Contracts on Interpersonal Trust. *Administrative Science Quarterly,* 47(3), 534–559.

24 Medvec, V. H., Madey, S. F., and Gilovich, T. (1995). When Less Is More: Counterfactual Thinking and Satisfaction Among Olympic Medalists. *Journal of Personality & Social Psychology*, 69(4), 603–610.

25 Larrick, R., and Boles, T. L. (1995). Avoiding Regret in Decisions with Feedback: A Negotiation Example. *Organizational Behavior and Human Decision Processes*, 63, 87-97; Kahneman, D., and Miller, D. T. (1986). Norm Theory: Comparing Reality to Its Alternatives. *Psychological Review*, 93(2), 136–153.

26 Spranca, M., Minsk, E., and Baron, J. (1991). Omission and Commission in Judgment and Choice. *Journal of Experimental Social Psychology*, 27(1), 76–105.

CHAPTER 6: NEGOTIATING RATIONALLY IN AN IRRATIONAL WORLD

1 Dawes, R. M. (1988). *Rational Choice in an Uncertain World.* New York: Harcourt, Brace, and Jovanovich.

2 Neale, M. A., and Northcraft, G. B. (1990). Experience, Expertise, and Decision Bias in Negotiation: The Role of Strategic Conceptualization. In B. H. Sheppard, M. H. Bazerman, and R. J. Lewicki (eds.), *Research in Negotiation in Organizations* (vol. 2). Greenwich, CT: JAI Press.

3 Stanovich, K. E., and West, R. F. (2000). Individual Differences in Reasoning: Implications for the Rationality Debate. *Behavioral and Brain Sciences*, 23, 645–665.

4 Kahneman, D., and Frederick, S. (2002). Representativeness Revisited: Attribute Substitution in Intuitive Judgment. In T. Gilovich, D. Griffin, and D. Kahneman (eds.), *Heuristics and Biases: The Psychology of Intuitive Judgment.* New York: Cambridge University Press, 49–81.

5 Chugh, D. (2004). Why Milliseconds Matter: Societal and Managerial Implications of Implicit Social Cognition. *Social Justice Research*, 17(2), 203–222.

6 Ball, S. B., Bazerman, M. H., and Carroll, J. S. (1991). An Evaluation of Learning in the Bilateral Winner's Curse. *Organizational Behavior and Human Decision Processes*, 48(1), 1–22.

7 Loewenstein, J., Thompson, L., and Gentner, D. (2003). Analogical Learning in Negotiation Teams: Comparing Cases Promotes Learning and Transfer. *Academy of Management Learning and Education*, 2(2), 119–127.

8 Kahneman, D., and Lovallo, D. (1993). Timid Choices and Bold Forecasts: A Cognitive Perspective on Risk Taking. *Management Science*, 39, 17–31.

9 *Ibid.*

10 Cooper, A., Woo, C., and Dunkelberg, W. (1988). Entrepreneurs' Perceived Chances for Success. *Journal of Business Venturing*, 3, 97–108.

11 Kahneman, D., and Lovallo, D. (1993). Timid Choices and Bold Forecasts: A Cognitive Perspective on Risk Taking. *Management Science*, 39, 17–31.

12 Lewin, K. (1947). Group Decision and Social Change. In T. M. Newcomb and E. L. Hartley (eds.), *Readings in Social Psychology*. New York: Holt, Rinehart, & Winston.

13 Lewis, M. (2003). *Moneyball: The Art of Winning an Unfair Game*. New York: W.W. Norton.

14 Thaler, R., and Sunstein, C. (2003, September 1). Who's on First? *The New Republic*, 229, 27.

15 Bazerman, M. H. (2006). *Judgment in Managerial Decision Making* (6th ed.). New York: John Wiley & Sons.

CHAPTER 7: STRATEGIES OF INFLUENCE

1 Cialdini, R. (1993). *Influence: Science and Practice*. New York: HarperCollins.

2 Cialdini, R. (Summer 2003). The Power of Persuasion: Putting the Science of Influence to Work in Fundraising. *Stanford Social Innovation Review*, 18–27.

3 The late Amos Tversky and Nobel Laureate Daniel Kahneman first noted that "losses loom larger than gains" in their work on "prospect theory" published in 1979. Kahneman, D. and Tversky, A. (March 1979). Prospect Theory: An Analysis of Decision Under Risk. *Econometrica* 47, 263–292.

4 Kalichman, S. C., and Coley, B. (1995). Context Framing to Enhance HIV-Antibody-Testing Messages Targeted to African American Women. *Health Psychology*, 14, 247–254.

5 Rothman, A. J., Salovey, P., Pronin, E., Zullo, J., and Lefell, D. (1996). Prior Health Beliefs Moderate the Persuasiveness of Gain and Loss Framed Messages. Unpublished raw data.

6 Meyerowitz, B. E., and Chaiken, S. (1987). The Effect of Message Framing on Breast Self-Examination: Attitudes, Intentions, and Behavior. *Journal of Personality and Social Psychology*, 52, 500–510.

7 In their seminal work on prospect theory, Amos Tversky and Daniel Kahneman explained that such preferences result from the way in which we evaluate the prospects of winning or losing relative to salient reference points (such as the status quo). Specifically, they argue that people have diminishing *marginal utility* associated with gains and diminishing marginal disutility associated with losses. Kahneman, D., and Tversky, A. (March 1979). Prospect Theory: An Analysis of Decision Under Risk. *Econometrica*, 47, 263–292.

8 Cialdini, R., Vincent, J., Lewis, S., Catalan, J., Wheeler, D., and Darby, B.

(1975). Reciprocal Concessions Procedure for Inducing Compliance: The Door-in-the-Face Technique. *Journal of Personality and Social Psychology*, 31, 206–215.

9 Taylor, T., and Booth-Butterfield, S. (1993). Getting a Foot in the Door with Drinking and Driving: A Field Study of Healthy Influence. *Communication Research Reports*, 10, 95–101.

10 Burger, J. M., and Guadagno, R. E. (2003). Self Concept Clarity and the Foot-in-the-Door Procedure. *Basic and Applied Social Psychology*, 25, 79–86.

11 Langer, E. J., Blank, A., and Chanowitz, B. (1978). The Mindlessness of Ostensibly Thoughtful Action: The Role of "Placebic" Information in Interpersonal Interaction. *Journal of Personality and Social Psychology*, 36, 635–642.

12 Cialdini, R. B. (January 2004). Everybody's Doing It. *Negotiation*, 7.

13 Festinger, L. (1954). A Theory of Social Comparison Processes. *Human Relations*, 7, 117–140.

14 James, J. M., and Bolstein, R. (Winter 1992). Large Monetary Incentives and Their Effect on Mail Survey Response Rates. *Public Opinion Quarterly*, 56, 442–453.

15 Malhotra, D. (2004). Trust and Reciprocity Decisions: The Differing Perspectives of Trustors and Trusted Parties. *Organizational Behavior and Human Decision Processes*, 94, 61–73.

16 Tversky, A., and Kahneman, D. (1981) The Framing of Decisions and the Rationality of Choice. *Science*, 211, 453–458.

17 Thaler, R. (1985). Mental Accounting and Consumer Choice. *Marketing Science*, 4, 199–214.

18 Bazerman, M. H. (2005). *Judgment in Managerial Decision Making*, 6th ed. New York: John Wiley & Sons.

CHAPTER 8: BLIND SPOTS IN NEGOTIATION

1 Feder, B. (2006, January 26). Quiet End to Battle of the Bids. *New York Times*, C1.

2 Feder, B., and Sorkin, A. R. (2005, November 3). Troubled Maker of Heart Devices May Lose Suitor. *New York Times*, A1.

3 Feder, B. (2006, January 26). Quiet End to Battle of the Bids. *New York Times*, C1.

4 Meier, B. (2005, November 10). Guidant Issues Data on Faulty Heart Devices. *New York Times*, C5.

5 Bajaj, V. (2005, December 28). F.D.A. Puts Restrictions on Guidant. *New York Times*, C1.

6 Feder, B., and Sorkin, A. R. (2006, January 18). Boston Scientific, with Abbott's Help, Raises Bid for Guidant. *New York Times*, C1.

7 Saul, S. (2006, January 25). J&J Passes on Raising Guidant Bid. *New*

York Times, C1; Feder, B. (2006, January 26). Quiet End to Battle of the Bids. *New York Times,* C1.

8 Harris, G., and Feder, B. (2006, January 27). F.D.A. Warns Device Maker over Safety. *New York Times,* C1.

9 Tully, S. (2006, October 16). The (Second) Worst Deal Ever. *Fortune,* 154 (8).

10 Bazerman, M. H., and Chugh, D. (2006). Decisions Without Blinders. *Harvard Business Review,* 84(1).

11 (1995, November 10). American Won't Make First Bid on USAir. *Charleston Daily Mail,* C4.

12 Akerlof, G. (1970). The Market for Lemons: Qualitative Uncertainty and the Market Mechanism. *Quarterly Journal of Economics,* 89, 488–500.

13 Ball, S. B., Bazerman, M. H., and Carroll, J. S. (1991). An Evaluation of Learning in the Bilateral Winner's Curse. *Organizational Behavior and Human Decision Processes,* 48(1), 1–22.

14 Bereby-Meyer, Y., and Grosskopf, B. (2002). *Overcoming the Winner's Curse: An Adaptive Learning Perspective.* AOM Conflict Management Division 2002 meetings, No. 13496. http://ssrn.com/abstract=324201.

15 Moore, D. A., and Kim, T. G. (2003). Myopic Social Prediction and the Solo Comparison Effect. *Journal of Personality and Social Psychology,* 85(6), 1121–1135.

16 Camerer, C., and Lovallo, D. (1999). Overconfidence and Excess Entry: An Experimental Approach. *American Economic Review,* 306–318.

17 Fox, C. R., and Tversky, A. (1998). A Belief-Based Account of Decision Under Uncertainty. *Management Science,* 44(7), 879–895.

18 Emphasis added. Brahimi's comments were made during a panel discussion at the Harvard Business School in October 2002.

19 Simons, D. J. (2003). Surprising Studies of Visual Awareness. [DVD]. Champaign, IL: VisCog Productions, http://www.viscog.com.

20 Neisser, U. (1979). The Concept of Intelligence. *Intelligence,* 3(3), 217–227.

CHAPTER 9: CONFRONTING LIES AND DECEPTION

1 Gladwell, M. (2005). *Blink: The Power of Thinking Without Thinking.* New York: Little, Brown.

2 Ekman, P. (2002). *Telling Lies: Clues to Deceit in the Marketplace, Marriage, and Politics.* New York: W.W. Norton.

3 Malhotra, D. (2004). Smart Alternatives to Lying in Negotiation. *Negotiation,* 7(5).

CHAPTER 10: RECOGNIZING AND RESOLVING ETHICAL DILEMMAS

1 Banaji, M. R., Bazerman, M. H., and Chugh, D. (December 2003). How (Un)Ethical Are You? *Harvard Business Review*.

2 Indeed, in most states, a seller's real-estate agent has a formal fiduciary responsibility to the seller.

3 Cain, D., Loewenstein, G., and Moore, D. (2005). The Dirt on Coming Clean: Perverse Effects of Disclosing Conflicts of Interest. *Journal of Legal Studies*, 34, 1–25.

4 Greenwald, A. G., McGhee, D. E., and Schwartz, J.L.K. (1998). Measuring Individual Differences in Implicit Cognition: The Implicit Association Test. *Journal of Personality and Social Psychology*, 74(6), 1464–1480.

5 Chugh, D. (2004). Why Milliseconds Matter: Societal and Managerial Implications of Implicit Social Cognition. *Social Justice Research*, 17(2), 203–222.

6 Gillespie, J. J., and Bazerman, M. H. (1997). Parasitic Integration: Win-Win Agreements Containing Losers. *Negotiation Journal*, 13(3), 271–282. We use the term "parasitic value creation" synonymously with Gillespie and Bazerman's term "parasitic integration."

7 The administrative law judge ruled in favor of the pharmaceutical firms. An FTC bipartisan panel overruled the administrative judge by a 5–0 vote. They, in turn, were overruled by an appeals court. The U.S. Supreme Court refused to hear the FTC's appeal of the appellate court ruling, helping create the blueprint for parasitic value creation that has become even more common in the pharmaceutical arena.

8 Murnighan, J. K. (1994). Game Theory and Organizational Behavior. In B. M. Staw and L. L. Cummings (eds.), *Research in Organizational Behavior*. Greenwich, CT: JAI Press.

9 Kim Wade-Benzoni, Ann Tenbrunsel, and Max Bazerman developed an experimental simulation based on this class of problems in which participants played the roles of representatives of various commercial and recreational fishing groups meeting for a conference to discuss the crisis. They found that the participants made self-serving interpretations of what was fair, and that these biased interpretations were an excellent predictor of overharvesting.

10 Caruso, E., Epley, N., and Bazerman, M. H. (2006). The Good, the Bad and the Ugly of Perspective Taking in Groups. In E. A. Mannix, M. A. Neale, and A. E. Tenbrunsel (eds.), *Research on Managing Groups and Teams: Ethics and Groups* (vol. 8). London: Elsevier.

11 Chugh, D. (2004). Why Milliseconds Matter: Societal and Managerial

Implications of Implicit Social Cognition. *Social Justice Research*, 17(2), 203–222.

CHAPTER 11: NEGOTIATING FROM A POSITION OF WEAKNESS

1 Subramanian, G., and Zeckhauser, R. (February 2005). "Negotiauctions": Taking a Hybrid Approach to the Sale of High-Value Assets. *Negotiation*.

2 Bazerman, M. H., and Neale, M. A. (1992). *Negotiating Rationally*. New York: Free Press.

CHAPTER 12: WHEN NEGOTIATIONS GET UGLY: DEALING WITH IRRATIONALITY, DISTRUST, ANGER, THREATS, AND EGO

1 Kennedy, R. (1971). *Thirteen Days: A Memoir of the Cuban Missile Crisis*. New York: W. W. Norton.

2 Malhotra, D. (2006). Is Your Counterpart Irrational ... *Really*? *Negotiation*, 9(3).

3 Mayer, R. C., Davis, J. H., and Schoorman, F. D. (1995). An Integrative Model of Organizational Trust. *Academy of Management Review*, 20, 709–734.

4 Dirks, K. T., and Ferrin, D. L. (2001). The Role of Interpersonal Trust in Organizational Settings. *Organization Science*, 12, 450–467.

5 *Thirteen Days*, 97.

CHAPTER 14: THE PATH TO GENIUS

1 Neale, M. A., and Northcraft, G. B. (1990). Experience, Expertise, and Decision Bias in Negotiation: The Role of Strategic Conceptualization. In B. H. Sheppard, M. H. Bazerman, and R. J. Lewicki (eds.), *Research in Negotiation in Organizations* (vol. 2). Greenwich, CT: JAI Press.

ACKNOWLEDGMENTS

The authors, and the ideas in this book, have been strongly influenced by our colleagues. We are really good at finding excellent people as colleagues. Many of these colleagues are or were part of the faculty and doctoral programs at two excellent institutions: Northwestern University and Harvard University—with large concentrations of colleagues in the Kellogg Graduate School of Management and the Harvard Business School, respectively. Both universities are leading centers for research and teaching in the area of negotiations and many of the ideas in this book were developed by—or in collaboration with—the excellent scholars we interacted with while at these schools. From our days at Kellogg, we would like to acknowledge the insights of Sally Blount, Jeanne Brett, Tina Diekmann, Craig Fox, Adam Galinsky, Dedre Gentner, Andy Hoffman, Michael Jensen, Mark Kennedy, Laura Kray, Gillian Ku, Terri Kurtzberg, Rick Larrick, Beta Mannix, Doug Medin, Victoria Medvec, David Messick, Don Moore, Keith Murnighan, Maggie Neal, Tetsu Okumura, Holly Schroth, Pri Pradhan Shah, Harris Sondak, Ann Tenbrunsel, Leigh Thompson, Cathy Tinsley, Tom Tripp, Kimberly Wade-Benzoni, Mark Weber, and Lauri Weingart.

At Harvard University, we are both fortunate to be professors in the Negotiations, Organizations, and Markets Unit of the Harvard Business School, where we have been surrounded by excellent colleagues who improve the quality of our work: Nava Ashraf, George Baker, Gregory Barron, Yoella Bereby-Meyer, Peter Coles, Francesca Gino, Jerry Green, Brit Grosskopf, Brian Hall, Lorraine Idson, Kathleen McGinn, Simone Moran, Al Roth, Jim Sebenius, Ravi Singh,

William Simpson, Guhan Subramanian, Andy Wasynczuk, Michael Watkins, Toni Wegner, and Michael Wheeler.

We are also both associated with the Program on Negotiation at the Harvard Law School, which has been a tremendous source of social and intellectual support. Our affiliation with the Program on Negotiation, a variety of doctoral programs at Harvard, and with other schools and departments at the university, has allowed us to benefit from the ideas and insights of many others during our time at Harvard, including Modupe Akinola, Mahzarin Banaji, John Beshears, Iris Bohnet, Hannah Riley Bowles, Daylian Cain, Eugene Caruso, Heather Caruso, Dolly Chugh, Luke Coffman, Nick Epley, Steve Garcia, Dan Gilbert, Joshua Greene, Fiona Grieg, Susan Hackley, Karin Kassam, David Laibson, Jolie Martin, Mary Carol Mazza, Wendy Mendez, Katy Milkman, Jason Mitchell, Bob Mnookin, Sendhil Mullainathan, Neeru Paharia, Jeff Polzer, Todd Rogers, Ben Shenoy, Larry Susskind, Carmit Tadmor, Mike Tushman, and Dan Wegner.

We also have learned a great deal from Jon Baron, Linda Babcock, Art Brief, Jenn Lerner, George Loewenstein, Brian McGrath, Madan Pillutla, Phil Tetlock, and many other colleagues and friends whom we will later be embarrassed for forgetting.

We would also like to thank the thousands of executives from around the world who have been our students or clients. Some of your experiences have found their way into this book. Many of your problems, questions, and stories have motivated the substance of this book. And all of you have inspired us to write it.

When it came to the task of actually writing, we were extremely fortunate to have absolutely fantastic editorial help. Katie Shonk, Max's longtime research assistant, spent countless hours reading, editing, and commenting on every word, sentence, and chapter. Her help was invaluable. Our excellent faculty assistants, Alyssa Razook and Elizabeth Sweeny, proofread, fact-checked, and generally fixed stuff in the book. Our editor at Bantam, Toni Burbank, knew exactly when to push us, and when to trust our judgment. The process of writing the book was vastly improved thanks to her assertiveness, enthusiasm, and collegiality.

Finally, we would like to acknowledge the support of our families. Deepak's parents, Chander and Sudesh Malhotra, and his brother,

Manu Malhotra, read multiple drafts of the book and provided innumerable helpful suggestions. Deepak's wife, Shikha, not only read and edited every page of the book, but also provided the encouragement and support necessary to push the project through to the end. Max's spouse, Marla Felcher, always provides a thorough critique of all of Max's ideas, and refines his arguments in the process. We would also like to thank Shikha and Marla for clarifying—by being a part of our lives—that the best things in life require no negotiation.

INDEX

ABOUT THE AUTHORS

Deepak Malhotra is an Associate Professor in the Negotiations, Organizations, and Markets Unit at the Harvard Business School. Deepak teaches Negotiation courses in the MBA program and in a wide variety of executive programs.

Deepak's research focuses on negotiation strategy, trust development, international and ethnic dispute resolution, and the dynamics of competitive escalation. His research has been published in top journals in the fields of management, psychology, and conflict resolution. Deepak has also won numerous awards for both his teaching and his research.

Deepak's professional activities include training and consulting with firms across the globe in a multitude of industries, including banking, education, energy, financial management, health care, hospitality, information technology, manufacturing, media, newspaper, nonprofits, pharmaceuticals, printing, real estate, retail, and telecommunications.

For more information about Deepak, please go to: http://pine.hbs.edu/external/facPersonalShow.do?pid=189290

Max H. Bazerman is the Jesse Isador Straus Professor of Business Administration at the Harvard Business School. In addition, Max is formally affiliated with the Kennedy School of Government, the Psychology Department at Harvard University, the Institute for Quantitative Social Sciences, the Harvard University Center on the Environment, and the Program on Negotiation.

Max's research focuses on decision-making in negotiation, and improving decision-making in organizations, nations, and society. He is the author of 180 research articles and chapters, and the author, co-author, or co-editor of fifteen earlier books, including *Judgment in Managerial Decision Making* (2005, Wiley, now in its 6th edition), *Predictable Surprises* (2004, Harvard Business School Press, with Michael Watkins), and *You Can't Enlarge the Pie: Six Barriers to Effective Government* (2001, Basic Books, with Jon Baron and Katie Shonk). He is a member of the editorial boards of the *American Behavioral Scientist, Perspectives on Psychological Science, Journal of Management and Governance, Mind and Society, Negotiations and Conflict Management Research,* and *The Journal of Behavioral Finance.* Also, he is a member of the international advisory board of the *Negotiation Journal.*

From 2002 to 2005, Max was consistently named one of the top forty authors, speakers, and teachers of management by Executive Excellence. While at Kellogg, he was named "Teacher of the Year" by the Executive Masters Program of the Kellogg School. In 2003, Max received the Everett Mendelsohn Excellence in Mentoring Award from Harvard University's Graduate School of Arts and Sciences. In 2006, Max received an honorary doctorate from the University of London (London Business School), the Kulp-Wright Book Award from the American Risk and Insurance Association for *Predictable Surprises* (with Michael Watkins), and the Life Achievement Award from the Aspen Institute's Business and Society Program.

His former doctoral students have accepted positions at leading business schools throughout the United States, including the Kellogg School at Northwestern, the Fuqua School at Duke, the Johnson School at Cornell, Carnegie-Mellon University, the Stern School at NYU, Stanford University, the University of Chicago, Notre Dame, Columbia, and the Harvard Business School.

His professional activities include projects with Abbott, Aetna, Alcar, Alcoa, Allstate, Ameritech, Amgen, Apex Partners, Asian Development Bank, AstraZeneca, AT&T, Aventis, BASF, Bayer, Becton Dickinson, Biogen, Boston Scientific, BP, Bristol-Meyers Squibb, Business Week, Celtic Insurance, Chevron, Chicago Tribune, City of Chicago, Deloitte and Touche, Dial, Ernst and Young, First Chicago, Gemini Consulting, General Motors, Harris Bank, Home Depot, Hyatt Hotels, IBM, John Hancock, Johnson & Johnson, Kohler, KPMG, Lucent,

The May Company, McKinsey, Merrill Lynch, Monitor, Motorola, National Association of Broadcasters, the Nature Conservancy, PriceWaterhouseCoopers, R. P. Scherer, Sara Lee, Siemens, Sprint, Sulzermedica, Unicredito, Union Bank of Switzerland, Wilson Sporting Goods, World Bank, Xerox, Young Presidents Organization, and Zurich Insurance. Max's consulting, teaching, and lecturing have spanned over twenty-five countries.

For more information about Max, please go to:
http://people.hbs.edu/mbazerman/